Computer Assisted Mass Appraisal

An International Review

Edited by
WILLIAM J. McCLUSKEY
ALASTAIR S. ADAIR
School of the Built Environment
University of Ulster

Routledge
Taylor & Francis Group

LONDON AND NEW YORK

First published 1997 by Ashgate Publishing

Reissued 2018 by Routledge
2 Park Square, Milton Park, Abingdon, Oxon, OX14 4RN
711 Third Avenue, New York, NY I 0017, USA

Routledge is an imprint of the Taylor & Francis Group, an informa business

Publisher's Note
The publisher has gone to great lengths to ensure the quality of this reprint but points out that some imperfections in the original copies may be apparent.

Disclaimer
The publisher has made every effort to trace copyright holders and welcomes correspondence from those they have been unable to contact.

A Library of Congress record exists under LC control number: 97071714

ISBN 13: 978-1-138-61748-3 (hbk)
ISBN 13: 978-1-138-61752-0 (pbk)
ISBN 13: 978-0-429-46169-9 (ebk)

Contents

Figures and tables

ix

Contributors

R. Almy
Almy, Gloudemans & Jacobs, Chicago, United States

S. Anand
University of Ulster, Northern Ireland

M. Cusack
Cook County Assessor's Office, Chicago, United States

K. Dyson
University of Ulster, Northern Ireland

R. Gloudemans
Almy, Gloudemans & Jacobs, Chicago, United States

S. Gronow
University of Glamorgan, Wales

G. M. ten Have
De Boer Den Hartog Hooft B.V., Amsterdam, The Netherlands

J. Horbas
Cook County Assessor's Office, Chicago, United States

H. James
University of Portsmouth, England

J. E. Janssen
NVM, Nieuwegein, The Netherlands

D. Jenkins
University of Glamorgan, Wales

A. Kirby
Department of Lands, Queensland, Australia

L. S. Leng
Inland Revenue Authority of Singapore, Singapore

W. J. McCluskey
University of Ulster, Northern Ireland

D. McFall
University of Ulster, Northern Ireland

A. H. Nawawi
University of Glamorgan, Wales

A. Pearce
British Columbia Assessment Authority, Canada

A. Pegler
Valuation New Zealand, New Zealand

W. Riley
Maryland Assessment Office, Maryland, United States

R. Stevenson
Rating and Valuation Department, Hong Kong

A. Sundquist
National Land Survey, Sweden

D. Thomas
Hydro Property Services, Tasmania, Australia

A.G. op't Veld
TNO Beleidsstudies, Delft, The Netherlands

Acknowledgements

We would like to thank all the contributors to this book for their consideration, hard work and undoubted patience. Special thanks are due, in particular, to Rosemary Clelland who prepared many of the graphics, Roisin McCluskey for typesetting and all those others who supported us throughout the preparation of this work.

Preface

The rationale for this book arose from the need to establish a forum to publish material on the research and development, use, and application of mass appraisal techniques as used in ad valorem property tax systems. The development of such techniques clearly is of international interest and concern to those involved in mass appraisal. What is significant is the range of techniques which are currently being applied or being field tested. From the established, statistically based, multiple regression approaches to developments in artificial intelligence and machine learning. The main paradigms covered include various forms of regression (additive, multiplicative, hybrid), base home technique, adaptive estimation procedure, comparable sales analysis, expert systems and artificial neural networks

What conclusions can then be drawn from the wealth of information contained in this book? Diversity of approach in applying broadly similar techniques is evident. This demonstrates that such factors as volatility of property markets, availability of property data, presence of cadastres, the expertise of those applying the techniques and the available funding for system development are all relevant in the design and application of systems. A common objective to all the systems reviewed is to achieve assessment fairness at an economic cost. In addition, the integration of geographic information systems and CAMA is an extremely important development. The next generation of mass appraisal systems will need to incorporate the spatial dimension, again leading to enhanced performance in assessment and taxpayer acceptability. One has to suggest that the days of 'manually' appraising or valuing several hundred thousand or millions of parcels is now gone. Mass appraisal processes are now an integral part of the overall property taxation administrative processes.

This book represents an attempt to bring together leading experts and researchers who are linked with the common theme of developing more rigorous, more objective and more cost effective appraisal approaches to the determination of property values. There was also the underlying theme, to specifically ensure that as many property types were addressed. To this end, chapters cover residential, condominiums, retail, office and industrial property as well as agricultural and forestry land. Much of the material could be described as 'cutting edge' or 'state of the art', and therefore it is hoped that it will be of direct benefit to students, researchers, property tax valuers and appraisers.

1 A critical review of computer assisted mass appraisal techniques

W. J. McCluskey

Mass appraisal

Mass appraisal has been defined as the systematic appraisal of groups of properties as of a given date using standardized procedures and statistical testing (IAAO, 1978). It differs from single property appraisal only in terms of scale. In mass appraisal modelling the aim is to try and replicate the market within which real estate is traded and to derive a representative mathematical model which achieves this aim. Thus, valuation models developed for mass appraisal purposes must represent supply and demand patterns for groups of properties. The model must be firmly established within micro-economic theory which would support the underlying rationale of the model. Appraisal judgements for mass appraisal must relate to large groups of properties rather than to single properties. The ultimate objective is, however, the same whether the approach is mass or single valuation that is, an accurate assessment of the value of many properties or of a single property. The methods of valuation which the valuer utilizes are essentially the same, the main differences between the approaches are in the areas of market analysis and quality control.

Quality control is measured differently across the two approaches. In mass appraisal given the scale of valuations, statistical methods are used to measure accuracy and variations in the assessed values from actual sale prices. For most mass appraisal models if the average deviation from sale prices falls within a predetermined range, the model and quality is considered good. In single property appraisal, quality can usually be measured by direct comparison with specific comparable sales. In both approaches the valuer will be required to defend his assessment of value, and as one would expect this is somewhat easier in the single property appraisal than in the mass appraisal situation. Nonetheless the model needs to be capable of explanation to demonstrate how the value was achieved.

1

Shonk (1982) asked the question, 'Why? ... does the profession have to come to grips with mass appraisal at all? Why won't the time hallowed methods of assessment serve us as well into the future?' A number of statements were made by Shonk which aptly answer the questions he posed;

> We as a profession have to contain our costs and keep our product competitive.

> We have to stretch one value and find ways of extending a single valuation decision to all properties with similar characteristics.

Mass appraisal in essence evolved out of the need to provide uniformity and consistency in ad valorem valuations. An equally important aspect was the ever increasing financial burden of undertaking single manual appraisals, particularly at times of revaluations where several millions parcels needed to be assessed at the same time. According to Silverherz (1936) the reappraisal of St Paul, Minnesota, marked the beginning of scientific mass appraisal. Developments in mass appraisal accelerated in the 1950s with the introduction of computers. Renshaw (1958) had this to say about scientific appraisal;

> While it may be hopeless to isolate all the factors which buyers take into consideration when purchasing property, it is possible to establish a correlation between real estate values and a select subset of determining variables. Although the choice of the function and its mathematical form is somewhat arbitrary, it is not necessary to choose the best possible function, but only the one which predicts real estate values with sufficient accuracy in a statistical sense, for the type of appraisal under consideration.

Since then, hardware and software developments have meant that most property tax assessing departments have access to relatively inexpensive mass appraisal systems. Within the mass appraisal system the dual components of predictive accuracy and explainability are extremely important. Predictive accuracy can be assessed through quality control measures as noted previously, however, explainability, not being capable of being statistically measured, is therefore more difficult to assess. Gloudemans (1982) suggested that there are at least seven issues related to explainability within a mass appraisal system, they are; (i) simplicity of the design of the models in terms of functional form and rationale of the variables used in the models; (ii) the reasonableness of the monetary value assigned to the property attributes; the effect on the estimated price of a property of a particular attribute must conform with a priori expectations; (iii) there should be consistency between sub-models which means that sub-model equations produce accuracy between as well as within property groups in terms

2

of the values assigned to particular attributes; (iv) consistency of time ensures that values for individual properties do not change inexplicably from one year to the next; (v) decomposition of value between land and improvements which may be important in those jurisdictions where land and buildings are taxed at different rates; (vi) ease of explanation of the underlying models to the tax payer, or rather demonstrating in simplistic terms how the assessed value was arrived at rather than showing the mathematical functional form of the models; and finally (vii) explainability is enhanced through comparable transactions, which have traditionally provided the main source of evidence in defending assessments.

Therefore explanatory mass appraisal systems enhance taxpayer understanding and general acceptance of the property tax system through concepts such as fairness and equity.

The mass appraisal process

Figure 1.1 describes the key components of the typical mass appraisal process.

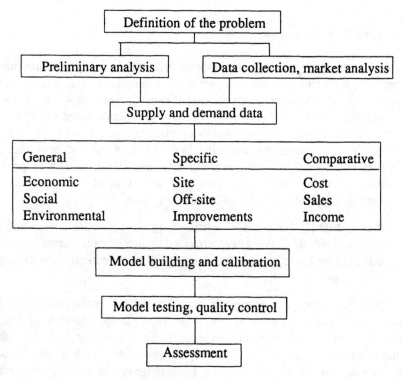

Figure 1.1 The mass appraisal process

Mass appraisal techniques

Mass appraisal modelling techniques can take a number of forms all of which have the same dual objectives firstly, to attain acceptable standards of predictive accuracy and secondly, to facilitate explainability of the assessed values. The main models achieve these objectives with varying degrees of success, some scoring highly in both whilst others forego one to achieve better than average results in the other. It could be argued that, predictive accuracy is more important and therefore, models should be as comprehensive as possible in achieving high levels of accuracy notwithstanding that such models are not tax payer friendly in explaining how the values were determined. Ultimately the application and use of particular modelling techniques depends largely on data availability, data characteristics, the value base and the objectives of the assessment jurisdiction.

The following section outlines, some of the main modelling paradigms which are currently used internationally for determining real estate values for property taxation. It cannot be totally comprehensive, since with continuing research new modelling techniques and hybrid approaches are continually being developed.

Rule based expert systems

A rule based expert system is a computerized technique representing human expertise which can emulate and perform the functions of an expert and/or perform tasks which require a certain level of expertise (McCluskey et al., 1996). Curtis (1989) states that the general objectives of any rule based expert system are to ascertain a body of knowledge in a particular domain, to be able to apply this knowledge to given situations (often in situations of incomplete or uncertain information), to deliver effective and efficient solutions and to provide explanations and justifications for these solutions. Bonnet (1988) provides the following as a typical definition of an expert system;

> It is a program that contains a large body of knowledge concerning one specific field, this having been provided by one or more human experts in that field, and able to achieve the same performance in problem solving as those experts.

The knowledge elicitation process is central to the success or failure of a rule based expert system. Thus the system is not merely a representation of data but more accurately a simulation of the expertise and knowledge of the expert valuer. Unlike multiple regression analysis which begins with a predetermined model, the rule model discovers the expertise. Knowledge can be directly or indirectly derived from the expert or a team of experts.

The basic structure of the expert system comprises three features;

1   The Facts Base. This comprises the permanent facts of the field to which the problem belongs, together with any special facts concerning the particular problem which has to be resolved i.e. the database.

2   The Knowledge Base. This consists of rules or production rules which usually enable deductions to be made from the given facts.

3   The Inference Engine. This uses the knowledge base to reason about the problem, given the contents of the facts base.

Gronow and Scott (1986) argue that the greatest feature of rule based expert systems is their ability to encapsulate rules of thumb or heuristics and generalities. One of the problems of this technique is that they do not inherently learn but merely mirror the actions of an expert, therefore, provided the problem to be addressed is one in which information is already contained within the parameters of the elicited knowledge, then the expert system should be able to deduce a solution. One additional problem is that the behaviour of large rule based systems can be difficult to predict, because although individual rules may be easy to understand on their own, interactions between rules are not obvious.

Artificial neural networks

Artificial intelligence is a sub-field of computer science concerned with the use of computers in tasks that are normally considered to require knowledge, perception, reasoning, learning, understanding and similar cognitive abilities (Gevarter, 1985). Therefore, one could consider artificial intelligence to be concerned with intelligent behaviour involving complexity, uncertainty and ambiguity. It represent techniques which have strong problem solving components such as synthesizing a set of attributes to achieve a goal and powers of deduction. The ability of people to make accurate generalizations from a few scattered facts or to discover patterns from within a collection of observations is a primary research focus of artificial intelligence. The development of a number of conceptual tools have made it relatively easy to structure and manipulate symbolic databases. The notion of representing information in the form of networks or nodes and links is one of the major contributions of artificial intelligence research and in particular the development of artificial neural networks. Artificial Neural Networks (ANNs), a separate branch of artificial intelligence, builds upon the accepted theories of understanding what intelligence is and how to make machines more useful.

5

ANNs take their name from the network of nerve cells in the brain. Traditional neuroscience has identified two key functions of the brain firstly, the ability to learn from experience and secondly, the ability to create internal representations of the world in the form of internal data maps. Research has now been able to harness these powerful abilities into computer programmes, which are currently being applied to a wide range of practical problems. Neural networks excel at problems involving patterns including, pattern mapping, pattern valuing, financial prediction and so forth.

Neural networks utilize a parallel processing structure that has a large number of processing elements and many interconnections between them. A typical structure for an ANN would have on the left side the inputs to the processing unit. Each interconnection has an associated connection strength or weight, denoted as w_1, w_2, ... w_n. The processing unit performs a weighted sum of the inputs and then uses a non-linear threshold function (sigmoid function) normally utilizing a back propagation algorithm to compute its output. The calculated result is then denoted as the output of the network.

ANNs are not programmed but rather they 'learn' by example. A network is presented with a training set of data from which it can learn the underlying pattern. The most common approach to training the network is to process input data with its associated output, in other words property characteristics including the known sale price. The forward pass through the network will result in the connection weights being adjusted in an attempt to minimize the error between the output of the network and the actual desired result.

Regression analysis

Regression analysis is today a widely accepted technique applied successfully within the ad valorem assessment process. Numerous studies and research have been undertaken which demonstrate the potential of the technique in terms of both explanation and predictive capabilities (Brown, 1974; Gloudemans and Miller, 1978; Mark and Goldberg, 1988 and Cannaday, 1989).

It might be useful at this point to give a brief overview of the technique. Simple regression is concerned with describing how one factor or variable behaves in relation to another, in other words it seeks to study the statistical relationship between one dependant variable Y and one independent variable X. To study the relationship between Y and several independent variables, multiple regression analysis is used.

$$Y = a + b_1X_1 + b_2X_2 + ... + b_iX_i$$

6

Multiple regression will find the best numerical values for a, b_1, b_2 etc. by the method of least squares such that the sum of the squared errors $E(Y_i - \bar{Y}_i)^2$ is minimized where the Y_i's are the actual values and the $\bar{Y}_i$'s are the predicted values.

The basic objective therefore of MRA is to develop a strong predictive relationship between property characteristics and value, so that the latter can be estimated through knowledge of the former (IAAO, 1978). There are two broad types of multiple regression analysis i.e. non-stepwise and stepwise. Non-stepwise requires the user to specify all the predictors/variables which are to be used in the model regardless of their statistical significance (Eckert, 1985).

Stepwise

This procedure distinguishes between variables which are statistically significant in terms of prediction and those which are not. The model enters variables one by one and arranges them in rank order of significant coefficients. The stepwise model can take the form of one of the following: forward selection regression, backward selection regression, forward stepwise regression and backward stepwise regression.

In relation to forward selection regression, this technique enters variables until all of the significant predictors have been entered. The backward selection initially enters the full set of variables and subsequently eliminates those with little statistical significance until only those which are significant at predicting the dependant variable remain. Forward and backward stepwise regression refines the above process. Forward stepwise regression allows the elimination of any variable that entered the model at an early stage but has since become statistically insignificant. Backward stepwise regression allows the input of a variable which was deleted at an early stage but has since become statistically significant. Thus, both of these models allow for the possibility that the statistical significance of the variables may alter in subsequent stages of the process. Additionally backward stepwise regression considers the interactive effect of multiple variables which may be statistically significant if considered jointly, but which are of negligible significance if they were to be considered individually.

The various stepwise alternatives each attempt to isolate the best subset model by ensuring that all of the value predictors included in the model are statistically significant, and therefore important in the estimation of value. Usually, the results of the various stepwise alternatives will be mutually consistent with one another, but only when the predictors are essentially uncorrelated.

Other forms of regression can be applied in given situations where the standard linear regression models are not applicable, these would include constrained regression, ridge regression, nonlinear regression, constrained nonlinear, Gauss-Newton nonlinear regression and so forth.

7

Measures to evaluate regression performance

It is necessary to be able to evaluate the results produced by the regression analysis. The techniques used for this process can be classified into two categories, firstly, statistics which test the 'goodness of fit' which include (1) the coefficient of determination (r^2), (2) the standard error of the estimate (SEE), (3) the coefficient of variation (COV), and (4) coefficient of dispersion (COD); the first four statistics indicate how well the entire regression equation succeeds in minimizing the sum of the squared errors, i.e. in predicting sale prices and secondly, statistics which indicate the importance of the individual regression variables in predicting sale prices. These are (1) the coefficient of correlation (r), (2) the t-statistic, (3) the F-statistic, and (4) the beta coefficient.

Comparable sales analysis

The storage and rapid retrieval capabilities of computer databases can readily be used to select 'comparables' which are then used to determine the value of a subject property. The approach is for the system to select comparables closest to the subject which obviates the necessity of the valuer having to search through data sales to find comparables and secondly to adjust them for comparability. The computer based adjustments are made to the selected properties by deletions and additions of dollar amounts to make the comparable a notional physical replica to the subject. The approach utilizes distance to establish a measure of comparability between the subject and the comparable. This 'distance' (sometimes referred to as Mahalanobis distance) can be calculated as follows:

$$D = \lambda \sqrt{\sum_i \{A_i (X_i - X_{si})]^\lambda + \sum_j \{A_j \delta(X_j, X_{sj})]^\lambda}$$

where

λ	=	Minkowski Exponent Lambda
A_i	=	weight associated with the ith continuous characteristic
X_i	=	value of the ith characteristic in the sale property
X_{si}	=	value of the ith characteristic in the subject property
$\sum_i$	=	summation of terms of i characteristics
A_j	=	weight associated with the jth categorical characteristic
X_j	=	value of the jth characteristic in the sale property
X_{sj}	=	value of the ith characteristic in the subject property
$\sum_j$	=	summation of terms of j characteristics
$\delta(a,b)$	=	inverse delta function (0 if $a = b$; 1 if $a \ne b$)

8

The comparables with the lowest distance are selected. In calculating the distance the variables are allocated a factor weight (Borst and McCluskey, 1996). The weighting is used to balance the effect of variables according to the magnitude of the variable itself, so that a variable with larger numerical size has a smaller weight.

For each comparable property the sale price is adjusted to the comparable property by applying regression based adjustments as follows;

Adjusted sales price = Sales price - (Comparable MRA - Subject MRA).

The results of the comparables selection routine is to identify a number of closest comparables whose price is adjusted to reflect what the sale price of each would have been if the physical characteristics of the sale property were the same as the subject. This adjusted sale price, together with the adjusted prices of the comparables, is used to value the subject (Fraser and Blackwell, 1988).

The comparable sales analysis approach lends itself to produce defensible assessed values; its output is traditional in that actual comparables are used so one can see how the value of the subject was arrived at. This is in contrast to MRA where due to variable transformations the coefficients can be difficult to interpret.

Case based reasoning

Case based reasoning (CBR) is an artificial intelligence paradigm which uses past experience to solve current problems and in this respect mirrors the comparative method of valuation (O'Roarty, 1996). Barletta (1991) contends that the ability of CBR to reason from past cases is appealing because it corresponds to the process an expert adopts. In contrast to rule based expert systems, CBR is not founded on rules but rather on the premise that cases should be used as the foundation of the system. Essentially CBR utilizes a data set of 'comparables' termed the case library. This set of cases describe the features of past problems or events together with solutions or outcomes. With regard to residential valuation, each property characteristic would be represented with a field in the data set and price as an outcome field. A CBR system enables a hypothetical case to be presented and searches for similar cases with the objective of determining a reasoned output. CBR utilizes a system of case indexing from which it derives the power to remove relevant cases quickly and accurately. CBR can employ a number of case indexing techniques, the one most relevant to property assessment would be the 'nearest neighbour' technique.

The nearest neighbour approach enables weights to be placed against fields in respect of the input cases and retrieves cases from memory based on the weighted sum of the features. The goal of case retrieval is to present the most similar past cases that are relevant to the current input situation. CBR is an artificial intelligence application with the ability to learn from past problems and from the solution to those past problems.

It has been argued (Barletta, 1991) that CBR has distinct advantages over artificial neural networks:

1   it can learn from a wide range of feature types;

2   much shorter time is needed for training;

3   the output is more easily interpreted and understood by a nontechnical user;

4   it may be used to perform additional tasks other than the prediction of the selling price, whereas ANNs and rule based systems may only be employed to generate a specific output.

Adaptive estimation procedure

Adaptive Estimation Procedure (AEP) otherwise known as 'feedback' was developed by Carbone and Longini (1977). The method derives its name from the way in which the data is processed. In the case of estimating the selling price of real estate, sale transactions are processed one at a time in the sequence in which the sales took place. The feedback model is one that learns by experience. If the predicted value of the first property is higher than the actual value, it is reasonable to assume that the assigned weights and values for each attribute were too high and should be reduced. The model alters the assigned weights and the next sale is then processed, with the predicted value again being compared to the actual value. The two values will not match exactly, so again the coefficients in the equation will be adjusted to minimize the error. The coefficients are associated with various property characteristics such as lot size, number of rooms, garage, floor area etc. The alterations made to the coefficients are made in a way that extreme changes in the associated weights do not occur, therefore the modifications are smoothed out.

AEP can be visualized as 'curve tracking' with information constantly being fed into the model which alters in order to improve the level of accuracy. This is in contrast to MRA which involves 'curve fitting' with all data being processed simultaneously.

Within the AEP model, property characteristics are classified as being either qualitative or quantitative (Schrieber, 1985). For example lot size would be a quantitative variable and type of construction would be a qualitative variable.

Property characteristics are further differentiated as follows; general qualitative characteristics (GQ), building qualitative characteristics (BQ), land qualitative characteristics (LQ), quantitative building characteristics (QB) and quantitative land characteristics (QL). Quantitative variables are deemed to have an additive effect on value whereas qualitative variables tend to have a multiplicative effect.

The feedback equation tends to follow the following form;

$$\text{Estimated value} = \pi Q_G M_G [\pi Q_B M_B \ \Sigma f_B A_B + \pi Q_L M_L \ \Sigma f_L A_L]$$

where:

f_B = building quantitative variables
f_L = land quantitative variables
A = coefficient of each variable
Q_B = Qualitative building coefficient
Q_L = Qualitative land coefficient
π = the product of both the building and land qualitative coefficients
M_B = coefficient for continuous variables with a multiplicative effect (e.g. age of building)
M_B = continuous variable coefficient for land
Q_G = qualitative general factor (affecting both land and buildings)
M_G = multiplicative general factor (affecting both land and buildings).

It has been suggested that AEP has a number of advantages over MRA including the ease of the model to incorporate both types of variables which have an additive and a multiplicative effect on value. As a result the variable coefficients tend to have a realistic appearance which are more readily accepted by property owners/taxpayers.

The feedback system is not optimal in the sense of minimizing a pre-specified mathematical form. This is in contrast with regression analysis which seeks to fit an equation to data in order to minimize the sum of the squared errors.

Because AEP coefficients are continuously refined each time a sale is processed, it is considered that there is little likelihood of there being unexplainable year-to-year fluctuations in value estimates, a problem which can occur with MRA. Also, there is no need to store old sales data, since the prior year's formula can be easily updated using current sales. This feature makes it suitable in situations in which properties are not sold frequently or in large volumes.

Chapter reviews

The following section represents a brief summary review of each chapter included within the book. It is meant to focus on the main modelling techniques applied

11

and to highlight some of the problems which have been addressed by mass appraisal applications.

The chapter by Stevenson introduces two techniques which have been developed in response to the dynamic nature of the Hong Kong property market. They are regression based indexation and the reference assessment approach. Regression based indexation can have a wide based application provided there is sufficient data available; it is based upon the a priori assumption that the existing assessed value can be used to determine the new assessed value at a revaluation. The technique, as well as being applied as a predictive model, can be used to measure and analyse assessment equity as the previous assessed value is a variable within the model. The model based on multiple regression analysis operates to update the existing assessed value through the application of an index factor. The existing assessed value already represents an amalgam of property characteristics which have been modelled, estimated and weighted at a prior date. Therefore the assessed value can be easily updated by including a few major variables that can identify changing preferences or price movements over time.

The reference assessment approach is applicable when there are a significant number of similar properties located within the one building or within a geographical area. In the Hong Kong context there are substantial numbers of high rise residential apartments and offices which could be within predetermined homogeneous groups. The technique determines a reference assessment for a typical property within say one building and then using regression analysis determines percentage adjustments for the main differences between the reference assessment for example size, quality of accommodation, location, floor, presence of lift etc.

The chapter amply demonstrates the evolvement of specific techniques to meet the challenges of mass appraisal within a unique property environment.

McCluskey et al. in their chapter investigate the application of three mass appraisal techniques and evaluate their performance in terms of predictive accuracy. The techniques include multiple regression analysis, expert or rule induction system and artificial neural networks as applied to a data set of residential properties. In order to maintain consistency of analysis the dataset was randomly divided into two distinct subsets (on a 3:1 ratio). The larger subset was used to derive the models and the smaller holdout set was then used to test and verify the models. The results of all the models was broadly encouraging in terms of each's predictive accuracy. However, the best results were achieved by the artificial neural network (for which three different topologies were configured).

The artificial neural network approach has the advantage of modelling simplicity, in that, all the variables are used as multicollinearity is not a problem.

In fact, the greater the number of variables and data points the better, given that a neural network is as data hungry as multiple regression, but less constrained in terms of statistical assumptions. The neural network model is a robust, generalization technique but suffers from the lack of transparency or explainability. Unlike regression and rule induction models which have coefficients and rules neural networks have a series of hidden weight adjustments which cannot be easily translated to the layperson. This chapter highlights the future developing role of neural networks within the field of mass appraisal.

James focuses on the theoretical aspects of artificial intelligence and its application to mass appraisal. Machine learning technologies have a role to play within the mass appraisal community. Research into this area has only recently produced empirical evidence to support this. This chapter provides an in-depth investigation of artificial neural networks and explains the principles involved, network structure, topology and learning algorithms. In addition the author examines a further technique not as yet widely applied in real estate appraisal, that of Kohonen Self Organising Maps. As opposed to the supervised learning approach of back propagation the self organising maps applies unsupervised learning to resolve problems. The chapter highlights the potential application of this new breed of mass appraisal models derived from the machine learning environment.

An investigation of the potential for the application of a expert system for the property taxation of commercial and industrial property in Malaysia is undertaken in the chapter by Nawawi et al. The scope of the research is intended to cover office complexes, retail centres, shophouse/office/flat style properties and factories. The focus of the work is concentrated on knowledge elicitation from valuers, property managers and other building related experts, with the aim being to find those main attributes which affect the rental value of the properties. For example, location was determined as a main attribute and then first level sub-attributes of accessibility, siting, quality of neighbourhood etc. were derived. This process was completed for all the main property types. The next stage was to determine rental values of standard units based on the importance of the main attributes; a number of steps were involved with this (i) calculating a maximum score for each attribute, (ii) deriving a maximum score for each property as a percentage of the maximum score found in (i), (iii) applying regression analysis of rental value against the percentage derived in (ii) for each main attribute, (iv) calculating the hypothetical maximum rent.

The model is then used to predict the rental values which are checked against the actual rents. The authors have found that the use of point scores complement the expert's heuristic approach in selecting comparables and in making adjustments within the comparison process.

Pearce in her chapter provides an insight into the techniques applied by British Columbia Assessment Authority for the mass assessment of agricultural land.

13

The statistics amply demonstrate the size of the task undertaken. Approximately 6 million acres or 2.5% of the total land area of British Columbia is within land assessment. One of the real threats to agricultural land is highlighted i.e. the ever expansion of urban areas. Though not unique to British Columbia the threat of urbanism to high quality productive land is a world wide problem of immense scale. British Columbia's solution has been to establish an Agricultural Land Reserve (created in 1972) designed to protect the natural resource against the impact of urbanization. Another mechanism designed to preserve land is through preferential assessment policies.

Preferential assessment applies where the use of the land meets certain defined standards and also inherently recognises that a farming operation requires the use of larger proportions of land than other commercial activities. In essence the objectives of a farm assessment system as applied in British Columbia are (i) to implement a consistent approach to farm land classification and valuation, (ii) to support the family farm and (iii) to assist in the conservation and preservation of farm land. Preferential assessment requires land to be assessed in it's existing use notwithstanding that its Highest and Best use might be more valuable. This is particularly significant on the urban/rural fringe.

The key variables within the assessment system include soil characteristics, climatic conditions, topographical nature of the land and percentage of land within particular agricultural classes. It is accepted that the quality of the land is the logical foundation for equitable land assessment. To maintain fairness across assessments, the assessed value to sales value ratios are used.

With the chapter on Sweden, Sundquist focuses on the use of CAMA approaches in the appraisal of agricultural and forestry land. In Sweden the property tax is based on the assessed value which represents 75% of the market value of the subject property. One interesting feature of the tax system is the use made of 'rolling revaluations'. This approach involves valuing sectors of the property tax base at different times, for example in Sweden a year one revaluation would include apartment blocks, commercial buildings and industrial property, then two years later dwelling houses and holiday homes and a further two years later agricultural and forestry properties. This in effect means that each sector is regularly revalued on a six year cycle. During the intervening period the base value (assessed value) determined in the year of the revaluation is annually indexed to maintain relativity with open market values.

The main focus of this chapter has been to examine the mass valuation approach for agricultural and forestry land. Given the varying climatic conditions prevailing in Sweden resulting from its long length, the main approach adopted to the assessment of agricultural and forestry land reflects the problems of climate, accessibility, soil quality etc. The approach is based on the application of classes which represent varying levels of quality and productive capacity. Essentially

14

the mid-class is considered the average or the norm and if property is within a class on either side its assessed value is adjusted upwards or downwards accordingly.

For forestry land such factors as size (hectares), costs of production (transport, accessibility, type of terrain etc.) and types of trees are built into the econometric models. As with arable and pastoral land, forestry land is subdivided into five classes according to productive capability.

The application of GIS to data analysis and assessment has been considered a positive step forward in terms of achieving improved assessment uniformity and cost savings. The system is used to produce standard value maps for various districts known as valuation areas. These valuation areas would tend to include homogeneous properties within a specific geographical area. The chapter illustrates the role which GIS has to play within the assessment process and how it can assist in terms of data analysis and in measuring the spatial distribution of property values.

Given the federal system in Australia each state has been developing its own mass appraisal approach. Kirby considers the state of Queensland where a CAMA system has been in operation since 1981, developed to assist and support the change from a five year cycle to an annually based revaluation system. The basis of the system is designed around the identification of sub-market areas (SMAs), representing groupings of properties determined by geographical or physical features, and whose values will move similarly over time.

The CAMA algorithm applied to determine the new predicted value utilizes the 'old' value which is enhanced by the use of a factor multiplier. The 'new' value can be determined by one of four options available to the valuer, all of which are based on the additive effect of entering the 'old' values as independent variables. This approach is based on the assumption that the reassessed values can be easily determined by using the existing assessment as the base value. This assumption reflects the a priori condition that the existing assessment contains a great deal of useful information and therefore negates the need to continually develop new regression equations to determine the annual values, but rather only a factor to update the existing assessments.

The system's advantage is that it has proven to be cost effective and efficient in producing mass valuations. Current refinements include the linking of a GIS to the valuation system.

Valuation New Zealand has for several years been developing CAMA models; Pegler provides a review of the current state of the art in New Zealand. Research into mass appraisal in New Zealand has tended to focus on multiple regression analysis as the base statistical technique. Since 1979 MRA approaches have been widely used in determining capital values and improved values for residential property. Three separate regression based models have been designed.

15

Firstly, the Predict, which attempts to explain the variation in price by observed property characteristics. Secondly, the Index which examines the variation in the ratio of the sale price to the existing capital value, and thirdly, the ModIndex which is an amalgam of the variables used in the previous two techniques.

A further development has been to establish and value benchmark properties, against which other similar properties are compared in terms of actual and predicted values. In addition a system of indexation of values has been introduced to update both capital and land values. The index is simply the ratio of sale price divided by assessed value, and then applied across other similar properties.

Within New Zealand the application of CAMA has led to significant improvements in productivity, but it is also accepted that the role of the valuer is dominant in the process and not subservient to the CAMA system.

The approach to computer assisted mass appraisal in Tasmania has been towards the development of a proportionality model based upon multiple regression analysis. Research by Thomas has identified six categories of variables utilized in the model development, including, building characteristics, land factors, fiscal variables, neighbourhood characteristics and access variables. The generic model developed was based on the generic form of Price = Land Value + Building Value. From this basic form regression based additive and multiplicative models were determined including suitably transformed variables which best described the characteristics of the property market.

It was found that the proportionality model was suitable for both small and large heterogeneous neighbourhoods with low sales volumes. It represents a robust technique with distinct advantages over the more traditional regression approaches.

The chapter by Almy et al. provides a thorough analysis of mass appraisal and a review of some of the main techniques as applied in the United States. The chapter illustrates the application of the Base Home Approach (BHA) technique incorporating a case study from Arizona. In effect the technique operates to determine for each class of residential property a base home value, normally determined by regression analysis. From this value other properties can then be compared and differences reflected in the estimated value. The authors do note that the BHA represents no more than a repackaging of the regression model. What is highlighted however, is that the base home value represents a more stable reference value than the regression constant. The technique also, provides a more user friendly visualization of the results than MRA.

An interesting refinement in the model has been the determination of 'market areas' which constituted large geographical areas similar in terms of locational factors and market value. Each market area is then subdivided into smaller sub-areas; regression analysis is then used to determine a value for the sub-area.

The development of this approach has led to substantial improvements in equity and uniformity within the assessment process.

The second case study examined a further modelling refinement utilized within Cook County, Illinois i.e. determining neighbourhood linearized variables. A recognition of the explanatory effect of neighbourhoods on value resulted in capturing data used in the design of a linear desirability index based on average sales prices within neighbourhoods.

Within the chapter by Riley important issues concerning mass appraisal versus single property appraisal are addressed together with how they relate to the assessment of condominium properties. An interesting insight is given to the history and evolution of condominium development and ownership. Multiple regression analysis was the calibration model utilized to undertake the mass appraisal. The author examines in detail the advantages of integrated CAMA software in terms of efficiency, speed, performance and being able to test the quality of the results obtained. The case study investigated the valuation of some 3,463 condominium units. As some of the tables within the chapter demonstrate the number of variables collected for each unit was quite substantial. The model was derived from analysing 338 sales. The overall results achieved were encouraging in terms of coefficient of dispersion statistics.

The chapter by Ten Have et al. examines advances in mass appraisal that have been taking place in the Netherlands. Each of the main municipalities (Amsterdam, The Hague, Rotterdam and Utrecht) have independently developed their own CAMA systems. Somewhat unique to the Netherlands is the Multiple Listing System which has some 2,300 members, all of which provide transaction based data, which is assimilated within a mainframe database system, and which forms the basis of the CAMA system. The model used is a hedonic model calibrated by using multiple regression analysis.

In view of the large differences between regional housing markets, the country has been subdivided into a number of sub-areas of fairly homogeneous properties. The method employed in segmenting the properties is related to the selling prices and other characteristics. The groups of properties are continually broken down until a group of almost identical properties remain. The number of sub-divisions is limitless in terms of adequately describing the range of properties.

The algorithm used in assessing the value of the properties is based upon the 'closest' comparable. The data set base is interrogated to collate those comparable properties whose characteristics are the most similar to the subject being valued. MRA is then used to determine the predicted value of the subject property based on the range of closest comparables.

The challenges for the Singapore Valuation Authority (SVA) in developing a mass appraisal system are somewhat unique, being related to the extreme volatility of the property market. Leng illustrates the developments in applying mass appraisal techniques within a dynamic real estate market. Rapid economic and social changes in association with quickly changing property values created problems in maintaining a valuation list which is up-to-date. In view of these rather unique circumstances the SVA in choosing a mass appraisal system considered that the more established multiple regression models were not feasible. This conclusion was based on the increased likely costs involved in collecting and maintaining a detailed database, higher administrative costs and the need to regularly update coefficients to reflect new factors and changing market conditions.

The approach adopted was a much more modest and robust technique based on categorising property into specific groups and then to further segment them into sub-market groups (SMGs). The main groups decided were as follows, high-rise public residential apartments; high-rise private residential apartments, factories, warehouses and offices; private residential houses, landed factories, warehouses and shops; and others (hospitals, land etc.). The CAMA system in recognition of the valuers expert knowledge of market behaviour, stratified the main groups into SMGs (currently there are 341 SMGs). For each SMG a common base value or rate is determined, usually calculated by reference to a benchmark property, which is valued in the normal way. A relativity factor is then determined for the SMG which would reflect physical factors, economic criteria and expressed as a percentage of the base value. The basic formula is then simply;

> Estimated annual value equals the base value of the SMG multiplied by the relativity factor and multiplied by the floor area of the subject.

Given the simplicity of this mass valuation approach, all properties can be reviewed annually with less need to undertake ad-hoc reassessments.

Conclusions

From this brief international review of mass appraisal techniques it is clearly evident the importance placed on computer assisted approaches to ad valorem taxation. Since the 1940s with advances in computer hardware and software significant gains have been made in improving the assessment function for property taxation. CAMA systems are now well within the financial budgets of the smallest jurisdictions and countries. Equally important is the research being undertaken to improve systems and algorithms. This has resulted in new methodological approaches such as adaptive estimation procedure (feedback), artificial intelligence applications for example, artificial neural networks, expert systems and case based reasoning.

18

Mass appraisal systems by in large originated within the science of econometric modelling with the application of multiple regression techniques. Renshaw's (1958) work is often attributed as being the start of experimentations with MRA to appraisal problems. Hedonic models are representative of the characteristics of value in terms of the property attributes. By using statistically based analytical techniques such as regression, the effect on value of independent variables can be isolated which assists the explanation of value. The coefficients of each predictor variable can be tested for significance and the derived model can then be used to predict value. Such value predictions can then be tested by the application of parametric and non-parametric techniques to validate the model in terms of quality and performance.

As one would expect multiple regression applications in all the various forms remain the cornerstone of most mass appraisal systems reviewed in this book. The following countries utilize regression within their systems Hong Kong with regard to regression indexing, the United States in relation to standard regression models (additive, multiplicative and hybrid) and also as the basis of the base home technique, Australia, British Columbia, Sweden, New Zealand and the Netherlands.

The relatively less common techniques are still used to significant effect. Tasmania applies a proportionality model which in many respects is a hybrid model based on feedback with regression components Research in Malaysia is focused on applying an expert system and Northern Ireland is researching the application of artificial neural networks.

Several countries have recognised the importance of utilizing the 'old' assessed value as a predictor variable in terms of determining the 'new' value. Important information is contained within the 'old' value which can be applied to either index or update to derive the 'new' value. Currently Singapore, Australia and Hong Kong successfully apply this approach. Interestingly, these three countries have property tax systems which are more frequently updated than most other countries i.e. annually or at least every three years without delays, and in addition, by regularly indexing values the volatility of property markets, as in Hong Kong and Singapore can be quickly built into the ad valorem tax system.

It has long been recognised that mass appraisal techniques are better equipped to analyse and appraise large groups of homogeneous properties. Variability within property types can be modelled successfully but enhanced performance can be obtained if property is segmented or stratified. The benefit of mass valuing property located within small market groups (SMGs) has been recognised within the Netherlands, Australia, Singapore, Northern Ireland and United States. The mechanisms in determining the SMG is largely dependant upon physical characteristics of the properties and locational factors.

Linked to the last paragraph the application of geographic information systems has been making a significant impact within the mass appraisal environment.

SMGs based on geographic similarities can be effectively modelled within a GIS framework enhancing analytical capabilities. The GIS approach can be used to monitor value shifts within regions, to create value maps or value based contours, and to research distance related variables in a spatial setting. Mass appraisal systems which are utilizing GIS include Sweden, British Columbia and Australia.

This concluding section is not meant to be totally comprehensive in its analysis of the various country contributions, but rather to highlight the state of the art in relation to computer assisted mass appraisal systems and techniques. From an international perspective there is a growing trend in the application of mass appraisal within property tax systems. There are added benefits in having such computer assisted approaches including the obvious of mass valuing, but also data analysis, quality control, administrative, financial and economic efficiency arguments, as well as recognising that the future does not rest in manually based valuation systems. Notwithstanding that, mass appraisal models are tools which assist the valuer and complement his other appraisal skills. They equip him with the technical ability to perform his job more efficiently whilst also recognising that it is he who must stand up to defend the assessments before the taxpayer, valuation tribunal or court.

References

Mass appraisal

Cook, C.C. (1985), *The Future of Software for the Property Tax and Mass Appraisal*, paper presented at the Second World Congress on Computer Assisted Valuation, Lincoln Institute of Land Policy, Massachusetts.

Eckert, J.; Dotson, M. and Gloudemans, R (1983), 'Computer Assisted Appraisal Systems' in *Legends of CAMA*, Lincoln Institute of Land Policy, Massachusetts.

Gustafson, R.H. (1985), *An Introduction to Computer Assisted Mass Appraisal: Elements of a CAMA System*, paper presented at the Second World Congress on Computer Assisted Valuation, Lincoln Institute of Land Policy, Massachusetts.

Jensen, D.L. (1983), 'Alternative Modelling Techniques in Computer Assisted Mass Appraisal' in *Legends of CAMA*, Lincoln Institute of Land Policy, Massachusetts.

Jensen, D.L. (1983), 'Coping with Abnormally Large Sales Data Bases in Computer Assisted Mass Appraisal' in *Legends of CAMA*, Lincoln Institute of Land Policy, Massachusetts.

Multiple regression analysis

Bland, R.L. (1984), 'The Implicit Price of Housing Attributes: An Explication and Application of the Theory to Mass Appraisal Research' *Property Tax Journal*, vol. 3.

Borst, R and McCluskey, W.J. (1996), *An Evaluation of Multiple Regression Analysis, Comparable Sales Analysis and Artificial Neural Networks for the Mass Appraisal of Residential Properties in Northern Ireland*, paper presented at IAAO Conference in Assessment Administration, Houston, United States.

Brown, R.J. (1974), 'On the Selection of the Best Predictive Model in Multiple Regression Analysis', *The Appraisal Journal*, vol. 42.

Cannaday, R.E. (1989), 'How Should You Estimate and Provide Market Support for Adjustments in Single Family Appraisals?', *The Real Estate Appraiser & Analyst*, Winter.

Dilmore, G. (1974), 'Appraising Houses', *The Real Estate Appraiser*, July-August.

Eckert, J.K. (1990), *Property Appraisal and Assessment Administration*, IAAO, Chicago.

Eisenlauer, J.F. (1968), 'Mass versus Individual Appraisals', *The Appraisal Journal*, October.

Fibbens, M. (1995), 'Australian Rating and Taxing: Mass Appraisal Practice', *Journal of Property Tax Assessment & Administration*, vol. 1 no. 3.

Fraser, R.R. and Blackwell, F.M. (1988), 'Comparable Selection and Multiple Regression in Estimating Real Estate Value: An Empirical Study', *Journal of Valuation*, vol. 7 no. 3.

Gibson, B. (1989), 'Computer Assisted Mass Appraisal of Rural Property in New Zealand', *New Zealand Valuers' Journal*, June.

Gloudemans, R.J. and Miller, D.W. (1978), 'Multiple Regression Analysis Applied to Residential Properties: A Study of Structural Relationships Over Time', *Decision Sciences*, vol. 7.

Handley, J. (1987), 'A Case Study of Mass Computer Assisted Valuation', *The Valuer*, January.

IAAO, (1978), *Improving Real Property Assessment: A Reference Manual*, International Association of Assessing Officers, Chicago.

Jackson, M. (1991), 'Regression Analysis Application to Rental Assessments in Dunedin', *New Zealand Valuers' Journal*, March.

Jensen, D.L. (1983), 'Constrained Regression Analysis in Computer Assisted Mass Appraisal' in *Legends of CAMA*, Lincoln Institute of Land Policy, Massachusetts.

Jensen, D.L. (1983), 'The Use of Multiple Linear Regression in Residential Land Valuation' in *Legends of CAMA*, Lincoln Institute of Land Policy, Massachusetts.

Lockwood, A.J. (1985), 'Computer Assisted Valuations - Further Model Developments', *The Valuer*, July.

Lockwood, A.J. and Reynolds, W.J. (1992), 'Computer Assisted Valuations', *The Valuer & Land Economist*.

Mark, J.H. and Goldberg, M.A. (1988), 'Multiple Regression Analysis: A Review of the Issues', *The Appraisal Journal*, vol. 56, pp. 89-109.

McCluskey, W.J. and Adair, A (1994), 'Assessment Techniques and Advances in Mass Appraisal for Property Taxation' in Franzsen, R.C.D. (ed.),*Regional and Local Taxation in a Future South Africa*, Centre for Human Rights, University of Pretoria, South Africa.

Meacham, A. (1988), 'Applying Regression Analysis to Real Estate Appraisals', *The Real Estate Appraiser and Analyst*, Summer.

Miller, N.G. (1982), 'Residential Property Hedonic Pricing Models: A Review', in Sirmans, C.F. (ed.), *Research in Real Estate*, vol. 2.

Millington, A. (1994), *An Introduction to Property Valuation*, 4th edition, Estates Gazette Ltd, London.

Pendelton, W. (1965), 'Statistical Inference in Appraisal and Assessment Procedures', *The Appraisal, Journal*, January.

Renshaw, E.F. (1958), 'Scientific Appraisal', *National Tax Journal*, December.

Smeltzer, M.V. (1986), 'The Application of Multi-Linear Regression Analysis and Correlation to the Appraisal of Real Estate', *The Appraisal Review*, vol. 28.

Stenehjem, E. (1974), 'A Scientific Approach to the Mass Appraisal of Residential Property', in *Automated Mass Appraisal of Real Property*, IAAO, Chicago.

Administration, IAAO, Chicago.

Wise, J.O. and Dover, H.J. (1974), 'An Evaluation of a Statistical Method of Appraisal of Rural Property', *The Appraisal Journal*, January.

Rule based systems

Bonnet, A.; Haton, J.P. and Truong-Ngoc, J.M. (1988), *Expert Systems: Principles and Practice*, Prentice Hall, UK.

Boyle, C. (1984), 'An Expert System of Valuation of Residential Properties', *Journal of Valuation*, vol. 2 no. 3.

Kidd, A. and Welbank, M. (1984), *Knowledge Acquisition Expert Systems: State of the Art* Report 12:7, Pergamon Infotech Ltd., Oxford.

Nawawi, A.H. and Gronow, S.A. (1991), 'Expert Systems in Rating Valuation', *Journal of the Society of Surveying Technicians*, vol. 18 no. 6.

Nawawi, A.H., Gronow, S.A. and Hizam, R.B. (1993), 'The Role of an Expert System in Rating Valuation of Commercial Properties in Malaysia', *Journal of the Institute of Surveyors*.

Case based reasoning

Barletta, R (1991), An Introduction to Case Based Reasoning, *A I Expert*, vol. 6, August.

Kolodner, J.L. (1993), *Case Based Learning*, Kluwer Academic Publishers.

O'Roarty, B. (1996), *A Critical Assessment of the Rental Valuation of Retail Property*, Unpublished DPhil Thesis, University of Ulster, Northern Ireland.

Watson, I. and Mari, F. (1994), 'Case-based Reasoning: A Review', *Knowledge Engineering Review*, vol. 9 no. 4.

Comparable sales analysis

Borst, R and McCluskey, W.J. (1996), *An Evaluation of Multiple Regression Analysis, Comparable Sales Analysis and Artificial Neural Networks for the Mass Appraisal of Residential Properties in Northern Ireland*, paper presented at IAAO Conference in Assessment Administration, Houston, United States.

Detweiler, J.H. and Radigan, R.E. (1996), 'Computer Assisted Real Estate Appraisal: A Tool for the Practising Appraiser', *The Appraisal Journal*, January.

Diaz, J. (1990), 'The Process of Selecting Comparable Sales', *The Appraisal Journal*, October.

Fraser, R.R. and Blackwell, F.M. (1988), 'Comparable Selection and Multiple Regression in Estimating Real Estate Value: An Empirical Study', *Journal of Valuation*, vol. 7 no. 3.

Gau, G.W.; Tsong-Yue Lai and Ko Wang (1992), 'Optimal Comparable Selection and Weighting in Real Property Valuation: An Extension', *Journal of American Real Estate Urban Economics Association*, vol. 20 no. 1.

Moliver, D. and Boronico, J. (1996), 'Unit Selection and the Sales Comparison Approach', *Journal of Property Valuation & Investment*, vol. 14 no. 5.

Shenkel, W.M. and Eidson, A.S. (1971), 'Comparable Sales Retrieval Systems', *The Appraisal Journal*, October.

Skaff, M.S. (1975), 'The Search for Comparable Sales: A New Approach', *Assessors Journal*, April.

Tchira, A. (1979), 'Comparable Sales Selection - A Computer Approach', *The Appraisal Journal*, January.

Vandell, K.D. (1991), 'Optimal Comparable Selection and Weighting in Real Property Valuation: An Extension', *Journal of American Real Estate Urban Economics Association*, vol. 19 no. 2.

Feedback references

Carbone, R. and Longini, R (1977), 'A Feedback Model for Automated Real Estate Assessment', *Management Science*, vol. 24 no. 3.

IAAO, (1978), *Improving Real Property Assessment: A Reference Manual*, International Association of Assessing Officers, Chicago.

Schreiber, J (1985), 'A Feedback Primer' in Woolery, A. and Shea, S. (eds), *Introduction to Computer Assisted Valuation*, Oelgeschlager, Gunn and Hain, United States.

Sauter, B. (1985), *Solving today's Computer Assisted Valuation Issues using the Adaptive Estimation Procedure and Bayesian Regression*, paper presented at the Second World Congress on Computer Assisted Valuation, Lincoln Institute of Land Policy, Massachusetts.

Whitted, M.E. and Opfer, W.A. (1993), *AEP - An Alternative Market Approach*, paper presented at Conference on Assessment Administration, IAAO, Chicago.

Artificial neural networks

Borst, R.A. (1995), 'Artificial Neural Networks in Mass Appraisal', *Journal of Property Tax Assessment & Administration*, vol. 1 no. 2.

Borst, R.A. and McCluskey, W.J. (1996), 'Artificial Neural Networks' in Flaherty, J.; Lombardo, R; Morgan, P and De Silva, B (eds), Quantitative Methods in Property, Royal Melbourne Institute of Technology, Australia.

Borst, R and McCluskey, W.J. (1996), *An Evaluation of Multiple Regression Analysis, Comparable Sales Analysis and Artificial Neural Networks for the Mass Appraisal of Residential Properties in Northern Ireland*, paper presented at IAAO Conference in Assessment Administration, Houston, United States.

Do, A.Q and Grudnitski, G. (1992), 'A Neural Network Approach to Residential Property Appraisal', *The Real Estate Appraiser*, December 1992.

Evans, A., James, H. and Collins, A. (1995), 'Artificial Neural Networks: An Application to Residential Valuation in the UK', *Journal of Property Tax Assessment & Administration*, vol. 1 no. 3.

Gevarter, W.B (1985), *Intelligent Machines*, Prentice Hall Inc., Englewood Cliffs, NJ.

McCluskey, W.J. (1996), 'Predictive Accuracy of Machine Learning Models for the Mass Appraisal of Residential Property', *New Zealand Valuers' Journal*, July, pp. 41-47.

McCluskey, W.J.; Dyson, K.; McFall, D. and Anand, S. (1996), 'Mass Appraisal for Property Taxation: An Artificial Intelligence Approach', *Australian Land*

Economics Review, vol. 2 no. 1 pp. 25-32.

Tay, D.P. and Ho, D.K. (1994), 'Intelligent Mass Appraisal', *Journal of Property Tax Assessment & Administration*, vol. 1 no. 1.

Worzala, E., Lenk, M. and Silva, A. (1995), 'An Exploration of Neural Networks and its Application to Real Estate Valuation', *The Journal of Real Estate Research*, vol. 10 no. 2.

2 The use of mass appraisal techniques for rating valuation in Hong Kong

R. Stevenson

Introduction

The following discussion centres on two valuation techniques used in Hong Kong, the Regression Based Indexation and the Reference Assessment Approach. Regression Indexing has widespread application to the valuation of many types of property providing that there is sufficient market evidence available. It is based on the assumption that there is a significant amount of information embedded in the existing rateable or taxable value, and that regression analysis can be used to satisfactorily update these values. Building in Hong Kong is dominated by high-rise, multi-unit development. The Reference Assessment approach is suitable for application where there are a number of similar, related assessments, e.g. many assessments within a common building or development. Due to physical proximity and similarity, the relationship between these assessments must be carefully considered, and changes in relative values need to be strictly controlled. Both Regression Indexing and the Reference Approach can have significant valuation productivity, accuracy and data minimization advantages.

Historical development

In Hong Kong the basis of the property tax[1] or 'rates', is the annual rental value. The imposition of rates in Hong Kong based on rental value, dates back to 1845. They were originally introduced to pay for a police force, but later, additional rates were levied to pay for street lighting, water and a fire brigade. Rates now have a wider purpose, contributing to both central and local government revenue. Rateable values will also play a part in the resumption of sovereignty by China. Virtually all private land in Hong Kong is held on long leases from the

27

Government, many of which are due to expire in 1997. Under the Joint Declaration on the Future of Hong Kong, these leases will be renewed for 50 years, subject to the payment of ground rents at 3% of 'rateable' (i.e. rental) value, which includes the contribution from both land and improvement elements.

The Hong Kong Government Rating & Valuation Department also has a Capital Valuation role in the real property transfer tax process. All sale prices are scrutinised by the department, and stamp duty or transfer tax is levied on the actual sale price, or on the capital valuation if the price is deemed to be low.

Both the rental (rateable) valuation and capital (sale price) valuation involve computer assisted valuation processing.

Need for computerization

Hong Kong has experienced high economic growth rates, and this has led to a significant increase in the Department's workload.

Table 2.1
Major changes in workload & values 1981-94

1 April	No. of Assessments	New Entries	Deletions	Stamp Duty Valuations	Rateable Value (million)	Rates Revenue HK$ (million)
1981	604,426	53,009	7,313	43,600	12,307	1,491
1994	1,338,475	70,965	10,950	154,586	257,146	12,625
	+121%	+34%	+50%	+254%		

The increases in volume of work between 1981 and 1994 are shown in brackets. The total number of assessments affects the size of the 3 yearly revaluation or reappraisal exercises (+121%). Recurrent annual work consists of new entries (+34%), deletions (+50%), and capital or sale price valuations for stamp duty (+254%). It is difficult to precisely compare staffing levels in 1981 with those in 1994 because of changing functions. In broad terms, the total number of staff has increased less than 15% yet the workload has risen significantly.

History of computerization

The first computer system was implemented in April 1971. The valuation process was still manual. The computer system was initially administrative and used for rates billing and collection, and was part of a central Treasury bureau service. In

1981, the system was rewritten to facilitate the automatic payment of rates through the banking system (autopay), and provide an on-line enquiry service. A limited, or ad hoc, computer assisted valuation capability was first developed for the 1984 revaluation. In 1986 a comprehensive computer assisted valuation system was incorporated to assess rateable (rental) values for most residential, office and industrial properties. The new valuation system was based on the concept of nominating a representative or reference assessment within each multi unit building. The statistical processing was done via SPSS on a government mainframe bureau service.

Current computer development

In 1992 a system was implemented to automate the entry of new rating assessments and provide computer assistance for capital valuations relating to the transfer tax on real property sales. The computer assisted valuation process for estimating sale prices exploits the data that has been collected for the rental based property tax. Tables were set up for all lots, streets, and buildings. The relational data base is ORACLE with the statistical processing in SAS. This began the transition from a COBOL based index sequential file to a relational data base.

The main business problems were that data was fragmented over a number of systems. The underlying data encompassed a database of property values and characteristics, property and billing addresses, occupiers' names and property market information on stock, supply sale prices and rents. The system was difficult to change, and fortnightly batch updating led to difficulties in controlling workflow. The Rating and Valuation data is a major component in a modern land information system, and it is critical that it can be adapted to handle a variety of demands and changes in property tax administration.

In 1993 a comprehensive Information System review was completed and approved. The review recommended the concept of a central on-line property master relating to a number of valuation related systems:

• Revaluation

• Entry and Analysis of Rents (which form the basis for rateable values)

• Forecasting Future Property Supply

• Forecasting Rates Revenue

• Rates Billing and Collection

- Capital Valuation for Property Transfer Tax on Sale Price

- Property Market Analysis (price and rental indices etc.)

A central property database shares information between systems, and eliminates duplication. While this reduces storage, a more important advantage is that it eliminates duplicate maintenance thus facilitating data integrity. If information is duplicated in different systems there is a danger that it will become inconsistent. Modern data bases with fourth generation programming tools are relatively efficient to programme, and more easily adapted as the business problem changes.

Data base system

The new Property Master is a relational data base management system (ORACLE). The production platform when fully assembled will comprise a data server HP H70 with 450 M/byte memory, three HP H50 applications systems, a total of more than 60 G/bytes of storage and some 330 terminals. Most terminal access will be accomplished with PC emulation on a Local Area Network (LAN). Chinese language software will also be installed to facilitate Chinese character display. Initial public access will be via interactive voice systems for automatic telephone enquiry on rates payment information. The statistical processing is via SAS on a SUN 10 platform. All major data and applications systems are UNIX based, with the PC front end using DOS or Windows.

Scope of computer assisted valuation activity

Hong Kong's computer assisted valuation activity centres on:

- rating, which is based on rents,

- scrutiny of sale prices in respect to the property transfer tax (Stamp Duty), and

- assessment and entry of new properties.

In Hong Kong, there are typically 80,000 new entries a year with an offset of approximately 11,000 deletions. It is therefore appropriate to apply computerization to ensure efficient initial entry of property characteristics, payment details, and calculation of property values.

Revising rateable values

Properties are currently revalued every three years. The philosophy is to have a common reference date for all properties in Hong Kong, and to issue all valuations at the same time. Separate rates percentage charges are applied within the Urban Council and Regional Council jurisdictions. The Urban Council Area basically encompasses Hong Kong Island and Kowloon and the Regional Council Area covers the balance of the territory which includes rural areas and the many outlying islands.[2] Agricultural land is exempt from assessment to rates, and indigenous villagers are exempt from payment of rates on their dwellings.

Work distribution

The decision to adopt a common reference date and to revalue all properties en masse has major implications. It is necessary to process and revalue all property types and districts, within a limited time. It would not be practical to achieve this manually. Computer assistance is applied to both the entry and analysis of rental evidence, and the setting and adjusting of new values for the relevant sub-populations of properties to be valued.

Valuation cycle

The major ongoing or current work relates to assessing new properties to rates, and the scrutiny of sales in respect to the property transfer tax. Even the 3 yearly revaluation load is not as cyclical as it first appears. Year 1 is the revaluation, Year 2 involves issuing the new values and dealing with appeals or objections. Year 3 activities relate to planning for the next revaluation, and court work for the complex appeal cases.

Philosophy and rationale for computerization

The principal tool for Computer Assisted Mass Appraisal (CAMA) is multiple regression analysis. Predictive variables such as quality, size, age, etc., are gathered for all properties to be valued. Rents or sales details are also entered for those properties recently sold or rented. Rental based regression models are generated for the rating application while sale price models are produced for Stamp Duty purposes. The regression models identify and quantify those attributes that affect value and these relationships are then applied to estimate values for all relevant properties.

One objective is to minimize both the number and subjectivity of predictive variables. The mathematical model form is only an approximation of the value determination process. There are limitations and bias in the samples of market data, on which the models are based. For example certain property types may be under-represented.

The methodology should be understood by the property valuer or appraiser and ideally support the approach that they would take. The reasons for this are to maintain staff acceptance, and to use their knowledge to critically examine not only the end result, the estimate of value, but also the treatment of particular factors within the model, e.g. how the model adjusts sale or rental value estimates for time, age or size. Staff can override the computer assisted valuation estimates, and can adjust the treatment for factors such as adjustment for time and discounts for size in the application of the predictive models.

In defending valuations the test is whether a particular value is fair and reasonable. The supporting evidence is based on appropriate, direct, comparisons from the property market and not arcane mathematical formulae.

Difficulties in applying CAMA to high-rise buildings

There are few single family residential houses in Hong Kong. The property tax valuation problem is dominated by high-rise residential, office and factory buildings, and typically there are many assessments or occupations in each building.

Increased focus on relative values

Single family house characteristics and values generally vary within a neighbourhood. Even when one particular developer has undertaken all the construction there are variations in materials, design, layout, orientation and access. Relative differences in the property values of adjacent assessments are therefore expected and emanate for a number of reasons. Minor random variations in value estimates arising from inappropriate interaction or extrapolation effects in regression or feedback models are somewhat masked by the variance in property attributes. However units within large high-rise apartment buildings are more homogeneous, and relative differences in values are more apparent. If individual high-rise unit values are based directly on regression models that include significant effects for floor level and size etc., then even minor random variation in relative values due to extrapolation, multi-collinearity or sample bias could be unacceptable. Within homogeneous high-rise buildings, value adjustments need to be tightly controlled.

Market evidence difficulties

There may be no rents or prices relating to particular units or influences in a building. Yet many value adjustments may have to be made, and it is necessary to have a precise reference for these relative adjustments.

Adopting a reference assessment in each building

The solution in Hong Kong has been to identify a reference assessment in most multi-unit or multi-assessment buildings and to tightly control the intra-building variation in assessment values. The reference approach generates values for 1.105 million assessments and reduces the number of major valuation decisions to the 20,432 buildings or reference assessments.

Table 2.2
Distribution of assessments & buildings in Hong Kong
(as at March 1995)

	Domestic	Shops & Commercial	Offices	Factories	Parking	Other	Overall
Reference Approach							
Assessments	943,118	24,467	55,567	81,832			1,104,984
Buildings	17,484	343	1,353	1,252			20,432
Assessments per Building	54	71	41	65			54
Non Reference Approach	52,057	80,495	42	1,191	121,347	33,231	288,263
Total Assessments	995,175	104,962	55,609	83,023	121,347	33,231	1,393,347

Alternative techniques - base home approach

The Hong Kong problem in valuing assessments within a development is similar to that addressed by Ward (1981) and Gloudemans (1982) in respect to condominium and town house valuations. However the Reference Assessment Approach adopts a specific assessment within the building and not a notional average. In the Reference Approach, effects are tightly controlled within the building and not automatically determined by the model; it is a formula approach, and is not necessarily tied to regression analysis.

33

The reference assessment approach

A reference assessment (unit) is identified within each building (domestic, office or factory).

Within buildings

The relative value difference between this reference assessment and each other assessment in the building is expressed in ± % terms. The relative % adjustments are broken into 3 types:

1   Discounts for size or Quantity Allowance (QA%) are separately identified.

2   Other influences are combined into a Composite Adjustment % (CA%).

3   Non-main floor area or ancillary value items are expressed as a % (AV%).

Within districts

Market evidence is analysed and an appropriate $m² rental value rate is applied to each building's reference assessment.

Within building valuation formula

The $m² rental valuation rate that is applied to the reference assessment in each building, can be estimated manually or through various CAMA techniques. But the value pattern for assessments or units within the building are set by the formula in (1) below.

$$RV_i = \$m^2 \times \text{Main Floor Area} \times (1 \pm QA\% \pm CA\% + AV\%) \tag{1}$$

where
RV_i =   Rateable Value for the *ith* assessment in the building
$QA\%$ =   Quantity Allowance % (size discount)
$CA\%$ =   Composite Adjustment % (net effect(s) of general influences)
$AV\%$ =   Ancillary Value % (balcony, roof area etc.)
$\$m^2$ = $ per square metre rental rate applied to the reference assessment (normally estimated via regression analysis)

All % adjustments are relative to the reference assessment and by definition $QA\% = CA\% = 0$ for the reference unit.

General influences - composite adjustments (CA%)

There are a wide variety of influences within a building e.g. view, absence of lift (elevator) service, problems with position or aspect such as poor outlook, proximity to motorway ramp, roof top with solar-heat-gain problems in summer etc. Instead of capturing these via a matrix of fixed variables, an alternative is to express these as a net composite ± % adjustment, and then describe each using free-format remark(s).

Example : Top floor flat with view (+10%) but without lift service (-7.5%)

Composite %   =   CA% = (+10% - 7.5%) = +2.5%

Stored Fields

CA%   =   +2.5%
Remarks   =   'View + 10%, No Lift - 7.5%'

These 'Composite %' adjustments are usually stable for a number of reappraisal cycles.

Under the new data entry system there will be a very comprehensive temporary set of standard adjustment factors for each unit. Appendix 2.1 lists approximately 120 different standard adjustments. Staff will assign an appropriate % to the applicable adjustments. The system will then sum these into a single composite % and also concatenate and compile the General Remarks. Staff can also incorporate nonstandard factors in the composite %, and also describe these in the Remarks field. When the new rateable values are finalised, the comprehensive temporary set of adjustments will be deleted and only the aggregated CA% and Remarks will be retained.

Discount for size or quantity allowance (QA%)

Size discounts may change between reappraisals. If this size discount or quantity allowance (QA%) is separately identified in the valuation formula then it can be automatically modified. Figure 2.1 shows a typical range of discounts for commercial and industrial property that might prevail during a market cycle.

General micro-economic theory would suggest a discount for quantity. A minor discount for size (coeff. = -0.05) would indicate a rising market and a shortage of space. A normal balance between supply and demand might be indicated by coefficients of around -0.12, and in a falling market deep discounts may appear (coeff. = -0.20). However when supply is limited and vacancy rates are low, tenants requiring a large amount of space may have to pay a premium i.e. in some circumstances there could be a premium for larger sized units. From a system's design standpoint the approach to size discounts should be flexible and easily effected.

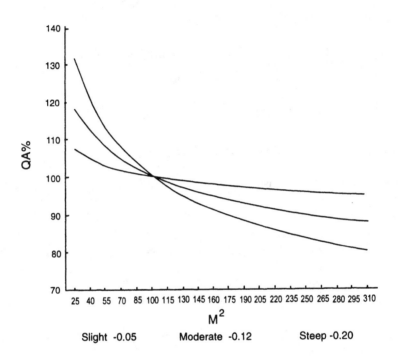

Figure 2.1
Typical range of size discounts (100 m² standard)

Estimating size discounts

Regression analysis can be used to estimate the relationship between rents and floor area. Linear and non-linear model forms and transformations can be tested to find the best fit. Other major predictor variables should be included to explain 'non size' effects and a careful check should be kept on variables that have a high correlation with floor area. The following equation (2) is of the log on log form and analyses Grade A office rents in the Tsim Sha Tsui district (on the peninsula opposite Hong Kong Island).

Model form

$$\text{Ln Rent } \$m^2 = a + b_1 X_1 + b_2 \text{ Ln } X_2 + b_3 X_3 + b_4 X_4 + b_5 \text{ Ln} \qquad (2)$$
per month

Table 2.3
Regression coefficients

Predictor Variables	B (Slope)	T	Correlation with Ln Floor Area
X_1 = Superior Location (0, 1)	0.27	14.6	0.066
X_2 = Year Built (Ln)	1.38	19.1	0.078
X_3 = District 212 & 214 (0, 1)	-0.18	-12.1	0.093
X_4 = Jan - Mar (0, 1)	0.11	7.2	0.019
X_5 = Floor Area (Ln)	-0.06	-6.3	1.000
a = Constant	-0.79	-2.7	

$R^2 = 0.52$ Std error = 0.156   Overall F = 174.4
Degree of Freedom - Regression = 5   Residual = 654

In these multiplicative models the coefficient (slope) for a continuous variable can be interpreted as an elasticity, thus a 10% increase in floor area results in approximately a 0.06 percent decrease in $\$m^2$ rent (rent per sq. metre per month).

Producing a quantity allowance schedule

The coefficient estimated for floor area in Table 2.3 above (-0.06) can be converted into a district schedule format based on say a 100 m^2 standard.

$$\text{QA\% for District} = \frac{(\text{Actual area} \div 100 \text{ m}^2)^b}{100 \text{ m}^2 \text{ standard}} \qquad (3)$$

where b = slope calculated in a generalized log on log model as per (2) above.

For example the 25m^2 QA% in Table 2.4 is calculated as follows:

$$\text{Discount QA\% @ 25m}^2 = (25/100)^{-0.06} = 1.087 = 1.09 = +9\%$$

A 25m² unit would be valued at +9% per m² more than a standard 100m² unit (assuming all factors except size were identical).

Table 2.4

Quantity allowance (size discount)

(Coefficient = -0.06 - 100 m² standard)

Floor Area	QA%
25	1.09
50	1.04
75	1.02
100	1.00
150	0.98
200	0.96
250	0.95
300	0.94
350	0.93

Calculating the QA% within the building

The size or quantity discount is initially estimated from rental evidence on a district basis for a particular property grouping. The slope is then re-centred (QA% = 0%) to the size of the particular reference assessment in each building. A relative QA% adjustment would be calculated for each assessment.

Example: if the district size discount in Table 2.3 is used then the coefficient for X_5, Floor Area, is -0.06. If the reference assessment in a particular building is 150m² in size, and the subject assessment in the building is 75m², the QA is 0% for the reference assessment (by definition) and QA = +4.2% for the smaller 75m² assessment $((75/150 - 0)^{-0.06} = 1.042 = + 4.2\%)$.

	m²	QA%
Reference Assessment	150	0%
Subject Assessment	75	+4.2%

Ancillary value (AV%)

Some assessments have ancillary items such as balconies, side roofs, top roofs, which could be open, enclosed or partly enclosed to a variety of standards. The value of these items can also be expressed as a simple % relative to the value of the main accommodation.

Ancillary value formula

$$AV\% = \frac{\text{\$ Lump Sum value of the ancillary item}}{\text{Subject Asst Main floor area x Reference Asst. \$m}^2} \qquad (4)$$

Example: Top Roof of 12.5 m² is valued at ½ the main rate.

$ Lump Sum for the top roof of the subject asst.
(12.5 m² x $80)/2   = $500

Main floor area of the subject asst.   = 50m²

$m² Rent applicable to the reference asst.   = $80 m²

$$\text{Ancillary Value \%} = \frac{\$500}{50 \text{ m}^2 \text{ x \$80 per m}^2} = 12.5\% \qquad (5)$$

Stored database fields

The database record of these calculations would be a numeric AV% field and an alpha numeric free format remarks field.

(a)   AV%   = 12.5
(b)   Remarks   = 'Top Roof, 12.5m² @ ½ Main $Rate'

Assumptions

The conversion of the $ lump sum to a percentage assumes that the value of the ancillary item will change at the same rate as the value of the main assessment. Normally these ancillary items do not comprise a high proportion of the total value (typically less than 20%), and this is a reasonable approach. There is also a facility to list unusually high or low %'s for review.

Parking value

The rental value attributable to a parking space is separately identified as a lump sum. It is not stated as a % relative to the units value in terms reference, because parking values and main accommodation values can change at different rates.

Applying the reference assessment approach

Step 1   Estimate the Reference Assessment Value

Regression techniques are used to estimate the $m^2 per month rental value ($m^2 Reference Rate) for the reference assessment within each building.

Step 2   Adjust the Reference Rate for Other Units

The $m^2 rental reference rate is then applied to every assessment or unit in the building, but modified by the formula in (1) to reflect value differences within the building.

Step 3   Consider any Parking Value Element

Add the value of any parking spaces to the Rateable Value calculation.

For Example:

Reference Assessment

$40m^2$ size flat @ $80m^2$, ground floor unit with no significant view, the building has no lift service.

Description of the Subject Assessment

The subject assessment is larger than the reference assessment ($50m^2$ versus $40m^2$), has a superior view, and a top roof. However because it is on a high floor the lack of lift service is a problem.

All % adjustments are relative to the reference assessment.

Upper floor unit with better view   (view = +10%)
No Lift or Elevator   (No Lift = -7.5%)
Composite Adjustment = CA% = +2.5% = (+10% view - 7.5% No Lift)
Quantity Allowance   = QA% = -5%   = (Larger Flat $50m^2$)
Ancillary Value   = AV% = -12.5% = (Top Roof as per example in
                                           (5) above)

Rental value of the subject assessment

$$\$RV = \$m^2 \ ref \ x \ (1 \pm CA\% \pm QA\% + AV\%) \ x \ Main \ Floor \ Area \qquad (6)$$

$$= \$80 \ x \ (1 + 0.025 - 0.05 + 0.125) \ x \ 50 \ m^2 = \$4400$$

where

RV = Rateable Value

$\$m^2 ref$ = rental value per metre square per month of the reference assessment which is $80

Analysis of comparisons

Market evidence (e.g. rents) can be adjusted to a common reference assessment basis using the formula:

$$\frac{Rent - Parking \ Value}{(1 \pm CA\% \pm QA\% + AV\%)} \qquad (7)$$

Standard size comparisons within the district

Within a district, for a particular grade or type of building, the floor areas of units (assessments) and the reference assessments may vary widely. By using size discounts or QA% curves as shown in Figure 2.1 and Table 2.3 above it is possible to convert $m² rents, prices or values to a particular standard size. For example convert all grade A office rents in a district to a common 100m² standard. This enables staff to concentrate on factors other than size in making value comparisons between buildings.

Eliminating the need for a large set of predictor variables

The adoption of an abbreviated free-format remarks field in combination with the CA% field, eliminates the need for a large matrix of variables to reflect value differences within buildings.

Some early applications of CAMA involved an extensive set of variables. These systems often involved both market driven (regression or feedback) and replacement cost less normal depreciation approaches (RCLND).

41

Estimating the reference assessment value

Statistical approach

Various CAMA techniques could be used to estimate the values for the reference assessments, such as multiple regression analysis or Carbone and Longini's (1977) feedback procedures, or techniques such as neural or adaptive networks that have been applied by Borst (1991 and 1994). The approach outlined herein emphasizes the use of multiple regression analysis to estimate the value for the particular reference assessment in each building. Three estimates are generated for each reference assessment from district based models for each property type (domestic, office and factory):

Estimate 1: Based on property characteristics such as grade, size, location, view, etc. and transaction details such as rent commencement date, fresh letting, etc.

Estimate 2: Includes the existing value as a predictor in addition to property characteristics and transaction details.

Estimate 3: Incorporates dummy variables to represent the effect of particular buildings, and includes rateable value, property characteristics and transaction details.

Regression indexation

Regression based indexation is used both as a major predictive tool and in analysing assessment equity. The present assessed or rateable value, which represents an amalgam of effects at a past date, is used to predict the current price or rent level. In a simple form, a regression model could be constructed as follows:

$$\text{Sale Price (or rent)} = a_0 + b_1 \text{ Assessed Value (or rental value)} + e \quad (8)$$

Where a_0 is the intercept, b_1 the coefficient for assessed value and e the error term. In a more complex form, other variables such as time, grade, year built, location etc., can be included as predictors, along with the assessed value.

Rental Value or Sales Price =

$$f \text{ (Assessed Value, Time, and the marginal effect of Building Grade, Age, Location, etc.)} \quad (9)$$

The regression indexation procedure updates the existing assessed value. If other predictor variables enter in conjunction with the assessed value then this indicates:

1   Changes in market preferences since the values were set and/or

2   Systematic assessment bias in estimating the original values.

3   Definitional or transaction related difference between Rent (or Price) and assessed value.[3]

The previous assessed value tends to dominate the model, and has a stabilizing effect reducing unexpected changes in relativities. Its inclusion nearly always improves estimating accuracy, sometimes quite dramatically.

Adjusting rents prior to model building

The variance within the building can be removed before model building, and rents adjusted to reference assessment terms (see equation (7)) with the reference assessment attributes being substituted for the actual e.g. the floor area of the reference assessment being used instead of the actual floor area.

An alternative approach is not to remove the variance within the building and use the unadjusted rent, and actual floor area etc. as predictors. In this approach it is necessary to include the limited set of predictor variables that explain the variation in value within the building.

Example of regression indexing

The following discussion of regression indexing relates to rents and rateable values, but can also be applied to sale prices and assessed values.

The analysis is based on 828 residential rents that were recorded in 1992 and 1993 in the popular Mid levels district on Hong Kong Island. The equation (10) is a basic double-log model which has a multiplicative form.

$$\text{Ln Rent } m^2 = a_0 + b_1 \text{ Ln Value} + e \tag{10}$$

where
Ln Rent m^2 = the natural log of Rent per m^2 (1992 & 1993 transactions)
Ln Value m^2 = the natural log of 1 July 1990 Rateable Value per m^2
a_0 = intercept
b_1 = coefficient for the value effect
e   = error term

Table 2.5
Equation 1

Variable	Coefficient	Standard Error	F	Prob > F
INTERCEPT	0.271	0.136	3.97	0.0467
LN VALUE M^2	0.954	0.024	1553.77	0.0001
Overall $R^2 = 0.65$ Regression 1 Total 826 DF Std Error 0.114				

Equation 1, in Table 2.5, illustrates that the 1 July 1990 Rateable Value is a reasonable predictor of 1992 rental levels. The coefficient of 0.954 can be interpreted as an elasticity. Independent of the intercept effect, a 10% increase in rateable value corresponds to a 9.54% increase in expected rent.

Table 2.6
Additional predictor variables

LN FLOOR_AREA	Size in m^2	Ln
COURT & POOL	Tennis Court & Swimming Pool	0, 1
LN FLOOR_LEVEL	3rd to highest floor	Ln
TIME 2	Nov 1992 = 1, Dec 1992 = 2 ...	C
POST-1987	Pre-1987 = 0, 1988 = 1, 1989 = 2 ...	C
TPU[4] - 140	District 140	0, 1
TPU - 141	District 141	0, 1

where
Ln   = natural logarithm
0, 1   = categorical; 1 = yes   0 = no
C   = continuous numeric

Equation 2 (Table 2.7)

Again the dependent variable is Ln Rent m^2 and in addition to Rateable Value this equation includes property characteristics and a time variable as co-predictors of rent.

Table 2.7
Equation 2: Property characteristics and rateable value

Predictor Variable(s)	Coefficient	Standard Error	F	Prob > F
Intercept	0.378	0.163	5.41	0.0202
Ln Flr	0.031	0.005	45.90	0.0001
Time 2	0.015	0.001	149.97	0.0001
Built Post-1987	0.011	0.003	14.72	0.0001
Ln Value	0.906	0.029	943.92	0.0001

Overall $R^2 = 0.72$ Regression 4   Total 827 DF   F = 535.31   Standard Error 0.10

Three additional predictor variables have entered in the presence of Rateable Value (Ln Value), and all except the intercept are significant at the 99% level. The coefficient for Time 2 (0.015) indicates that from November 1992 the rental market was probably rising 1.5% per month. Additional effects for floor level and newer building have also been detected in the rents; their entry can be attributed either to a change in market preferences since 1990, assessment bias in the 1990 rateable values, or a combination of both. For example the equation in Table 2.8 which excludes Rateable Value as a predictor, shows that rental values are approximately 4.2% higher for each year of construction since 1987 (1988 - 92). However in Table 2.7 the Built Post-1987 coefficient only indicates a 1.1% per year increase. The 1.1% per year is in addition to the age effects that are already reflected in the 1990 Rateable Values, and may indicate a slight change in preferences.

Improved accuracy

The inclusion of other variables, in addition to the rateable value, improves the standard error of estimate from 0.114 to 0.10. In this log based model a standard error of 0.10 can be interpreted such that 68% of estimates would be within approximately 10% of the actual rent.

Equation 3 (Table 2.8)

The dependent variable is Rent m^2 but this equation excludes Rateable Value as a predictor of rent levels.

Table 2.8
Equation 3: Property characteristics only

Predictor Variable(s)	Coefficient	Standard Error	F	Prob > F
INTERCEPT	5.573	0.045	15608.30	0.0001
LN FLOOR_AREA	-0.038	0.010	16.15	0.0001
COURT & POOL	0.108	0.012	87.06	0.0001
LN FLOOR_LEVEL	0.033	0.006	27.99	0.0001
TIME 2	0.016	0.002	89.68	0.0001
POST-1987	0.042	0.004	121.79	0.0001
TPU - 140	-0.195	0.017	132.30	0.0001
TPU - 141	-0.067	0.014	22.41	0.0001
Overall R^2 = 0.51 Regression 7 Total 827 DF F = 121.69 Standard Error = 0.14				

Comparing equation 2 and 3

Similar treatment for time

Both models have a similar coefficient for TIME 2, which gives confidence to the estimate of 1.5% per month for rental price inflation in late November 1992 and early 1993.

Overall predictive ability

Equation 2 which includes Rateable Value as a predictive variable is clearly superior and has an R^2 of 0.72 and standard error of 0.10 compared to 0.51 and 0.14 respectively for Equation 3.

Location effect - equation 2 versus equation 3

Location is represented by categorical (0, 1) Tertiary Planning Unit (TPU) variables. Each TPU represents a sub-district containing up to 10,000 assessments and 200 high-rise buildings. TPU 143 was deliberately excluded to prevent overspecification, and both TPU 140 and TPU 141 entered the model. The location effects in Equation 3 are summarised in Table 2.9.

Table 2.9
Location effects

Location	Coefficient	Transformed
TPU 143	-	100
TPU 140	-0.195	82
TPU 141	-0.067	94

TPU 143 (base 100) is the better location. Similar properties would be worth -18% less in TPU 140 and -6% in TPU141.

It would be unsatisfactory to apply a model such as Equation 3 that would give rise to sudden changes in value at the TPU boundary e.g. an 18% difference between TPU 140 and TPU 143.

The TPU variables were considered in Equation 2 (the regression indexing model that uses Rateable Value), but did not enter. The conclusion is that the 1990 Rateable Values adequately account for location differences between TPU's.

Advantages of regression indexing

Treatment of variables There is a problem in determining whether property or transaction characteristics have an additive or multiplicative effect. The existing Rateable Value, reflects an end adjusted appraisal weighting of value components. If the present values are properly established then each property's rateable value represents an amalgam of property characteristics that were appropriately combined and weighted at a prior date.

Acceptable basis Rateable and Capital Values have been the subject of internal and public scrutiny. Taxpayers are not only interested in the absolute correctness of the new value, but may also dispute the magnitude of any change from the previous level.

Constraining influence When the existing Rateable Value is included in the model it tends to be both a dominating and constraining influence.

Lack of sample size Limitations in market data may make it difficult to analyse a wide variety of influences. Yet it may be possible to efficiently update the existing values by including a few major variables that can identify changing preferences or price movements over time.

Limited data set By including the information in the current value, it may be possible to rely on a small set of relatively objective variables such as type of property, size, age, etc. and eliminate many subjective or qualitative variables that can be expensive and difficult to maintain.

Comparative accuracy of regression indexing

The summary of results in Appendix 2.2 is based on comparisons between two model forms for each district and property group (domestic, factory and office). The major difference between the model forms being the inclusion or exclusion of the existing Rateable Value as a predictor variable. These models are of the multiplicative form, and each pair of models has the same number of predictor variables (Regression and Total Degrees of Freedom are equal). The dependent variable for all models is the natural logarithm of rent per m^2 with a variety of independent or predictor variable such as view (Yes = 1, No = 0), natural logarithm floor area (m^2), or a series of untransformed continuous variables for the building age effect (see Appendix 2.3). The focus for comparison is the difference in predictive accuracy, as measured by the Standard Error of Estimate.

Appendix 2.2 shows that for some 34 out of 37 districts the estimating accuracy was superior when the 1990 Rateable Value was included as a predictor of current rental levels. Figure 2.2 below shows that the models that included rateable value as a predictor of current rent levels had a lower standard error of estimate. These comparisons are made between equations where all predictor variables are significant at the 95% level.

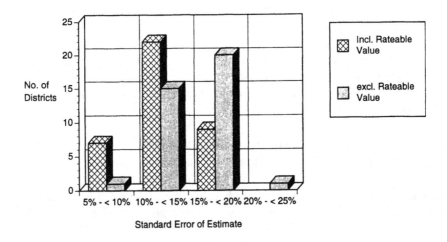

Figure 2.2 Comparison when rateable value is a predictor

48

The regression indexed based models that included Rateable Value have generally reduced the standard error of estimate by 2 - 3%. A 2% reduction means that 68% of estimates are within say 10% rather than 12% of the actual rent. In one case there was a 7% improvement. Figure 2.3 shows that the standard error of estimate reduction, or estimating improvement, from incorporating the Current Rateable Value was most marked for offices, and more advantageous for domestic than for factories. It appears that the property groups that are the most sensitive to location, benefit more from the regression indexing approach.

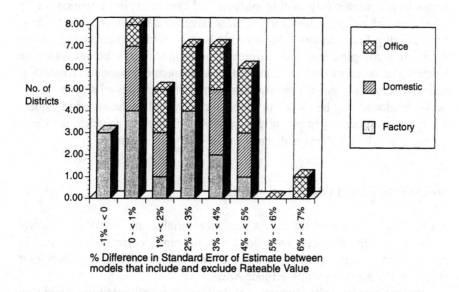

Figure 2.3 Effect of using rateable value as a predictor

Selecting the appropriate model

Three types of estimates are presented to operational staff - one based on property characteristics only and two regression index based estimates. The valuation staff select which model form to initially apply in the district, and are also presented with the three alternative estimates when they individually review the reference values for buildings in the district.

Check values

If the rental value estimate based only on property characteristics varies substantially from the regression indexed estimate then this would serve as a warning to review the building more carefully.

A low cost response surface

Regression Indexing may be appropriate for those jurisdictions that do not have access to geographic information systems and cannot exploit Location Value Response Surface techniques such as those developed by Eichenbaum (1989). If the existing Tax Assessment Values have been properly established then they represent a complex response surface. It may not always be necessary to disaggregate these values into land and improvement components. Analysing the total (historical) assessed value and property characteristics relative to current market evidence may be sufficient to satisfactorily update the assessed values. It is however necessary to periodically review the property values in the field, and there will be problems at discrete model district boundaries.

Avoiding unwanted interaction effects

Introducing the rateable value as a predictor variable may cause collinearity problems. If other predictor variables are significantly correlated, then it may be necessary to make suitable transformations. It is possible to construct joint variables e.g. Rateable Value ÷ Floor Areas.

A major alternative transformation to deal with this collinearity problem is to move rateable value across to the other side of the equation. The dependent variable then becomes rent (or price) divided by the rateable (assessed) value.

$$R = a_o + \sum_{i=1}^{n} b_i x_i + e_i \qquad (11)$$

where

R	=	ratio of Rent/Rateable Value for the ith transaction
a_o	=	intercept
b_i	=	coefficient for the ith predictor variable
x_i	=	ith predictor variable e.g. location, age, etc.
e_i	=	error term.

Simple manual indexation in this form has been a traditional tool for updating assessed values. Regression analysis is used to identify and quantify factors that influence the Rent/Rateable Value ratio. While the model is additive, it is inherently proportional in its application.

Regression indexing and analysis of equity

The equation in (8) above is a restatement or reversal of Paglin and Fogarty's (1972) pioneering work on valuation equity, with Sale Price as the dependent variable and Assessed Value the independent variable.

Paglin & Fogarty Model

$$a_i = B_o + B_1 S_i + e_i \qquad (12)$$

where

a_i = assessed value for the ith property

S_i = sale price for the ith property

and B_o, B_1 and e_i are the intercept, slope and the error term

Pao Lun Cheng's (1974) non-linear model for the analysis of equity focused on the dependency between ratio of Value to Sale Price and Sale Price.

$$Log\ R_i = B_o + B_1\ Log\ S_i + e_i \qquad (13)$$

where

R_i = Ratio of Assessed Value to Sale Price for the ith property

S_i = Sale Price for the ith property

B_o = intercept

B_1 = coefficient for the Sale Price

e_i = error term

Regression indexing in the form of Equation 2 (Table 2.7) of (11) builds on the work of Paglin and Fogarty and Pao Lun Cheng. It tests the assumption that the existing value can be updated. The notion is also advanced that other predictor variables can be introduced to assist in updating the assessed value, or to identify the cause of assessment bias.

Appraisal software

The process for analysing rents or sales, removing outliers, generating and applying models is highly automated. The software exploits the SAS AF[5] menu driven features; experienced appraisal or valuation staff who understand the basic statistics can be relatively insulated from the complexities of the computer system.

Evaluating performance

The adoption of the reference assessment approach for domestic office and factory assessments has enabled the department to value 12.5 reference buildings or 650 assessments per man-day and has dramatically shortened the elapsed revaluation time to a major core period of only 5 months in the 3 year revaluation cycle. The International Association of Assessing Office (IAAO) standards relate to Capital Value. Rental markets have their own characteristics and international assessment accuracy standards are not yet established for rental based property tax values. However, from a comparative standpoint the overall coefficient of dispersion in Hong Kong would be well within the IAAO Capital Valuation standards with an overall ratio of Value to Rent ratio of 0.97 and Coefficient of Dispersion (COD) of approximately 11%. Capital valuation productivity levels have doubled, and new entry efficiency has increased 50%. These improvements are not just due to computer assisted valuation; the review process also involves changes at the management and even legislative levels.

Notes

1. Rental income is also taxed and this is called property tax. Rates is an additional charge levied on the assessed value of both owner occupied and rented property.
2. The rates charged in each of these areas have two components, a charge for the particular council and a general rate which is paid into central government's revenue. The total percentage charge is currently the same for all districts.
3. Examples of definitional or transaction related difference are where some sale prices or rents reflect existing tenancies whereas the tax assessed value assumes vacant possession. Time is another source of difference with the rent and existing rateable value being at a different dates.
4. TPU is a Tertiary Planning Unit, which is basically a neighbourhood or census planning district.
5. SAS Statistical Software, SAS Institute Inc., Cary NC USA.

References

Borst, R.A. (1991), 'Artificial Neural Networks: The Next Modelling/Calibration Technology for the Assessment Community?', *Property Tax Journal*, vol. 10 no. 1, pp. 69-94.
Borst, R.A. (1994), 'An Evaluation of Abductive Networks for the Valuation of

Residential Property', *IAAO 60th Annual Conference in Assessment Administration, Seattle*, pp. 402-415.

Carbone, R. and Longini, R.L. (1977), 'A feedback model for automated real estate assessment', *Management Service,* vol. 24, pp. 241-248.

Cheng, Pao Lung (1974), 'Property Taxation Assessment Performance and Its Measurement', *Public Finance/Finances Publiques,* vol. 29, pp. 268-284.

Eichenbaum, J. (1989), 'Location as a Factor in Determining Property Values', *Property Tax Journal,* vol. 9 no. 1, pp. 103-114.

Gloudemans, R.J. (1982), 'Simplified Sales Based Models for Condominium/ Town House Valuation', *World Congress Computer Assisted Valuation*, Lincoln Institute of Land Policy.

Paglin, M. & Fogarty, M. (1972), 'Equity and the Property Tax: A New Conceptual Form', *National Tax Journal*, pp. 557-565.

O'Conner, P.M. & Eichenbaum, J. (1988), 'Location Value Response Surfaces: The Geometry of Advanced Mass Appraisal', *Property Tax Journal*, vol. 7 no. 3, pp. 277-296.

Ward R.D. (1981), *Development of Valuation Methodology For Condominiums*, IAAO Conference.

Appendix 2.1
Standard composite adjustment items description

Accessibility-Narrow Path	Lane Adjoining	Orientation
Accessibility	Latrin	Privacy
Accessibility-Lane	Lavatory	Quality
Accessibility-Vehicular	Lavatory-Near	Quantity Allowance
Age	Layout	Refuse Collection Point
Area Adjustment Factor	Level of Entrance	Refuse Collection Point-Near
Aspect	Lift-No Direct Lift Service	Repairs
Balcony Effect	Lift-No Lift on Top Floor	Security
Column	Lighting	Semi-Detached
Commercial Value	Lighting & Ventilation	Shallow Depth
Construction	Loading	Shape
Corner	Location	Shape-Irregular
Corner Influence-Lane/Lane	Mid-Terrace	Solar Heat
Corner Influence-Lane/Road	Nuisance-Airport	Stairs
Corner Influence-Lane/Street	Nuisance-A/C Plant Room	Tenant's Improvements
Corner Influence-Road/Road	Nuisance-Bus-Terminus	Top Floor/Leakage
Corner Influence-Street/Road	Nuisance-Car Dismantling	Unit-End
Corner Influence-Street/Street	Nuisance-Car Park	Unit-Front
Detached	Nuisance-Cargo Handling Area	Unit-Inner
Eyesore	Nuisance-Commercial Centre	Unit-Outer
Finishings	Nuisance-Container Depot	Unit-Rear
Floor-High	Nuisance-Factory	Ventilation
Floor-Low	Nuisance-Funeral Parlour	View
Flyover	Nuisance-KCR	View-Distant
Fronatge	Nuisance-Lavatory	View-Extra
Frontage-Return	Nuisance-LRT	View-Garden
Frontage/Depth Ratio	Nuisance-Market	View-Landscaped
Government Water Supply	Nuisance-MTR	View-Mountain
Grave	Nuisance-Noise	View-Open
Graveyard	Nuisance-Nullah	View-Outlook
Ground Floor Advantage	Nuisance-Overhead Cable	View-Sea
Ground-Vth	Nuisance-Pylon	Walking Distance
Head Room	Nuisance-Pigsty	Walkway
Head Room-High	Nuisance-Plane	Water Closet
Head Room-High H/R on Top Roof	Nuisance-Plant Room	Water Closet-Near
Head Room-Low	Nuisance-Playground	Water Closet-Without
Head Room-Part with Higher Head Room	Nuisance-Poultry	Window-Extra
Head Room-Part with Lower Head Room	Nuisance-Pump Room	Window-Rear
High H/R on Top Roof	Nuisance-Refuse Chamber	Window-Side
Internal Staircase	Nuisance-Roof Garden	Window-Without
	Nuisance-School	
	Nuisance-Ship Dismantling	
	Nuisance-Switch Room	
	Nuisance-Transformer Room	

Appendix 2.2
Comparisons between omitting or including rateable value as a predictor

District	Degree of Freedom		Property Characteristics and Rateable Value			Degree of Freedom		Property Characteristics only		
	Reg.	Total	R^2	Standard Error	Overall F	Reg.	Total	R^2	Standard Error	Overall F
Domestic										
Mid Levels	19	2,529	0.800	0.117	543.23	20	2,528	0.685	0.151	274.50
Peak	7	239	0.790	0.115	129.74	9	237	0.622	0.158	43.38
Pokfulam	6	653	0.450	0.098	89.68	6	653	0.400	0.107	72.90
Aberdeen	10	597	0.780	0.096	215.02	12	595	0.746	0.112	145.28
Island South	15	1,382	0.820	0.091	418.38	16	1,381	0.618	0.133	139.38
Western	18	1,932	0.840	0.140	583.49	20	1,930	0.774	0.175	330.49
Tsim Sha Tsui	7	703	0.680	0.151	188.74	13	697	0.615	0.165	85.58
Ho Man Tin	9	731	0.770	0.113	277.70	15	725	0.616	0.148	77.38
Hung Hom	10	1,330	0.800	0.164	545.38	19	1,321	0.814	0.172	304.56
Yau Ma Tei	15	1,342	0.810	0.169	390.21	15	1,342	0.810	0.170	390.21
Factory (Grade)										
Hong Kong (AB)	11	580	0.790	0.137	198.31	11	580	0.620	0.182	87.87
Hong Kong (CDE)	7	306	0.550	0.148	52.52	9	304	0.379	0.180	20.61
Kowloon (AB)	6	302	0.698	0.134	116.20	6	302	0.550	0.166	61.53
Kowloon (CDE)	3	228	0.584	0.164	106.77	7	224	0.603	0.192	48.59
Cheung Sha Wan (AB)	3	206	0.480	0.167	63.52	3	206	0.432	0.164	52.20
Cheung Sha Wan (CDE)	6	155	0.772	0.146	87.30	5	156	0.786	0.154	114.60
Kowloon Bay (AB)	8	461	0.572	0.137	77.15	8	461	0.571	0.135	76.83
Kwun Tong/Yau Tong (AB)	8	400	0.719	0.150	127.90	10	398	0.582	0.171	55.36
Kwun Tong/Yau Tong (CDE)	6	616	0.800	0.139	411.88	7	615	0.732	0.161	239.46
San Po Kong (CDE)	3	152	0.277	0.167	19.45	5	150	0.256	0.172	10.31
Shatin (AB)	8	498	0.453	0.159	51.48	8	498	0.443	0.162	45.55

Comparisons between omitting or including rateable value as a predictor

District	Degree of Freedom		Property Characteristics and Rateable Value			Degree of Freedom		Property Characteristics only		
	Reg.	Total	R^2	Standard Error	Overall F	Reg.	Total	R^2	Standard Error	Overall F
Tsuen Wan/Kwai Ching (AB)	13	1,167	0.749	0.143	267.50	14	1,166	0.733	0.147	229.09
Tsuen Wan/Kwai Ching (CDE)	10	906	0.691	0.161	202.61	11	905	0.590	0.188	118.29
Tuen Mun (AB)	6	538	0.745	0.135	262.20	3	541	0.681	0.148	384.62
Tuen Mun (CDE)	2	84	0.200	0.132	10.52	3	83	0.250	0.130	9.21
Office (Grade)										
West/Sheung Wan (AB)	8	564	0.724	0.110	184.70	9	563	0.414	0.155	44.12
West/Sheung Wan (CD)	9	1,614	0.786	0.138	659.70	14	1,609	0.586	0.198	162.46
Central (AB)	15	1,020	0.669	0.112	137.40	15	1,020	0.385	0.139	42.55
Central (CDE)	10	490	0.631	0.127	83.72	10	490	0.438	0.164	38.22
Wanchai/Causeway Bay (AB)	10	840	0.645	0.107	152.76	11	839	0.542	0.124	90.26
Wanchai/Causeway Bay (CD)	13	684	0.694	0.118	119.13	11	686	0.527	0.141	69.49
North Point/SKW (AB)	3	63	0.803	0.085	86.03	6	60	0.813	0.092	43.61
North Point/SKW (CD)	5	109	0.904	0.078	205.02	5	109	0.838	0.102	112.72
Tsim Sha Tsui (AB)	15	1,076	0.553	0.099	88.89	15	1,076	0.431	0.114	54.40
Tsim Sha Tsui (CD)	10	565	0.715	0.109	141.87	11	564	0.530	0.141	57.78
Kin Remainder (AB)	14	673	0.844	0.88	260.98	14	673	0.667	0.135	96.12
Kin Remainder (CD)	14	896	0.808	0.127	269.90	17	893	0.652	0.173	98.60

Appendix 2.3
Major predictor variables

Effect	Definitions	Type
Property Related		
Age	- 1950 <= Year Built <= 1969	C
	- 1970 <= Year Built <= 1979	C
	- 1980 <= Year Built <= 1987	C
	- Year Built after 1987	C
Air Conditioning	- Central Free-Standing, None	1, 0
View		1, 0
Floor Level	- Ln (Flr Level) - Lift	C
	- Floor Level - No Lift	C
	- Ln (Flr Level) - No Lift	C
Current Rateable Value	Ln ($M2 Current Rateable Value)	C
Location	Defined by Tertiary Planning Areas	1, 0
Building	Defined by Users	1, 0
Bay Window	Bay Window Area	1, 0
Balcony	Balcony Area	1, 0 or C
Amenities	Court, Swimming Pool, Court and Pool	1, 0
Ancillary Value	Other Non Main Floor Area Components	1, 0 or C
Building Grade	Office and Factory Residential A, B, C, D, & E Flat A = Superior Tenement E = Poor Miscellaneous	1, 0
Head Room	Ln (Head Room)	C
Loading Capacity	Light, Heavy, Super Heavy (Factories)	1, 0
Transaction Related		
Sale		
Date of Agreement	Time	1, 0 or C
Possession	Subject to Existing Tenancy	1, 0
Rental		
Status	Fresh Letting or Renewal	1, 0
Liability	Inclusive of Rates	1, 0
Date	Time	1, 0 or C

3 The mass appraisal of residential property in Northern Ireland

W. J. McCluskey, K. Dyson, S. Anand and D. McFall

Introduction

Property valuation can be seen as both an art and a science. According to Smeltzer (1986) real estate appraisal is an estimate or opinion of value of a specific property as of a specified date, supported by the presentation and analysis of relevant data. Examining this statement it is obvious that the reliability and validity of the appraisal of property is highly dependent upon two critical factors, the quality of the data being used and the experience of the appraiser. In practising the art of real estate appraisal, the appraiser has recourse to three main techniques: the cost approach, the income approach and the comparative sales approach. The comparative sales approach simply compares the subject to be valued with a number of similar properties which have recently been sold. Adjustments for differences between the subject and comparables being made by the appraiser in a subjective manner. As a means of introducing science into the art of real estate appraisal, regression analysis, and in particular multiple regression, has been used. Therefore over the last forty to fifty years real estate appraisal has had to take on board statistical techniques to assist the appraiser and counteract the criticisms of appraisals being highly subjective.

With the advent of such statistically based approaches the ability to mass appraise properties became possible. The traditional approach has been to provide a discrete value manually calculated for each individual property. It has to be accepted that this approach is probably the most accurate but also the most time consuming, and therefore the most expensive representing a greater drain on finite resources.

In relation to property tax systems which are ad valorem based it is essential to maintain relativities between individual properties and across property sectors. Therefore to achieve acceptable levels of equity and fairness, the property within

59

the taxable base must be regularly reappraised. Within most systems this reappraisal usually is undertaken every three, five or seven years. As one might expect such a reappraisal can be a daunting and extremely expensive operation, particularly if a manual approach is employed. As an example, in England during 1990 approximately two million commercial properties were valued for the non-domestic property tax and then in 1993 over 20 million domestic properties were valued for the residential property tax, commonly referred to as the Council Tax. Consequently, mass appraisal techniques have had the greatest impact within the area of property taxation, with many countries now reviewing manually based approaches in favour of computer assisted mass appraisal techniques.

Mass appraisal can be defined as the systematic appraisal of groups of properties as of a given date using standardized procedures and statistical testing (Eckert, 1990). Mass appraisal, unlike single property appraisal, requires the development of a single model capable of replicating the components of supply and demand over a large area. Therefore appraisal judgement must relate to homogeneous groups of properties rather than to a single property. In reality mass appraisal evolved as a response to the need to provide uniformity and consistency in ad valorem assessments (McCluskey, 1993). The mass appraisal or scientific approach advocates the use of statistical methods within the assessment process to assist the appraiser in two ways, firstly, in explanation of values and secondly, in the prediction of values (Mark and Goldberg, 1988).

The approach of using comparable sales to provide for the value estimation of similar properties has been accorded heavy weight by both law and appraisal theory (Eisenlauer, 1968). The basis of this approach is that if enough recently sold properties can be found with characteristics identical to those of properties not sold, the prices of the sold properties would represent proxies or evidence of value for the unsold ones. Therefore, the primary element of the comparative sales approach is the identification of variables with which to compare sold and unsold properties. The differences between variables give a measurable, positive or negative impact on value (Hinshaw, 1968).

On that basis the adjustment process has, however, been a source of criticism of the comparative sales approach. The selling prices of properties are market determined and therefore objective and finite adjustments for differences between properties cannot normally be extracted from sale prices. It is the role of the experienced appraiser to identify the value significant variables and to assess their impact on value. The traditional method used to adjust for differences in comparables is the cost-to-cure approach. In this case the appraiser estimates the cost of making the comparable identical to the subject being valued. To use an example, the comparable and subject are similar with the exception that the subject has an extra bedroom. The process would require the adjustment upwards of the comparable by adding the cost of an additional bedroom. This approach is not without problems, particularly from the point of view that cost and value are not necessarily equal (Radcliff and Swan, 1972).

The structure of this chapter is as follows: an examination of the various techniques available for mass appraisal, from multiple regression analysis through to artificial neural networks; methodological considerations relating to the dataset and evaluation of predictive accuracy are then discussed; the application of three of the techniques (neural networks, expert systems and multiple regression) are evaluated in an empirical analysis and finally, the robustness of two of the better techniques (neural networks and multiple regression) are examined under more stringent conditions.

Multiple regression analysis

In terms of mass appraisal one of the most important advances was the introduction of regression as a tool for the prediction of value. Multiple regression provides a statistically based approach for estimating (for a sample of fairly homogeneous properties) how selling price is related to the selected determinants of value.

Essentially one attempts to develop a linear equation ('line-of best fit') for the dataset available, and then utilize the coefficients derived for each independent variable in order to make predictions on the basis of a holdout sample. The basic equation is of the form:

$$Y_i = \alpha + \beta_1 X_{1i} + \beta_2 X_{2i} + \beta_3 X_{3i} + \ldots + \beta_n X_{ni} + \varepsilon_i$$

where
Y_i = Dependent variable
α = constant (intercept)
β_i = regression coefficient
X_i = independent variable
ε = error term

Pendelton (1965) suggests that if one can identify the determinants of real estate prices, multiple regression provides a means for estimating how much prices increase or decrease with the given changes in the determinants. Pendelton goes on to contend that the accuracy and hence the usefulness of the results depends upon the size of the sample, the accuracy of the data and the skill with which the independent variables have been selected. Renshaw (1958) was of the opinion that it might be impossible to isolate all the factors which buyers take into consideration when purchasing property. It is nonetheless possible to establish a correlation between real estate values and a select subset of determining variables.

Given the variety of multivariate regression techniques in terms of function and mathematical form, it is not always necessary to choose the best possible function, but rather the one which predicts real estate values with sufficient accuracy in a statistical sense for the type of appraisal under consideration (Stenehjem, 1974).

A major difficulty in applying regression models is in meeting the statistical assumptions underlying them. For example, since the regression model demands multivariate normality, it is often the case that the variables being used need to be transformed, for example using log, log-log, square root and other such transformations.

Adaptive estimation procedure

Adaptive Estimation Procedure (AEP) is a fairly recent development in the field of value prediction. AEP is seen as a potential alterative to regression analysis. One of the main differences between the approaches is that whereas regression aims to minimize the sum of the squared errors, AEP seeks to minimize the average absolute error. In effect AEP mirrors as closely as possible the real estate market, in other words it tracks the market, whereas regression forces a line of best fit to the market.

AEP is sometimes called 'feedback' by virtue of the way data is processed. Property sales information is processed one at a time in the sequence in which the sales took place. For each new sale processed the coefficients in the valuation formula are modified. The coefficients are associated with various property characteristicswhich are defined as being either qualitative and quantitative. Quantitative types are continuous variables such as living area, age, number of bedrooms whereas qualitative variables are discrete variables for example building condition, location, roof finish and so forth. Essentially the value of the property is estimated by summing the estimates of value of the land and improvement components of that property. The coefficients assigned to each of the qualitative and quantitative factors are determined by a curve tracking algorithm which uses a systemized trial and error approach to learn the contribution of each factor.

One of the advantages of the AEP approach is that the structure of the model need not be linear. In fact both additive and multiplicative variables can be included, and more importantly the variables need not be transformed. As a result variable coefficients tend to be reasonable in appearance and magnitude and more easily explained to the layperson.

Expert system

An expert system is a tool implemented in computerized form which performs the role of an expert or carries out a task which requires expertise. According to Curtis (1989) such a system would have the following attributes; has a body of knowledge in a particular subject area; can apply this knowledge to problem situations, often in conditions of uncertain or incomplete information: can deliver effective and efficient solutions such as the diagnosis of a problem, advice, planning or recommended courses of action; and is able to provide explanations and justifications for these solutions.

In general the expert system requires that an agreed set of rules be implemented as a computer program (Boyle, 1984). The method of discovering the rules varies from a team of professionals formulating the rules to a professional expert system developer making an informed guess on the basis of knowledge elicitation. The entire validity of expert systems depends on the capture of the true nature of how the expert undertakes a specific role. Only then can conversion of the rules into a form suitable for programming be undertaken.

Artificial neural networks

The Artificial Neural Network (ANN) attempts to mimic the processing capabilities of the biological brain. The human brain consists of a network of approximately 10^{11} neurons. Each biological neuron consists of a number of nerve fibres called dendrites connected to the cell body where the cell nucleus is located. The axon is a long, single fibre that originates from the cell body and branches near its end into a number of strands. At the ends of these strands are the transmitting ends of the synapse that connect to other biological neurons through the receiving ends of the synapse found on dendrites as well as the cell body of biological neurons. A single axon typically makes thousands of synapses with other neurons. The transmission process is a complex chemical process which effectively increases or decreases the electrical potential within the cell body of the receiving neuron. When this electrical potential reaches a threshold value (action potential) it enters its excitatory state and is said to fire. It is the connectivity of the neurons that give these simple devices their real power. Figure 3.1 shows a typical biological neuron.

Artificial Neurons (or processing elements, PE) are highly simplified models of the biological neuron (see Figure 3.1). As in biological neurons an artificial neuron has a number of inputs, a cell body (consisting of the summing node and the Semi-Linear function node in Figure 3.2) and an output which can be connected to a number of other artificial neurons.

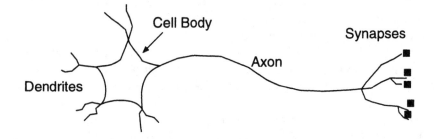

Figure 3.1 A biological neuron

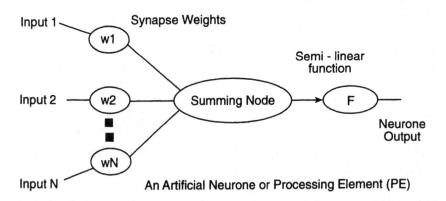

Figure 3.2 An artificial neuron or processing element (PE)

Neural Networks are densely interconnected networks of PEs together with a rule to adjust the strength of the connections between the units in response to externally supplied data. The strength of an ANN lies in its ability to learn, the finding of underlying patterns and the application of this new found information to a specific problem. With a back propagation network for example, the process is relatively straightforward. Data is exposed to an ANN which then, through a system of feedback, compares actual values with generated values with the size of the difference or error, being an indication of how well the ANN has been able to discern the patterns, linear or otherwise, underlying the data. The purpose of continually back processing the data is being able to reduce the error to an acceptable level. Once the error is reduced (not necessarily to a minimum) the network can then be used to classify other previously unseen data.

There are at present several types of ANNs and the behaviour of each type is determined by its connectivity rather than by the detailed operation of any element. Different topologies for neural networks are suitable for different tasks e.g. Hopfield Networks for optimization problems, Multi-Layered Perceptron for classification problems, Back Propagation for prediction and Kohonen Networks for data coding.

There are essentially three main ingredients to a neural network:

- the neurons and the links between them;
- the algorithm for the training phase;
- a method for interpreting the response from the network in the training phase.

This chapter will concentrate on the back propagation approach and the organization of this technique is shown diagrammatically in Figure 3.3.

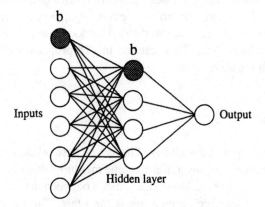

Figure 3.3 A three layered single processing neural network

65

Data for each property transaction in relation to the selected variables is passed through the hidden layers, with each input connected to each hidden layer node. Each node has an associated connection weight, which, depending upon their value, either enhances or depresses the inputs to which they are connected. Each hidden layer node sums up its inputs and feeds them to what is called a transfer or threshold function (normally a sigmoid function) to produce an output. The output could represent the capital value of the property, which in all probability will differ from the actual selling price. This will be because at the beginning of the training process the connection weights are set at random. The next property's attributes are then presented to the network, until all the properties comprising the training set have been processed. The process repeats itself many hundreds or indeed thousands of times, continually correcting the connection weights until the pattern has been learned. At this point the holdout data sample is presented to the network and the errors calculated will determine how well or otherwise the network has performed its function.

This research primarily focuses on the use of ANNs for the prediction of residential property prices. To enable a comparison of the results obtained by this technique, results are also presented on the basis of multiple regression and an expert system.

Data

Data for this research was obtained from the Valuation and Lands Agency and covered a two year period from August 1992 until August 1994. The data set consisted of 416 transactions mainly of detached and semidetached houses and bungalows. The properties were located within a defined but localized geographical area. The variable-set were as follows: price (dependent variable), ward, transaction date, size, bedrooms, class, age, type, heating, garage (independent variables). The sample was divided randomly on a 2:1 basis between training data and holdout data. This resulted in 278 properties in the training data set, and 138 in the holdout set.

Predictive accuracy

In order to evaluate the predictive ability of the neural network and other methods from a statistical perspective, one requires some measure which incorporates an indication of the strength of the linear relationship between the actual sale price and forecasted sale price. Such a measure is the t-test. The t-test determines whether any linear relationship between two variables is significant. Effectively, one tests to substantiate or refute the null hypothesis (H_0), that the correlation coefficient between the two variables is zero, with the alternative hypothesis (H_1) that it is not equal to zero. The t statistic is as follows:

$$t = \frac{r}{\sqrt{\frac{1 - r^2}{n - 2}}}$$

With r calculated as follows;

$$r = \frac{n\Sigma XY - \Sigma X\Sigma Y}{\sqrt{[n(\Sigma X^2) - (\Sigma X)^2]}\sqrt{[n(\Sigma Y^2) - (\Sigma Y)^2]}}$$

where:
r = correlation coefficient
n = sample size
Y = actual house price
X = forecasted house price

The t statistic, in effect, measures the number of standard deviations r lies from zero.

Hypothesis

H_0 : Corr = 0
H_1 : Corr ≠ 0
α = 0.01

Decision Rule

If t >=$t_{critical}$ = reject H_0
If t <=$t_{critical}$ = accept H_0

Otherwise, do not reject H_0

Back propagation (ANN) application

The back propagation ANN was implemented using Clementine, a data mining toolkit developed by Integral Solutions Ltd. Three different neural network configurations were used to investigate the effect of different network topologies on predictive accuracy. These topologies were as follows:

(a) Network 1:   Input Layer (22 nodes)
                      Hidden Layer (6 nodes)
                      Output Layer (1 node)

(b) Network 2:   Input Layer (22 nodes)
                      Hidden Layer 1 (10 nodes)
                      Hidden Layer 2 (4 nodes)
                      Output Layer (1 node)

(c) Network 3:   Input Layer (22 nodes)
                      Hidden Layer 1 (18 nodes)
                      Hidden Layer 2 (2 nodes)
                      Output Layer (1 node)

All of these network topologies were trained separately utilizing the training sample. Once trained, the network was operated in predict mode with the holdout sample. The results for each network topology is given in Table 3.1.

Table 3.1
Predictive accuracy for neural network topologies

	Network 1	**Network 2**	**Network 3**
Minimum Error	£24.00	£12.00	£37.00
Maximum Error	£98,168.00	£76,874.00	£64,803.00
Mean Error	£1,219.90	£589.64	£326.45
Linear Correlation	0.64	0.87	0.76
t-statistic	9.75	13.50	16.96
t-critical	2.33	2.33	2.33

As can be seen in Table 3.1, the most successful network topology for predictive purposes was network 2. This four layered network (two processing layers) had a predictive accuracy of 87% on the basis of the Pearson correlation coefficient for actual and predicted house prices. Networks 3 and 1 had a predictive accuracy of 76% and 64% respectively. All three network configurations where highly significant at the 1% level on the basis of the t-statistics calculated. The mean error (absolute) between actual and predicted house prices was £326.45, £589.64, and £1219.90 for networks 3, 2, and 1 respectively. The minimum error achieved was £12.00 for network 2, with the maximum error figure obtained being £98,168.00 for network 1. All the network topologies, but in particular networks 2 and 3, provided good predictive ability with regards to the house prices.

Expert system application

As with the neural network, the expert or rule based system was developed in Clementine. The rules utilized in the expert system were derived by Clementine 'mining' the training set available, and not via knowledge elicitation as is the norm. Such an approach was utilized because of the many widely recognised problems with regards to knowledge elicitation and derivation of both implicit as well as explicit rules. The results of prediction on the basis of the holdout sample are presented in Table 3.2.

For the rule based system developed, the mean error (absolute) figure obtained was £1,089.70, a difference of £500.06 over neural network topology 2, and indeed only network 1 produced a worse mean error figure of £1,219.90. However, the predictive accuracy of the system was high, with a significant Pearson correlation coefficient of 75%. Also, the minimum error obtained was £00.00, in other words the system for one property or more from the holdout sample, accurately predicted the true selling price. The maximum error figure of £70,000.00 was also better than both neural networks 1 (£98,168.00) and 2 (£76,874.00), but not network 3 (£64,803.00).

Table 3.2
Predictive accuracy for the expert system

Expert System (Rule Based Approach)	
Minimum Error	£00.00
Maximum Error	£70,000.00
Mean Error	£1,089.70
Linear Correlation	0.75
t-statistic	13.04
t-critical	2.33

Multiple regression analysis application

The Multiple Regression Analysis was carried out utilizing the commonly available statistical package, SPSS for Windows. Initially, all of the independent variables where included in the model. However, examination of the correlation matrix for the variables, indicated that certain independent variables such as class and heating, and size and bedroom were highly correlated.

This examination, combined with a step-wise regression procedure resulted in four independent variables being utilized within the regression model, namely class, garage, size and transaction date. The functional form of the model, was therefore as follows:

$$Y_j = \alpha + \beta_1 X_{1i} + \beta_2 X_{2i} + \beta_3 X_{3i} + \beta_4 X_{4i} + \varepsilon_i$$

where:
Y_i = dependent variable (house price) for the ith observation
α = constant (intercept)
β_i = coefficient for variable i
X_i = independent variable i
ε_i = error term

The variable coefficients and associated statistics for the model may be found in Appendix 3.1. The results for the hold out sample in predictive mode are detailed in Table 3.3.

Table 3.3
Predictive accuracy for multiple regression analysis

Multiple Regression Model	
Minimum Error	3.51
Maximum Error	71,645.91
Mean Error	644.75
Linear Correlation	0.81
t-statistic	15.96
t-critical	2.33

The Multiple Regression model developed had a predictive accuracy of 81% on the basis of the Pearson correlation coefficient and again was highly significant at the 1% level. Thus, the regression model outperformed both the expert system (75%), and neural networks 1 (64%) and 3 (76%), but not neural network 2 (87%). The mean error (absolute) figure of £644.75 lies in the mid-range of those figures obtained for the neural network topologies, and is well below the figure of £1,089.70 obtained for the expert system.

Summary

Of the three neural network topologies, the best predictive accuracy obtained was 87% with network 2, and indeed of all the approaches tested here (neural networks, expert system and multiple regression) this network was superior. The second best performance was achieved with the multiple regression model with a predictive accuracy of 81% on the basis of the Pearson correlation coefficient, compared with 75% for the expert system. The neural network topologies also produced the lowest mean error (absolute) figures, with £326.45 for network 3, and £589.64 for network 2, compared with £644.75 for the multiple regression model and £1,089.70 for the expert system. Only for the minimum error figure did the expert system outperform both the neural network topologies and multiple regression model with a figure of £00.00 for one or more houses, compared with £3.51 for the regression model and £12.00 at best for a network topology (network 2).

Consequently, for the holdout sample as a whole, the best predictive accuracy was obtained firstly by a neural network, namely network 2 with 87%, followed by the multiple regression model with 81%, thirdly. neural network 3 with 76%, and finally, the expert system with 75%. Thus, the neural network approach and multiple regression modelling technique appear to provide the best approaches at this stage with regards to house price prediction. The predicted and actual house price for each holdout sample observation may be found in Appendix 3.2 for the neural network topologies, expert system and multiple regression approach.

Conclusions

In this chapter the theoretical underpinnings of a number of mass appraisal techniques have been examined. In an empirical study, three of these techniques (multiple regression, expert systems and artificial neural networks) have been applied to a dataset made available by the Valuation and Land Agency for

71

Northern Ireland. The results of the study tend to indicate that neural networks provide superior predictive ability in comparison to the other commonly used techniques. The application of neural network paradigms to mass appraisal, therefore appears to warrant further investigation.

References

Boyle, C. (1984), 'An Expert System for Valuation of Residential Properties', *Journal of Valuation*, vol.2, pp. 271-287.

Curtis, G. (1989), *Business Information Systems: Analysis, Design and Practice*, Addison Wesley.

Eckert, J.K. (1990), *Property Appraisal and Assessment Administration*, IAAO, Chicago.

Eisenlauer, J.F. (1968), 'Mass verus Individual Appraisals', *The Appraisal Journal,* October.

Mark, J.H. and Goldberg, M.A. (1988), 'Multiple Regression Analysis: A Review of the Issues', *The Appraisal Journal*, vol. 56, pp. 89-109.

McCluskey, W.J. and Adair, A (1994), 'Assessment Techniques and Advances in Mass Appraisal for Property Taxation', in Franzsen, R.C.D. (ed.), *Regional and Local Taxation in a Future South Africa*, Centre for Human Rights, University of Pretoria, South Africa.

Pendelton, W. (1965), 'Statistical Inference in Appraisal and Assessment Procedures', *The Appraisal Journal*, January.

Radcliff, R. and Swan, D.G. (1972), 'Getting more from Comparables by Rating and Regression', *The Appraisal Journal*, January.

Renshaw, E.F. (1958), 'Scientific Appraisal', *National Tax Journal*, December.

Smeltzer, M.V. (1986), 'The Application of Multi-Linear Regression Analysis and Correlation to the Appraisal of Real Estate', *The Appraisal Review*, vol. 28.

Stenehjem, E. (1974), 'A Scientific Approach to the Mass Appraisal of Residential Property', in *Automated Mass Appraisal of Real Property*, IAAO, Chicago.

Appendix 3.1

Multiple regression variable coefficients and associated statistics

Variables	Coefficients
Class	-9,483.567 (-8.122)[*1]
Garage	2,955.145 (2.966)[*1]
Size	314.405 (13.684)[*1]
Transaction Date	7.525 (3.074)[*1]
Constant (Intercept)	-239,449.653 (-2.863)[*1]
Adjusted R^2	0.647
F Test	(127.948)[*1]

Note: *1 = Significant at the 1% level

Appendix 3.2

Actual and predicted house prices for the neural network topologies, expert system and multiple regression approaches

		Predicted Prices for Hold Out Sample			
Actual Price	**Expert System**	**ANN 1**	**ANN2**	**ANN 3**	**MRA**
58000	62685	61017	61355	60000	26918
41000	38322	45210	39114	38025	21182
43500	42537	49972	43808	39517	41966
50000	47062	52908	46789	43513	30747
47000	46695	52859	46374	43513	37070
33850	37555	43525	50953	33974	34034
44000	37977	52393	34905	50500	27992
46000	50989	57017	53073	51750	22836
29000	36859	41246	31577	34500	28133
39000	45496	49492	45132	43513	34192
50000	40412	50024	40750	39517	24879
35870	35930	38674	34643	20000	36071
46500	47259	55762	48123	46836	19809
33500	31605	31800	32662	34734	27080
34250	36097	39545	35400	34994	30082
42269	36102	40294	35266	46836	21382
35790	31512	30906	30871	34973	31299
36110	36421	40752	36602	34975	30305
44556	44350	45660	46690	46816	26086
32125	31729	32365	34017	34734	28980
45465	44975	46309	46902	46816	30519
28950	30127	31100	28077	29725	27027
32950	30171	31819	29318	45250	29315
42950	54193	52860	54219	51969	30415
40306	54859	52326	55765	51969	35614
41250	40682	39240	37445	33950	31595
44500	38363	54430	38646	42000	28958
65500	41521	56934	46946	50500	31303
70338	63791	60012	64930	51950	32826
47802	45329	56668	50265	42572	34807

Actual Price	Expert System	ANN 1	ANN2	ANN 3	MRA
48600	55347	57902	55712	59679	29807
44932	45226	43444	45498	45246	21950
58598	51221	58388	53770	61875	31773
69355	68516	60699	70179	66500	32693
31950	34117	34908	31913	32225	28983
29000	34514	32450	31497	32225	28502
24500	34200	40041	31871	34975	32379
28000	33368	42280	30429	32000	35449
33500	33697	41140	30563	36950	35798
30000	30490	40475	30253	25000	33468
56811	56161	58511	57410	58714	33287
56000	55389	56995	60115	64800	34848
58291	52202	55332	54636	54062	34735
62982	62108	59138	64620	51950	41250
54187	52548	57730	54605	59326	36936
55000	59638	52393	61531	68000	37703
51500	52418	52447	52419	53575	29394
33000	30552	32019	30354	30500	36215
65500	57496	57290	62615	73350	38005
26600	28999	31217	26010	23900	32149
28500	31436	33134	26951	14000	42363
24000	32202	31430	27367	14000	31400
31000	28192	27426	26030	36500	32838
58512	51982	55961	56841	51750	37921
34180	30506	29091	34507	29000	39305
36341	33515	32379	40891	30500	34514
56500	60361	55950	57091	51969	31241
55000	55178	52055	56559	51969	38461
58250	55434	55200	52897	51969	36889
28500	33224	32718	32018	14000	33011
39563	34925	38750	32820	34994	35274
130000	53126	31832	65197	60000	32642
51000	52357	41172	50353	41000	32433
29950	29433	32471	28515	30950	32905
28950	28848	31120	26517	30000	39304
28250	31062	34468	27635	26950	41183
29000	32061	39052	26828	20000	33402

Actual Price	Expert System	ANN 1	ANN2	ANN 3	MRA
23500	31751	39229	26364	20000	44043
33000	29828	30899	29156	15625	31431
34500	29371	36778	26001	26950	30738
27500	27751	27779	24756	11250	38706
28000	31723	28878	35548	36000	36252
32500	29626	26950	26988	29125	44503
26500	27559	26869	23602	25267	21681
38000	46887	50281	45005	39517	36036
36500	32595	29543	37273	36000	33701
37000	47194	51688	42767	38977	34749
29500	29391	31883	28243	30950	39184
36000	40533	38420	34166	33950	32589
40000	47297	52285	42366	38977	41034
25950	29262	30153	25189	27363	34253
37500	30597	34144	30443	39517	39776
14000	29838	26989	27435	35019	42842
57110	57098	50671	58630	64950	46736
37950	38371	39750	40150	42906	41745
42250	38249	39466	39390	42906	47406
37405	44592	41248	38879	42951	38456
14600	41824	39893	38656	29000	42045
33000	40249	37794	32591	33950	38379
38000	30189	32696	26130	11812	38841
14000	27510	27294	23617	11250	39634
61500	52559	55172	57853	73350	45549
36000	31283	30914	29529	33500	45675
45500	40911	39584	50530	52975	47134
33500	31344	30777	29596	35950	36108
33500	31344	30777	29596	35950	34633
35000	43108	41773	36804	46816	45670
47500	61715	42038	65175	49650	44592
45250	45640	54023	45208	46836	46106
95000	71470	64195	73269	66551	47912
57000	57481	57168	53629	59679	47919
36250	34419	31969	36847	37567	48717
37000	34329	31315	34333	35000	43970
35250	34386	31803	36215	37567	46332

Actual Price	Expert System	ANN 1	ANN2	ANN 3	MRA
43950	44567	55172	44436	60000	48163
40000	44274	43313	43568	36500	43106
39500	34419	31969	36847	37567	51669
36000	34360	31638	35584	37567	44379
77000	59159	52321	57639	64950	49375
35000	34330	30846	32520	35133	59217
46000	45871	44294	44703	47850	48954
20875	34323	30999	33111	20875	40876
37519	34329	31316	34340	20875	43264
38000	35045	37611	34102	46950	47505
38000	30256	31684	29805	15625	51411
48000	45194	55825	45075	42572	52638
16500	33644	36541	31546	20000	53512
48950	46522	44890	44986	49500	51115
37950	33401	32109	41111	15625	53632
25050	34330	30845	32514	35133	53929
46500	47066	57477	46401	42572	50714
38000	37271	40224	38167	39942	54304
40000	41909	38082	33528	39000	61593
34250	43646	39269	35185	39000	50974
39500	42333	40568	37943	39000	59226
36950	40791	39149	36524	39000	48026
39950	40157	38130	31521	33500	58583
55300	60263	53893	56078	64950	54570
34000	40526	37963	31976	39000	54838
35500	53054	38949	42163	38125	55621
35500	45151	40165	42588	33974	61799
33950	41818	38900	33226	39000	39902
16500	38677	37391	30114	33500	56325
40500	51744	38288	41843	38125	73868
26000	35011	34322	33538	32225	62874
30730	33436	36707	31001	20000	52513
27000	29562	29850	25611	35133	92854
28500	29576	29998	25665	14500	58354

4 The application of artificial intelligence to mass appraisal systems

H. James

The application of artificial intelligence

Historical development of the system

Local services such as waste disposal, minor works, and the support of local infrastructure are in most countries financed largely by local taxes, perhaps with some subsidies from central government. Methods of raising such local revenue vary, but in many countries, local businesses and local residences are usually the objects of taxation by local government.

Business taxation

The taxation of businesses is complex. Principles of natural fairness suggest that the more profitable a business is, the more that should be paid by the business in local taxes, but assessors may find difficulty in defining profit, and certainly, business owners may be reluctant to declare it. Moreover, taxation should be a legitimate overhead of a business and would be included in the expected expenses of any business, irrespective of its level of profitably. Consequently, business taxes are frequently linked to the premises which the company occupies; presumably, a company rents or owns a commercial property of a size and quality bearing some relation to its commercial success and turnover, so a tax related to its premises does not seem too unreasonable. Furthermore, the size of the building it occupies probably bears some relation to the quantity of local facilities it uses.

The level of taxation of a business, therefore, being based on its premises, must be adjusted to reflect the size, quality, and location of the premises. Thus a high quality construction close to road, rail, and air links would generate greater revenue than a similar building remote from communication links, or more than a neighbouring property of the same quality but smaller in size. Often, the level of taxation is arrived at by a formula which applies an addition or subtraction to an average taxation figure depending on the physical description of the property. The derivation of this formula is an expert task for a taxation specialist, based on experience and discussion with expert colleagues to arrive at a workable formulae.

Having applied a formula to increase or decrease the standard taxation based on characteristics of the company premises, the problem still remains of setting a standard taxation figure. Since most businesses are in rented properties, rental value is a frequently used basis. Conversely, when business premises are bought, the sales figure can form a reference point for fixing the standard taxation level. The problems are that few business premises are sold, and that rental levels and how they are arrived at by the owners are sometimes hard to uncover. Commercial secrecy is often a major obstacle to determining a sensible standard taxation value.

Residential taxation

In spite of, or because of, disastrous political experiments in trying to raise revenue by personal taxation, by far the most usual method of local non-commercial taxation is a residential property tax. The complications are fewer than for business taxes, because freehold ownership is common, and the various lease agreements, rental voids, and variations which complicate business premises rarely apply in the case of residences. Thus actual property sales in the market can form a basis for fixing the level of taxation to a fairly reliable reference point. From a standard level of taxation, determined by a political or policy decision, formulae can be used to adjust taxation levels for individual properties. Locality, size, and building specification all provide parameters for the adjustment of the tax demanded.

Characteristics of the current system

The process of fixing a standard valuation level for premises upon which taxation is based and then using a formula to adjust the level to suit individual cases, seems sound and in practice it works. The formulae used are often based upon the opinion of experts in the field, and if the resulting taxation seems unjust after the application of the adjustment formulae, then the level can be modified. The method may sound rather unscientific, so various ways have been used in the past to find improved formulae for interpolating property values for taxation purposes. The use of repeatable, logically consistent and agreed methods are much more sustainable if the case for a taxation level has to be defended in arbitration or in a court action. The problem therefore is to find the fundamental principles which operate to influence market value, because market value is the reference by which local taxation is calculated.

Approaching the problem

This section is devoted to the consideration of determining market value, and so relates principally to residential properties. Similar principles apply to commercial properties and finding their rental values, but there are complications such as lease conditions. Work on the effects of contributing factors which influence rental levels on commercial premises is continuing.

Property values are determined by the amount which was received on the sale of the properties. The actual price paid is determined by negotiation, in which attributes of the properties being sold were probably considered in the price negotiations. Property value relates in part to the characteristics of the property, including location, size, type, age, quality, facilities, and amenities. If such characteristics determine value, it is possible to quantify them and use mathematical language to encapsulate the relationship between value and property characteristics in the following manner: that value is a function of the property characteristics, plus some other factors which are not included, and which we probably do not have access to, such as the particular reasons for sale and purchase by the vendor and purchaser. These inaccessible characteristics appear as a random variation which can be added in to the equation:

$$\text{Value} = f(\text{characteristics of the property}) + e$$

where the $f(\ldots)$ denotes a function of the numericized characteristics of the property, and e is the addition of a random variable to take account of influences which are not available and so cannot be taken into account.

Previous studies of valuation estimation

Regression analysis has been used to estimate the values of properties from characteristics (Donnelly, 1990; Nellis, 1981). Using past sample data on sales of comparable properties and a knowledge of the property characteristics, the linear ordinary least squares method provides values of β_i in:

$$V = \beta_0 + \beta_1 X_1 + \beta_2 X_2 + \beta_3 X_3 + \beta_4 X_4 + \ldots + \beta_k X_k + e$$

where x_i are the characteristics of the property, k is the number of characteristics being considered indexed by i, and V is the value of the property. β_i are determined from a sample of previous sales of properties using the least squares method to minimize e over the data set. A target property value can be estimated by substituting its characteristics into x_i, using the $ß_i$ values gained from the sample to obtain a value of V for the property. The method is only usable if the target property is comparable to but not necessarily identical to the properties in the sample that was used to determine $ß_i$.

Shortcomings of regression

Useful and convenient though regression is, it fails to give the best possible estimate of value from the sample data which was used to determine the coefficients $ß_i$. Linear regression implies the assumption that the relationship between the causative variables x_i and the response V is approximately linear. In real life data, this is rarely the case, but multiple linear regression is so easy to use (personal computer spreadsheets offer the facility) that such concerns are often ignored, or tolerated (Donnelly, 1990). Figure 4.1 shows in principle how four variables may each affect value in a linear manner. The lines assume that as one variable is changed, the others are held at average values. The gradient of each line is the weight value associated with each attribute.

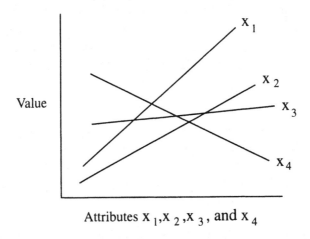

Attributes x_1, x_2, x_3, and x_4

Figure 4.1 How linear regression gives the effect of each variable on the value

The linear problem can be overcome, partially, by applying a transforming function to each value of x_i in order to make it linear and hence amenable to linear regression. For example, if the underlying shape of the effect of a variable on a response is a gradually increasing curve, then finding the logarithm of the variable can make it linear (Figure 4.2), so that:

$$V = \beta \log x$$

would be the functional form for a particular characteristic x. Linear regression can then be used to determine ß. The disadvantage of this approach is that if there is a large number of inputs, then each one would have to be transformed by a function, possibly a different one for each variable. The task then becomes a mathematical problem rather than an activity of an appraiser whose job is to make an analysis and give an estimate as quickly as possible with as high a degree of reliability as possible.

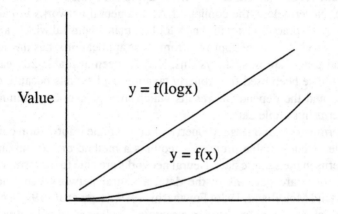

Figure 4.2 The logarithms of an increasing function can linearize it

A further disadvantage of linear or semi-linear regression is that not every sample of data on past sales can produce the required values of ß. The mathematical method used by the regression program in the computer inverts a matrix. If many of the input characteristics are logistic variables (i.e. they are either 1 or 0 to represent say the presence or absence of a garage) then the inversion of the matrix is not possible and the method fails, so ß cannot be found and the model cannot be created.

Analytical systems for determining values from a sample of comparable properties must be easy to use, non-linear, reliable, and robust in cases where the data is largely logistic. Fortunately, a new technology, Artificial Intelligence, obviates many of the drawbacks of regression.

Whilst it may be argued that linear regression is good enough for most cases, there are applications where non-linearity is essential in the solution of a problem; see for example (Donnelly, 1990; Baxt, 1993; Ripley,1994). We cannot say that there will not be occasions in valuation when non-linearity will be necessary to give the required degree of accuracy for the problem.

Artificial intelligence and mass appraisal

Many apparently new technologies have a firm base in history. Artificial Intelligence (AI) is certainly new to applications in the mass appraisal of property, but in fact, the ideas are now quite mature. One problem has been the lack of computing power available in the past, but now that is changing. Modern computers are now well able to cope with the demands of AI. As a prelude to presenting AI and its application to appraisal, we should consider a problem which arises in recommending AI methods. They have not had the mass usage which would recommend them for mass appraisal systems on the basis of experience. Nevertheless, the coming of AI and neural networks in particular has presented the practitioner with a new tool for mass appraisal which, although it has not yet had the seal of approval from mass applications, has the potential to be a vital procedure in such systems. Had AI been available 20 years ago, they would have been used for property taxation applications because of their ease of use and the dependable results which they give in determining non-linear patterns in sample data.

The determination of a target property value from the information contained in a sample of comparable properties requires a method of recognizing non-linear patterns in the sample data. Neural networks are able to perform that task. In fact, if there are patterns in the data, a neural network can find them (Rumelhartand McLelland, 1986; Funahashi, 1989; Hertz et al., 1991). A neural network which has found patterns in a sample is called a trained network, and the process of pattern recognition is called training. A trained neural network has an internal representation of the relationships in the data, and so can be used as a model to find the probable value of a target property.

This chapter now continues with a description of the underlying principles of neural networks applied to data analysis, and the means by which such methods can form the basis of practical taxation systems. Case studies are described and the principles of the application are presented. Finally, the chapter attempts to give a pointer towards likely developments of AI in the future, and how these can be utilized to advantage for professionals who have the task of creating and operating dependable mass appraisal systems.

The valuation task

Valuation is an expert task which depends on rules and judgement. Rules are useful, but they are often contradictory so that judgement has to be exercised to decide which rule takes precedence over others. Judgement is very different. Judgement takes all things into account: rules, 'feelings', social factors, the political situation, and the local and global economy. It is a heuristic activity in which the professional person has learned, by experience, the market forces and relationships, taking into account the various influences which have relevance to the valuation.

The human being therefore works in two ways: by rules and by heuristics. Rules are powerful but they conflict and are not always rigidly applicable to every situation. Heuristics are powerful too, but it is often difficult to give a reason for a decision taken on heuristic grounds. A decision may have to be justified later if it is questioned. Rules may have to be used in conjunction with heuristics, a scenario which is considered in a further section.

Rules and heuristic activities come from the two sides of the brain: left for rules and symbols and right for spatial and heuristic. Humans thus have a powerful weapon in the solution of problems - symbolic logic on the one hand, and heuristics on the other. A particular decision may depend purely on one or the other, but mostly a decision arises from a combination of both, so rules and their refinement by experience give the human a powerful combined tool for the solution of complex interaction problems, of which appraisal is an example.

There was a time when the heuristic mode of decision-making was considered to be less respectable, scientifically or mathematically than a purely rule-governed or formula prescribed decision. It was, and still is, thought to be questionable if a formula cannot be applied to solve a practical problem. Any other to many people is not acceptable because it is not explainable. Arguments to challenge such a position are not difficult to find.

Heuristic approaches are the only way that nature solves the problem of managing the complexity of life. For example, the recognition of a face is very rarely done by symbolic description or rules. We can recognize a face from 'knowing' someone. The process of recognition is never doubted. It is easy, and yet, it is a very complex process which is not possible to implement on a computer with a conventional program. Nor is it a formula. Facial recognition is learned very easily, and we are soon able to link up a name with a face: the process of association. We have the same ease of recognition of voices, smells, and touch. From experience, we develop the power to associate a certain input of senses with a name or an activity. For an interesting discussion of various levels of processing, see Smolensky, (1986).

Harnessing the brain's methods

Given that one activity of heuristics in the brain is recognition, there is another powerful operation that the brain can manage easily: mapping. It is recognized that certain actions that we make tend to be mirrored by the stimulation of neurons in particular regions of the brain. In fact, parts of our body are 'mapped'

85

to particular locations in the brain. Similarly, we literally have an internal geographical map in our brain of the area where we live. It forms automatically by experience, but is a powerful tool for thinking ahead and finding our way. Once we have an internal map as a representation of the world, we can use it to plan a route or to decide on a course of action because the problem is internalized; we have a model of the world which can be tested with various possibilities.

Then two activities of the brain are powerful problem-solvers - the ability to associate one thing with another, and the ability to make internal, often two-dimensional, representations of the world. Such activities are described in AI terminology as subsymbolic. This is separate from our ability to use language and to deduce a set of rules to handle a particular set of circumstances, or to communicate with others. The linguistic facility is called symbolic activity: the manipulation of letters and numbers to model the world, explain it, and communicate with other humans.

Recently, the heuristic ability of the brain has been modelled in computer programs which, though they run under rigidly determined programs, are able to simulate the adaptive behaviour of the brain. These programs are capable of associating certain attributes with others, and are able to make automatic classifications of data. The methods are now being applied along with traditional symbolic routines (i.e. statistical techniques) to achieve a goal which is to obtain the maximum amount of information from data. Given this proposition, if we can obtain the maximum information and classification from data, we are then able to provide the most satisfactory basis for making a decision about property valuation from the sample data of comparables. Once we can be satisfied that this is the maximum amount of information available, the valuer can then modify the valuation figure in the light of other external factors such as the social, political and economic situation. We can imitate, in the interaction between computer and human, the activities of heuristic judgement along with the implementation of rules.

Background to AI technology

The ability of the animal brain to solve problems is impressive. Without any knowledge of science, an animal can survive the most complex of natural threats even though the underlying factors are extremely complex. Animals, including humans, have impressive abilities which cannot be matched by the most advanced computers. Facial recognition, language ability, creative skills, forecasting and organizational ability are all attributes which are all too obviously lacking in computers.

Traditional neuroscience has identified two abilities of the brain which help in animal survival: the ability to learn from experience, and the ability to create

86

internal representations of the world, often in the form of internal data 'maps'. Recent research has now discovered not only how to engineer these powerful abilities into computer programs, but also how to actually put them to work in all branches of industry and commerce, and, of special interest to us in property appraisal.

The first inroad into engineering a brain-based machine was the understanding of the basic structure of the brain. The underlying repetitive element of the brain consists of neuron cells consisting of a tree-like (dendrite) structure. Neurons are arranged in layers, and are in contact with each other. The branches (axons) of the neurons in one layer appear to touch the dendrites (roots) of neurons in upper layers. The contact points between the neuron axons and dendrites of neurons in the next layer are a major feature of the brain and are called synapses. There are billions of them in the brain (Figure 4.3).

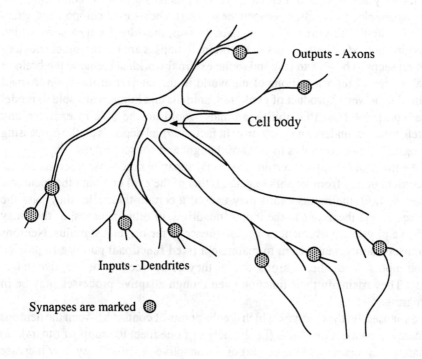

Figure 4.3 Diagram of a neuron with the dendrites

The neuron layers in the brain appear to be what we would term data processors. The input of electrical pulses, say from the retina, are linked into an initial layer of neurons, work their way across perhaps three or four layers, and emerge at neurons in the top layer. The top layer neurons determine some kind of response such as muscular movement. These may be motor neurons which cause the animal to react in some way to the stimulus which enter the layers. Thus the brain seems to consist of many modules of layered neurons in which we can identify the outside layers as inputs and outputs. Processing occurs in the internal neurons of the synapses.

What is the special purpose of neurons? They clearly exist in the body, mostly in the brain, for the purpose of data processing, there is little doubt about that. They gather electrical pulses from nerves and other neurons, and they pass these on to other neurons via the synapses. Neurons appear to pass electrical pulses that they receive on to other neurons if the incident pulses exceed a certain intensity. The intensities are modulated by the synapses - they can either inhibit or amplify the pulses. Synapses serve the crucial purpose of controlling the passage of electrical pulses between the neurons. They are the components which modify their ability to pass on signals. In fact, they are the means by which learning and adaptivity occurs in the brain. Synapses are the biological devices which seem to be able to respond to the external world, and enable the brain to make internal representations of the world in the interior of the brain. Armed with this powerful product of evolution, animals and humans are able to model the world. Without this ability, animals would not be able to exercise any intelligence or understand the world. In fact, survival depends on the processing of data in the brain, and is the seat of thought and consciousness.

Neurons and synapses perform distinctly separate functions. Neurons collect electrical pulses from sensors (e.g. the retina of the eye) or from other neurons. They sum up the inputs and if they exceed a certain threshold, they pass the pulses on via the axons to the inputs, dendrites, of other neurons, or they may effect a physical movement as a consequence of the original stimulus. Neurons themselves in general seem to maintain a fixed functional purpose in passing their inputs on to other neurons; that is, they do not seem to be adaptive in any way. They maintain their function even though adaptive processes may be in progress.

Synapses, on the contrary, which are the points of contact between the neurons where axons meet dendrites (i.e. branches of one meet the roots of others), do change their characteristics as part of the adaptive process. They may increase or decrease their ability to enhance or inhibit the train of pulses which pass between the neurons. They change in response to external stimuli in ways which are not fully understood for the brain. For artificial neural networks, however, rules of adaptivity have been discovered in recent years, and it is these which have led to a breakthrough in adaptive programming, and now enable artificial neural networks to be used in applications throughout industry and commerce, taking on the brain-like role of being adaptive to inputs, and to map multivariate data on to a simplified scale or area.

It is, therefore, in the nature of the adaptive synapses, controlling the responses of the neurons, that underlies the ability of the brain to respond to complex inputs. The observed adaptivity of synapses results in learning ability. Given a high degree of connectivity between processors, and given an adaptive rule for the for the strengths of their connections, there is the basis for making an effective artificial adaptive device which mimics some of the properties of the brain. Such is the inspiration for the neural network research that has advanced to the stage where artificial neural networks are making an impact in the field of data analysis, as well as other applications such as machine control and time series prediction. The ability to learn from experience and to map the external world on the basis of sample data, is thought to lie in the synapses which connect the neurons to each other. The synapses are considered to be the adaptive elements in the brain, and hence account for the ability of the brain to learn from experience and to represent the external world in the form of internal maps. The data processing and memory elements therefore are integrated into the whole structure of the neural system that constitutes the brain.

The brain does not have specific cells set aside for memory and others for processing. Memory and processing are distributed amongst the billions of neurons and synapses. Brain processing is not done in series like the conventional computer, but in parallel. As data passes forward from the input layer across the internal layers to the output layer, millions of neuron cells and synapses are active simultaneously. Although each individual action of a neuron is slow, the fact that it happens to millions at a time, in parallel, makes the brain a very fast processor. The connectionist architecture allows brains to, say, recognize a face in a matter of tenths of a second, even though facial recognition is a very difficult problem for a conventional computer.

As a consequence of the distributed nature of the processing in the brain, and the fact that data processing occurs simultaneously in parallel rather than consecutively in series, the mode of data handling in the brain is often termed Parallel Distributed Processing (PDP). Such is the title of the seminal work on this subject published in 1986 (Rumelhart, 1986). The work in that book describes a process in which the learning ability of the brain, neurons and the adaptive synapses, is simulated in the form of a mathematical algorithm which can be implemented in computer software. In another work of equal significance to the artificial intelligence community, the author T. Kohonen (1988) describes a mapping system which is able to make representations of data in the form of a conceptual two dimensional map. Thus in two different fields, we have the genesis of an engineered counterpart to the two learning abilities of the brain: learning by example and the self-organizing map.

This chapter now proceeds by explaining the principles underlying artificial intelligence, and neural networks in particular, and their application to the types of numerical methods and recognition activities relevant to the determination of property values for taxation purposes. Next, case studies are assessed and various scenarios for the practical implementation of neural networks are proposed. The methods are critically examined and recommendations are made for practical implementations. The chapter concludes with the likely outcome of present research and commercial developments in the artificial intelligence field relevant to the mass appraisal process.

The principles of neural networks

The device in an artificial neural network which imitates the neuron of the brain is called a perceptron. The 'intelligence' of the system comes from the connections between perceptrons, or the counterpart to synapses which in the artificial case are called weights. The various streams of research into artificial intelligence can be put to good use in the appraisal professions. Three streams of research are identified in this chapter as being:

1   Supervised neural networks in which connection weights are varied in response to a training set of independent variables and a dependent variable. The training set consists of past examples from which the neural network forms a model. The model then becomes the basis upon which future valuations are made;

2   The Kohonen Self-Organizing Map in which a special algorithm is employed to construct a one or two-dimensional map of the independent variables. Properties of similar types are grouped together in the two dimensional map, and outliers or exceptions are isolated. The resulting map forms the basis of a classification of the data which may be useful in the production of a banding model. The method accomplishes a considerable reduction in dimensionality from all the characteristics of the properties, which could number six to twenty, down to two dimensions or even down to one. So effectively, this is a data simplification or clustering technique.

3   Genetic Algorithms (GAs). Some applications in appraisal may require the production of a much more complex model than is normally handled by a neural network. Business valuation, with all the lease and rental complexities, may become so complex that the solution may be to use genetic algorithms. We do not describe GA applications in this chapter,

but the principles are mentioned. The techniques are certainly not for the faint-hearted, but as software implementations of AI progress, they will probably be commonplace in a few years' time.

Back propagation neural networks

By far the majority of applications of neural networks adopt the supervised algorithm, i.e. back-propagation, category 1 from the classification presented above. They use past data, which, in appraisal terms, is the reference to a sample of comparables. The technique thus applies itself quite naturally to the appraisal modelling application. So here we examine the particular techniques that allow these methods to be applied to the modelling of the patterns in comparables.

Neural networks work at the subsymbolic level and not the symbolic level. Neural networks accept numbers as relative levels of a variable, give numbers as outputs, and correct their own numerical weights by incremental numerical adjustments using the back propagation algorithm. As the weights are corrected, the network fits better and better to the underlying patterns, with tests being made from time to time of how well they are modelling.

Artificial neural networks (ANNs) consist of interconnected layers of neurons. The interconnections between neurons in the brain are modulated by synapses. In ANNs, the connections are weights. A typical layout of a network is shown in Figure 4.4. There are three layers: an input layer, a hidden layer, and an output layer. Each layer is fully connected to the next one by the weights. The number of inputs depends on the number of characteristics being modelled, and the number of outputs, one in this case, represents the value of the property. The number of hidden units depends on the complexity of the problem. If there are too many, the ANN will not learn the underlying patterns, simply each set of inputs and the related output. With too few hidden units, the ANN will not pick up the full detail of the underlying patterns in the data. A compromise has to be reached in each case by a process of experimentation.

When a neural network is set up in software ready to start training, all the connection weights are given random values. Each hidden layer neuron and output neuron takes its inputs and modifies them by an equation as shown in Figure 4.5.

The training process

The process of training on a sample of data proceeds as follows. The first comparable in the training set is presented to the network input. The data feeds forward from input to output through the hidden layer, using the weights and

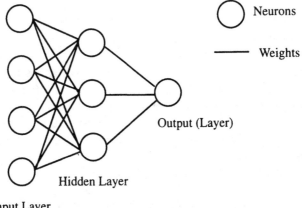

Neurons

Weights

Output (Layer)

Hidden Layer

Input Layer

Figure 4.4 A back propagation neural network with four inputs, three hidden units and one output

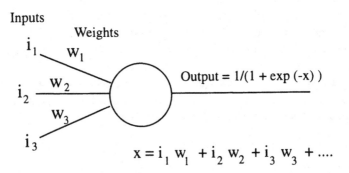

Inputs

Weights

i_1

w_1

Output = $1/(1 + \exp(-x))$

i_2

w_2

w_3

i_3

$x = i_1 w_1 + i_2 w_2 + i_3 w_3 + \ldots$

Figure 4.5 The mathematical structure of a neuron

equations already described. The output gives a value which will almost certainly be different from the true value (the target) of the property. The difference between the target value and the network output is taken and fed into an equation which calculates the amount which each weight must be changed to make the network output incrementally closer to the correct value. It is important to understand that the change made to each weight is only small, and only takes the network output a very small amount nearer to the correct value. This process of weight updating is carried out in a direction from output to input, a process which has been appropriately called back propagation.

Now the next comparable property is applied to the ANN input and the above process is repeated. When all the cases in the sample have been processed, the sample is fed through again. Gradually, the network builds up an internal representation of the patterns in the data in terms of the connection weights in the network. Once the optimum level of training has been reached, the network can then be used to provide values of comparable properties, even though these new presentations did form a part of the training sample.

In reality, the process of feeding back the error after each presentation of a comparable is wasteful of computer processing time. In fact, it is usual to feed n cases through the network, accumulating the errors for each case, and then invoking the back propagation routine. The quantity n is called an epoch, and may or may not be equal to the size of the training sample. Where an epoch is smaller than the training sample size, the network is less likely to reach a point where the error can no longer be reduced. This is called a false minimum, a state which has to be avoided in ANN training. The science of network training is advancing rapidly with some new, fast-training algorithms (see Johansson, 1992).

Validation

If a neural network were to be trained on all the cases in a sample, it would not be possible to know whether the ANN had found false patterns (overfitting), or had not been run long enough to pick up the full complexity in the data (underfitting). In order to increase the chance of finding the correct patterns, current practice is to section off a part of the sample and exclude it from network training. The excluded cases are called the validation set. During the training process, at regular intervals, training is suspended and the validation set is applied to the network without back propagation. The error on this set (compared with the known values) is measured; the network weights are also recorded. Training is now resumed on the training set, and after a preset number of sessions, the validation set is applied again to the network. The error is measured. If this error is less than from the previous measurement on the validation set, the previously saved network weights are deleted and the new weights recorded. After a few thousand cycles of the training set, training is stopped and the trained network used as the model is the one which gave the lowest error on the validation set (which may have been produced early on in the training cycle).

The Kohonen self-organizing map (SOM)

Back Propagation is classed as a supervised algorithm because the response of the inputs is used as examples for the network. In the SOM, however, the inputs are taken without the responses and the algorithm produces a classification of the characteristics of the properties in the sample. The algorithm does not have the responses to teach the network what the outputs should be, so the algorithm is called unsupervised. Strange though this may seem, it is probably quite a common algorithm in the real biological brain.

There are only two layers of neurons in the SOM: the input layer and the Kohonen layer. Every neuron in the input layer is connected to every neuron in the Kohonen layer. The Kohonen layer is usually in two dimensions, but other dimensions are possible, though above three dimensions, the results may be difficult to interpret. The Kohonen layer is both the calculation layer and the output. Its nature is often described as competitive, because the first condition in the algorithm is that only one neuron, the winner, can be 'on' or active at a time.

When the first case in the sample is presented to the input, the algorithm compares the inputs with the values of all the weights. Since the weights are given random values initially, as in back propagation, there will be one set of weights to a particular Kohonen layer neuron that is closer to the inputs than any other set. This is the winning neuron. The algorithm then proceeds to make not only the winning neuron's weights closer to the inputs, but also the weights in the neighbourhood of the winning neuron (see Figure 4.6). The next pattern is presented and the procedure is repeated on all the training sample a large number of times. As the training process continues, the size of the neighbourhood around the winning neurons is decreased gradually from all of the neurons in the layer at the start, to just the winning neuron towards the end of the training. The total and rather surprising result of this process is that the Kohonen layer has become a feature map of the data. For example, the algorithms may have found three general clusters of the data as shown in Figure 4.7.

Genetic algorithms

It may not be unreasonable to conclude from the story so far that since neural networks have been inspired by the brain, there may be other biological systems that can be copied and which may be useful additions to our armoury of analytical

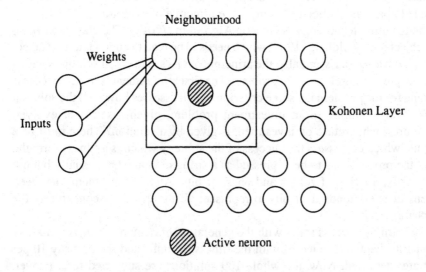

Figure 4.6 A Kohonen self-organizing map showing three inputs which are connected to every node in the layer, an active node which is closest to the input, and a neighbourhood around an active node

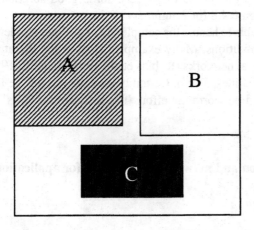

Figure 4.7 A trained Kohonen layer in which three layers, A, B and C have been organized by the algorithm to classify the input data

techniques. Since nature seems to have been successful in the production of species which have survived and adapted to their environment, perhaps we may be able to base an artificial system on the principle of evolution.

The resulting technology is Genetic Algorithms (GA's). The classic work on the subject is by Goldberg (1989) which needs to be read to appreciate the subject in all its intricacies. Essentially, the principle of GA's is to breed solutions which have adapted themselves to the problem. The first requirement is to have a fitness formula for the problem i.e. some criterion which assesses how well the solution works. For example, in an investment problem, given a series of evolved procedures, what return on investment is given by a solution? There must be a formula which can assess the success of the strategy which is a fitness formula. Next, the problem has to be expressed as a string of characters, usually but not necessarily, a string of zeroes and ones, or bits. A typical problem may need dozens or even hundred of bits to represent all the variables constituting the problem.

The learning process starts with the generation of random strings of bits, say about 100. Each one is tested with the fitness formula, and the best say 10 per cent are identified. Now, the whole 100 solutions are subjected to crossover, which is biological terms is sexual reproduction. Sections of strings are interchanged with sections of other strings to produce new ones which are made up of sections of the originals, however, the better fitting ones have a greater chance of 'mating' for crossover than the other less fit ones. The result of the crossover process is a new generation, which is now assessed by the fitness formula. And so the process continues for perhaps a hundred generations. The total effect of the process is to produce some good solutions to the original problem. See Figure 4.8 for a summary of the process.

GA's are well able to handle the complexity of difficult problems with awkward constraints or conditions. Many examples exist in the literature of the use of GA's to train neural networks (Robins et al., 1993; Radcliff, 1993; Dracopoulos and Jones, 1994; Jones, 1993). Certainly they are not for the faint-hearted, but the rewards could be worth the effort. The software for GA's is fairly cheap to buy!

Data preparation and network optimization for applications

Back propagation

The literature on the application of back propagation neural networks to property valuation has blossomed over the last two years (Evans et al., 1992; James et al., 1994; Quang,1992; Tay and Ho, 1991; Casdagli, 1989). Results achieved by many reported works have shown that the method has been an improvement on

```
1     Define a problem in terms of a string of 0's and 1's:

2     'Breed' random solutions:

      1000111010010111010111100011 01
      0011001011100010011001100011 01
      1100110111000110001001110100 01
      etc...

3     'Breed' new generations by crossover :
      i.e. take parts of one and exchange with others, and breed a
      new generation.

4     The more successful solutions have abetter chance or
      reproduction.

5     After many generations, a solution evolves. It works!!!
```

Figure 4.8 Summary of the process by which a problem can be solved by genetic algorithms

the previously-used regression techniques and considering the ease of use of neural networks and the existence of software which sets up the appropriate networks for the user (James, 1995), the use of such networks in valuation is likely to increase with time as appraisers realize that here is a new technique which can add accuracy and savings of time in the analysis of comparables. In one case (Collins and Evans, 1994) the results from neural networks have shown conclusions which were different from the results of regression.

The secret of good results from ANN's is proper data preparation and preprocessing. For the purposes of learning patterns in comparables, there are two types of data: analogue and logistic. Analogue variables are easy to handle in that they can have any value between a maximum and a minimum, and represent a quantity which is continuous, such as the age of a property. Age, although usually given an integer value, is nevertheless continuous variable and so can be represented by a single input into the neural network. In fact, neural network inputs are scaled between either 0 and 1 or -1 and +1 .

In the case of logistic variables, however, care must be taken. For example, a house may or may not have parking space. The absence of a parking space can be represented by a zero, and a parking space by a one. Such a logistic input must be represented by one input neuron. In the case of an attribute such as location, however, there are many ways of inputting it to a network. If the properties are from unconnected parts of a city, then it would be wise to have an input for each district being considered. All the location inputs would be zero except for the district that the property is in, and that would be presented to the network as a one in the appropriate column for that district. In the case of locations which are connected and some pattern is thought to exist as a function of district, then two inputs could stand for the grid reference of the properties.

Another problem with data may be that for a particular input, there is a cluster of properties around a particular value say of age, and then perhaps very old property, so that values presented to an input may mainly be in the range 1945 to 1993, but there are one or two properties built in 1698. This would tend to distort the range, so it may be prudent in this case to present the logarithm of the age of the property to the network.

Clearly the whole question of data preparation to a network is important and may be decisive in the success or failure of the method in an application. Reference should be made to the literature to discover standard practice. The DTI publish a best practice guide for neural networks which is being revised at the present time.

An important use of neural networks is in time series forecasting. For property valuation, it is frequently useful to model the trend of prices of houses or financial indices over a period of time, and hazard an estimate of the likely future value of the quantity. The techniques is often called windowing. A series of consecutive values of the series is presented to the network. The outcome is the next value of the series (see Figure 4.9). The window is moved randomly over the past values of the series until the network models the patterns. Once trained and validated, the network can be used as a model to predict the future course of the series. There are many examples of this kind of prediction in the literature (Casdagli, 1989; Azoff, 1993; Azoff, 1994; Hoptroff, 1993; de Groot and Wurtz, 1991).

The Kohonen self-organizing map

The potential of this algorithm is still to be realized, but there are some interesting papers appearing on the subject. In the work by Martin-del-Brio (1994), various characteristics of banks were recorded and applied to a self-organizing map training session. The inputs distributed themselves over the map. It was discovered that banks which were subsequently found to be solvent were clustered in one part of the map, and others which later became insolvent were clustered at another point on the map. Thus clustering, in such a manner may be helpful.

Work by the author James (1994) describes how a one-dimensional Kohonen map can be used to classify property data. The difference between the weights

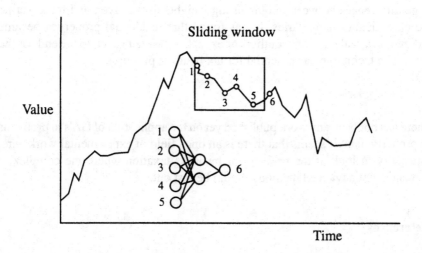

Figure 4.9 A five-input feed-forward multilayer perceptron is being used here to learn the trends in a time series. When trained, the network can be used to extrapolate the series into the future

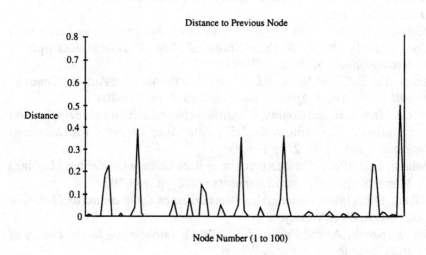

Figure 4.10 The distance between weights in a one-dimensional Kohonen layer can define the classification boundaries

in the record were recorded as shown in Figure 4.10. The peaks are positions of large differences between neighbouring weights in the layer, and these define the classification boundaries. It was found that residential properties became ordered on a scale, and that outliers or exceptions were pushed to the ends of the layer. The technique has potential for tax banding purposes.

Genetic algorithms

There has not been any work published yet on the application of GA's to problems of property data. It seems that there is an open field of experimental work here, especially to look at the problem of business taxation where the complexity demands that advanced methods should be test out.

References

Azoff, E.M. (1993), 'Reducing Error in Neural Network Time Series Forecasting', *Neural Computing & Applications*, vol. 1 no. 4, pp. 240-247.

Azoff, E.M. (1994), *Time Series Forecasting*, John Wiley Donnelly, W.A. (1990),

Baxt, W.G. (1993), 'A Neural Network Trained to Identify the Presence of Myocardial Infarction Bases Diagnostic Decision on Nonlinear Relationships Between the Input Variables', *Neural Computing & Applications* vol. 1, pp. 176-182.

Casdagli, M. (1989), 'Non-Linear Prediction of Chaotic Time Series', *Physica*, D 35, pp. 335-356.

de Groot, C. and Wurtz, D. (1991), 'Analysis of Univariate Time Series with Connectionist Nets: A Case Study of Two Classical Examples', *Neurocomputing*, vol. 3, pp. 177-192.

Dracopoulos, D.C. and Jones, A.J. 'Neuro-Genetic Adaptive Attitude Control', *Neural Computing & Applications*, vol. 2 no. 4, pp. 183-204.

Evans, A.; James, H. and Collins, A. 'Artificial Neural Networks: an Application to Residential Valuation in the UK', *Journal of Property Valuation and Investment*, vol. 11 no. 2, pp.195-204.

Funahashi, K.I. (1989), 'On the Approximate Realisation of Continuous Mappings by Neural Networks', *Neural Networks* vol. 2, pp. 183-192.

Goldberg, D.E. (1989), *Genetic Algorithms in Search Optimization and Machine Learning*, Addison Wesley.

Hertz, J.; Krogh, A. and Palmer, R.G. (1991), *Introduction to the Theory of Neural Computation*, Addison-Wesley.

Hoptroff, R.G. (1993), 'The Principles and Practice of Time Series Forecasting and Business Modelling Using Neural Nets', *Neural Computing & Applications*, vol. 1 no. 1, pp. 59-66.

James, H. (1994), 'Software Reviews', *The Economic Journal 104,* (January) pp. 180-196.

James, H. (1994), 'An Automatic Pilot for Surveyors', *London RICS The Cutting Edge.*

James, H.; Collins, A. and Lam, E.T.K. (1995), *The Principles and Practice of Artificial Neural Networks in Property Valuation Studies,* Paper presented at International Conference on Property Taxation, Dublin, 1994.

Johansson, E.M.; Dowla, F.U. and Goodman, D.M. (1992), 'Backpropagation Learning for Multilayer Feed-Forward Neural Networks Using the Conjugate Gradient Method', *International Journal of Neural Systems,* vol. 2 no. 4, pp. 291-301.

Jones, A.J. (1993), 'Genetic Algorithms and their Application to the Design of Neural Networks', *Neural Computing & Applications* vol. 1 no. 1, pp. 32-45.

Kohonen, T. (1988), *Associative Memory and Self-Organizing Maps,* Springer-Verlag.

Martin-del-Brio, B. and Serrano-Cinca, C, (1994), 'Self-Organizing Neural Networks for the Analysis and Representation of Data: Some Financial Cases', *Neural Computing & Applications,* vol. 1 no. 2, pp. 193-206.

Nellis, J.G. and Longbottom, J.A. (1981), 'An Empirical Analysis of the Determination of House Prices in the United Kingdom', *Urban Studies,* vol. 18 no. 1, pp. 9-21.

Radcliffe, N.J. (1993), 'Genetic Set Recombination and Its Application to Neural Network Topology Optimisation', *Neural Computing & Applications,* vol. 1 no. 1, pp. 67-90.

Ripley, B.D. (1994), 'Neural Networks and Related Methods for Classification', *Journal of the Royal Statistical Society* B vol. 56 no. 3, pp. 409-456.

Robbins, G.E. et al., (1993), 'Generation and Adaptation of Neural Networks by Evolutionary Techniques (GANNET)', *Neural Computing & Applications,* vol. 1 no. 1, pp. 23-31.

Rumelhart, D.E. and McLelland, J.L. (1986), (eds), *Parallel Distributed Processing,* MIT Press.

Smolensky, P. (1986), 'Information Processing in Dynamical Systems', in Rumelhart, D.E. and McLelland, J.L. (eds), *Parallel Distributed Processing,* MIT Press, pp. 194-281.

Quang, Do and Grudnitski, Gary (1992), 'A Neural Network Approach to Residential Property Appraisal', *The Real Estate Appraiser,* pp. 38-45. December.

Tay, D.P.H. and Ho, D.K.H. (1991), 'Artificial Intelligence and the Mass Appraisal of Residential Apartments', *Journal of Property Valuation & Investment,* vol. 10, pp. 525-540.

5 Expert system development for the mass appraisal of commercial property in Malaysia

A. H. Nawawi, D. Jenkins and S. Gronow

Introduction

The subject of this chapter is to investigate the use of knowledge from a number of experts in developing an expert system for rating valuation of commercial and industrial properties in Malaysia. This chapter examines (1) a review of the background to the research (2) the process of eliciting the knowledge (3) the knowledge that has been elicited (4) a description of the prototype (i.e. the system that represents the knowledge) and its evaluation and (5) the conclusions drawn from the research.

Regular revaluations have always been difficult for local authorities in Malaysia. Whilst political pressures may sometimes be contributory to revaluation delays, a shortage of qualified personnel is also significant. Replacement of the property tax with a poll tax (Hizam, 1991), delegation of the revaluation task to the Valuation and Property Services Department of the Ministry of Finance and the private sector (Low, 1986) have been seen as potential external solutions, but these have not really addressed the issue of increasing productivity of personnel and giving full autonomy and responsibility to the local authorities in revaluation work (as stipulated by the Local Government Act 1976).

In increasing productivity of personnel, besides the more qualitative human factors (Chow et al., 1988) such as attitude, experience, confidence, managerial/supervisory skills, motivation and the need for supportive superiors, more objective work systems geared towards deadline oriented work and 'signing powers' to local authorities' valuers, the potential role of computerization to increase productivity of personnel by utilizing computerized recording systems has also long been identified.

In Malaysia, current computerization exercises in local authorities mainly concentrate on the storage and retrieval of property records and for billing purposes (City Hall of Kuala Lumpur, 1990). The current information technology strategy to a certain extent is thus on a loose and piecemeal basis more concerned with speeding up certain routine works without an integrated and coherent attempt to elicit (acquire) and integrate the knowledge of valuers in the technology at the various stages of the valuation process. The latter could be achieved through development of expert systems which were being marketed as a means of 'deskilling' areas where 'experts' were in short supply (Jenkins, 1992).

Expert system

An expert system can be defined as 'a computer system which contains knowledge pertaining to an area of human specialization. The system can also implement that knowledge in such a fashion as to be able to act as a consultant expert in that field of specialization. Such a system typically requires the user to provide answers to relevant questions in order to supply advice based on those responses. In addition the system is able to justify or explain the reasoning behind a course of action it recommends, in order to defend its deduced solution'. (Scott, 1988).

The development of an expert system is thus centred on the elicitation of the knowledge from an expert or experts, analysis of the knowledge and representation and validation of the knowledge in a computer program.

Mass appraisals and expert systems

Most current systems on mass appraisal valuations have been associated with the traditional statistical approach of Multiple Regression Analysis (MRA). However, notwithstanding its importance, this method is not easily understood by valuers without a strong foundation in econometrics (Wiltshaw, 1991).

Alternatively, an expert system which embodies the knowledge of a valuer (or valuers) including heuristically determined values based on knowledge and experience, may provide a system capable of assisting in rating valuation including mass appraisal (Scott and Gronow, 1987; Nawawi and Gronow, 1991(a), 1991(b), 1992; Nawawi et al., 1993, 1994).

Nature of properties in the research

The scope of properties in the research includes purpose-built office complexes (of more than 5 storeys), shopping complexes, shop-house/office/flat and industrial properties that is factories. The wide spectrum of commercial and industrial properties were purposely selected rather than the more traditional approach by previous researchers to concentrate on just one particular type of property. This is unique to this current research involving the explanation of the variability of reasoning strategies within the same generic class of property (i.e. commercial and industrial) and the significance of knowledge blending in the context of multiple experts for different types of commercial properties.

The core principle of rating valuation in Malaysia is Annual Value. The current basis of assessment of rates in Malaysia is provided in the Local Government Act 1976. The Act which succeeded several important major enactments namely the Valuation of Land Enactment 1922 and the Town Boards Enactment 1930 had its roots from England as it was derived from the English's East India Act IX 1848 which was itself related to the Parochial Assessment Act 1836.

Based on its historical origin, the concept of 'annual value' forms the basis for rating assessment in Malaysia (except for the Johor state which uses the 'improvement value' i.e. capital value). The concept envisages a hypothetical tenancy leading to a hypothetical rent fixed by a hypothetical owner and a hypothetical tenant which in itself is guided by legal principles in the English rating law such as rebus sic stantibus and tenancy from year to year.

The objective of rating valuation in Malaysia thus is to arrive at an opinion of 'Annual Value' which can be interpreted from Section 2 of Part XV of the Local Government Act 1976 (for the valuation of buildings) as the estimated gross annual rent at which the holding might reasonably be expected to let from year to year having no regard to any restrictions or control on rent and also disregarding enhanced rent resulting from use of machinery for certain purposes.

The knowledge to be elicited from the experts in this research thus is all subsets of knowledge related to the process of estimation of the gross annual rent in accordance with the interpretation of Section 2 of the Local Government Act 1976. This involves using the comparison method of valuation i.e. a method of formulation of opinion of value (in this case rental value) at a particular date (date of revaluation or date of tone of the list) based on comparison of market rentals and characteristics of the subject property and other comparable properties.

The knowledge elicitation process

The research commenced with knowledge elicitation from valuers from the City Hall of Kuala Lumpur, the City Hall being the main collaborating local authority in this project, having the largest number of commercial holdings among the local authorities in Malaysia. Due to the complex nature of the main commercial properties and industrial properties in Kuala Lumpur and the range of experience and exposure of the valuers in valuing these properties, it was decided that the main source of knowledge of 'core valuers' would come from the City Hall.

Their knowledge would then be complemented and supplemented by the knowledge of other local authority valuers. The main reason for eliciting knowledge from other local authorities' valuers was related to the need for bridging the gap of contextual knowledge and contextual second opinion from valuers from other geographical and market conditions. Some examples of the contextual knowledge that could be elicited from the other local authorities' valuers includes; how valuation of shopping complexes should be undertaken where there was scant evidence or even no comparable shopping complex especially in relatively new smaller urban centres, the spatial influence of the siting of shop-house/office/flat on its rental in towns which predominantly consisted of such properties and valuing plant and machinery in a local authority that had heavy industrial properties.

Within the valuation process, an element of forecasting needed to be carried out, especially when there was a significant gap between rental evidence dates and the date of enforcement of valuation. Market knowledge (including technical knowledge of forecasting) of private valuers, who are generally more in touch with the market, could be useful in providing assistance to the valuers in making the forecast and so private valuers would form a distinct group within the knowledge elicitation process.

The legal knowledge of the rating valuers was mainly embodied in their working practice in terms of selecting suitable rental evidence and the application of the concept of rebus sic stantibus. An academic was included in the knowledge elicitation strategy to bridge any possible gap in the legal knowledge of the rating valuers in complying with the definition of 'Annual Value' provided by the Local Government Act 1976. Other local authorities' valuers, private sector valuers and academics are referred to as 'complementary valuers' in this research.

For the more complex commercial properties, namely the purpose-built office complexes and shopping complexes, it was found that certain gaps in the knowledge of the core valuers existed in making objective comparisons on factors related to building characteristics and in the case of shopping complexes, the status and tenant mix. The concept of class of purpose-built office complexes (City Hall of Kuala Lumpur, 1992) was appreciated by the City Hall of Kuala Lumpur's valuers but it was rather broad, rather unstructured and at times based too much on 'gut feeling'. Throughout the knowledge elicitation with the valuers, it was agreed that a more structured (and preferably more objective and detailed) means of comparison would be useful in giving explanation, notwithstanding the practicality for the rather broad heuristic comparison and adjustment.

For these reasons the elicitation process was further broadened to encompass supporting specialists, property managers, building related experts, a transport officer and an economic planning unit officer.

106

Knowledge representation

Valuers seemed to show a high level of confidence in making 'reasoned adjustments' (heuristically) for differences in factors using the comparison method in the case of shop-houses and industrial properties. Even in comparing between properties located in different areas, the level of confidence of valuers was high in making 'reasoned adjustments' in terms of the general rental difference between the properties in the different locations - quoting from experience in the market. Certain rules regarding the different 'multiplier' to adjust for location was clearly evident. The valuers agreed on the 'multiplier' although very small differences existed (which could be reconciled in most instances). This could be related to the rather low complexity of the building structure and design of the properties and implied a clearer heuristic in terms of concentrating more on location.

In the case of purpose-built office complexes in Kuala Lumpur City, the practice has been to classify them according to broad criteria. The relevant heuristics involved were the selection of market rentals, analysis and comparison between the subject property and comparable properties taking into account the differences in terms of location and physical aspects of the buildings (and tenant status in the case of shopping complexes). Figure 5.1 illustrates the general diagrammatic representations of the heuristic structure of the valuation process. Besides the detailed heuristical approach, the research has also attempted to investigate the application of simple regression analysis to be incorporated in an expert system model (as adopted also by other researchers e.g. Jensen and Wadsworth, 1990) using attributes ascertained from the knowledge elicitation process. The 'weightings' of the location and building as the two classes of attributes were based on statistical regression. The philosophy underlying this model thus was not strictly heuristic and was intended to serve as an empirical comparison and possibly complementary to the heuristic approach currently being developed in the research.

Incorporation of the simple regression model in the knowledge-base

The incorporation of the regression model in the knowledge-base was applied specifically to the more complex commercial properties (i.e. purpose-built office and shopping complexes). Only properties in Kuala Lumpur city were considered as it had a large number of the commercial properties. The purpose of the model was to establish and provide a detailed comparison of the standard lot's rental per square foot of the individual properties. Based on the earlier knowledge elicitation sessions, the standard lot of an office complex had been defined by

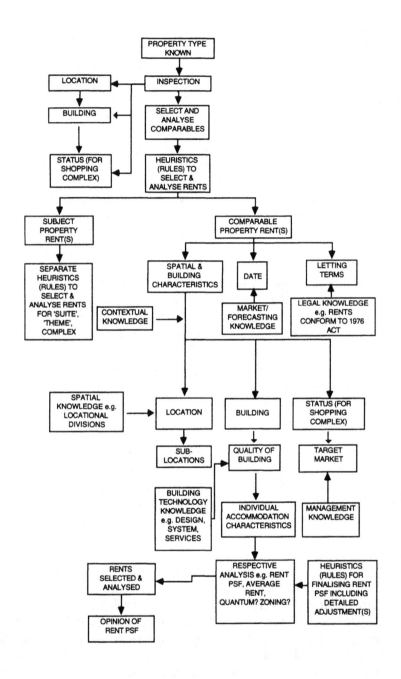

Figure 5.1 General representation of the knowledge in the valuation process

the valuers as the space used as offices on the second floor and above. For the shopping complex, a standard lot was more difficult to define but it was agreed with the valuers that it was an intermediate shop lot (ground, first, second and third floors) with the standard size (within a particular shopping complex) and not close to the main entrance but nor to the escalators, the latter for the upper floors.

As an illustration, the framework of the comparison model for the valuation of office complexes could be illustrated by Figure 5.2.

The development of this model (for the purpose of making comparison between the office complexes and between the shopping complexes) comprised several stages.

Stage 1 : Knowledge representation and identification of rental value-laden attributes from the knowledge elicitation

The first stage involved structuring and constructing the knowledge-base. This involved an initial identification of the main attributes affecting the rental values based on earlier knowledge elicitation from the experts. For example, in the case of purpose-built office complexes (as illustrated by Figure 5.2), location and building were highlighted as the main attributes by the valuers. The first level sub-attributes of location were then decided by the core valuers to be accessibility, siting, proximity to the conveniences and quality of neighbourhood. The first level sub-attributes of building were decided to be the age of building, design, system and services.

In the case of shopping complexes, the main attributes were location, building and the status of the complex (generally in terms of tenant mix). The first-level sub-attributes of location were then decided with the core valuers to be accessibility, siting, proximity to other users, and neighbourhood. The first-level sub-attributes of building were general condition, design (internal and external), system and services. The status had tenant status as the first-level sub-attribute. The views of complementary valuers and supporting specialists were also canvassed at this stage.

The second level sub-attributes were then worked out with the core valuers. The knowledge of the property managers and building related experts were accommodated flexibly. For example, in the case of purpose-built office complexes (as illustrated by Figure 5.2), the second level sub-attributes such as siting in terms of traffic flow; siting in terms of position and siting in terms of layer were decided more by the valuers' expertise whilst the more detailed aspects of building systems such as lift system interval, waiting time, security access, fire control system and air-conditioning control system were more in the realm of the property managers and building related experts with continuous comments

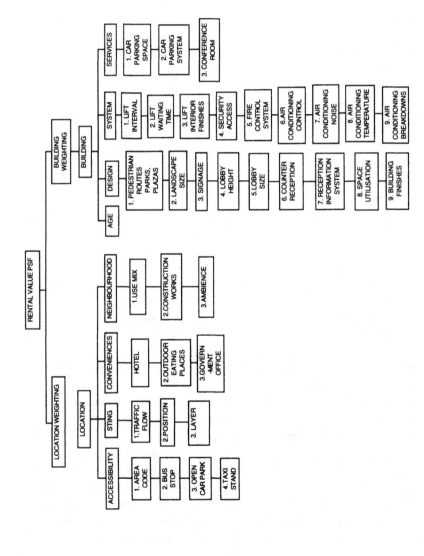

Figure 5.2 Framework of the comparison model for the valuation of office complexes

110

made by the core valuers along the way. The same applied for the shopping complexes, where general aspects of location were decided substantially by the valuers whilst aspects of building design knowledge both external and internal were mainly at the initial stage provided by the property managers which were then 'suited' to the valuation context by the core valuers. Refinement took place based on a valuer's specialized feel for the market. For example, in the case of second level sub-attribute 'distance from the city core' for the office complex the classes were further refined into different area cores of purpose-built office complexes within the Kuala Lumpur City (based on a valuer's specialized knowledge of the market agreed by the team of valuers) namely Golden Triangle Sultan Ismail Road Core; Golden Triangle Ampang Road Core; City Centre Core (Banking Belt) and City Fringe. The second-level sub-attribute 'distance from the city core' was finally changed to 'distance of area core'. The advantage of eliciting knowledge from several experts allowed for rechecking of the knowledge-base more rigorously.

For the office complex model, there are thirteen second level sub-attributes to location and twenty-two second level sub-attributes to building. For the shopping complex, there are thirteen second level sub-attributes to location, forty-two second level sub-attributes to building and seven second level sub-attributes to complex's status. Tables 5.1 and 5.2 provide examples of the main attributes, first level sub-attributes and second level sub-attributes of the office complex and shopping complex respectively.

Stage 2 : Establishing classes of situations

The second stage of the model construction was more rigorous. Basically it attempted to refine the granularity of the knowledge-base and to try to emulate in a more structured way and in more detail the 'feel for the property' in relation to other properties in the comparison process. For example, in the case of one of the purpose-built office complexes' second level sub-attributes for location e.g. distance from city core, discussion with valuers individually and as a group had arrived at three classes of situations namely the building located 'within the city core', 'up to 1 kilometre' and 'more than 1 kilometre'. The same applied in the case of shopping complexes e.g. in the case of second level of sub-attributes distance from the city core it had been decided by the valuers that the classes of situations to be not as detailed as the office (as this was how valuers perceived the pattern of value to be in the context of location of shopping complexes) i.e. just 'within the core' and 'edge of the core'.

A whole series of classes of situations were elicited with the valuers both for the second level sub-attributes for location and building in the case of purpose-built office complexes and for location, building and complex status in the case of shopping complexes.

Table 5.1

Example of main attributes, first level sub-attributes and second level sub-attributes of office complex

Main	1st level sub-attributes	2nd level sub-attributes
Location	Accessibility	Area core distance Bus stop distance Public car parking distance LRT distance (subject to completion)
	Siting and traffic flow	Traffic flow Position Layer
Building	General	Age
	External design	Pedestrian routes/parks/plazas distance Landscaping size Nature of signage
	Lobby	Height Size Nature of counter/reception Type of information system at counter
	Air conditioning system	Control system Noise level Comfort zone (temperature) Maintenance
	Car parking	Number of car parking spaces Type

Table 5.2
Example of main attributes, first level sub-attributes and second level sub-attributes of shopping complex

Main	1st level sub-attributes	2nd level sub-attributes
Location	Accessibility	City core distance Bus stop distance Public car parking distance Taxi stand distance LRT distance (subject to completion)
	Proximity to other users	Closest hotel distance Outside eating places distance Closest office complex distance Closest outside cinema distance
Building	General	Age Size
	External design	Pedestrian routes/parks/plazas distance Nature of signage Facade/external decorations Visibility of complex
	Interior design	Atrium (skylight) area Internal cinema/cineplex Recreation area Sitting area Children's play area
	Escalators	Arrangement of escalators Nature of escalators Visibility of escalators
	Car parking	Number of car parking spaces Type

Stage 3 : Eliciting valuers' opinions (in terms of point scores) on classes of situations and combining them with tenants' opinions

The third stage of the process involved eliciting opinions from the core valuers on the importance of each class of situations for each second level sub-attribute. The objective was to elicit the opinions in some numerical measurement context. Research into the measurement of subjective opinions by previous researchers (e.g. Husin, 1993) have indicated the practicality of using the two traditional methods of Likert Scaling (a method of measurement of opinion based on numbered scales) and Thurnston Scaling (a method of finding an index of opinion based on individual comparison between items). It was decided that a method more akin to the Likert Scaling should be adopted based on the nature of the many second level variables and the different number of classifications for each sub-attribute making the Thurnston comparison rather complex. Moreover, based on the discussion with the valuers, their approach in making subjective comparison may be represented in the form of point scores relating to how important a class of situation is compared to other classes of situations.

In line with the objective of obtaining tenants' opinions on the importance of relevant locational and building attributes in their decision of selecting office and shopping complexes, two separate sets of questionnaires of Tenants' Stated Preference Study (TSPS) were designed in accordance with the knowledge-base, one each for the purpose-built office complexes' tenants and the shopping complexes' tenants. The TSPS questionnaires were divided into three sections. The first section comprised general questions such as name of the tenant, address, telephone number, amount of rent that they are currently paying and the terms and service charge. Data on name of tenant, address and telephone number were relevant to make follow-ups whilst data on letting such as rental evidence were useful for checking level of rents at different times which could be utilized by valuers in carrying out their valuation in test cases as well as in finding weights of the main attributes that is location and building. The second section requested the tenants to state their opinions on the degree of importance of all the second level sub-attributes of location and building in deciding the location of their offices or shops. This was based on a Likert Scale of 0 (lowest rating) to 10 (highest rating). For example, a rating of 10 of second level sub-attribute access would mean that the tenant was of the opinion that access was very important and this will be 'translated' as full 100% importance and equivalent to multiplier 1.0. It followed that the middle and lower end of the rating would have multipliers of 0.5 and 0 respectively. The tenants' opinions expressed in terms of multiplier ranging from 0 to 1.0 may facilitate combination of valuers' opinion and tenants' opinions on the importance of the sub-attributes. The third section of the questionnaire requested the tenants to state any other important factors (that is second-level sub-attributes) that they thought relevant. In addition, the tenants were also requested to give their opinions on the weightings of location and building when they select the office or shopping space.

A random sample of 75 purpose-built office buildings were selected throughout Kuala Lumpur (about 60% of the total number of purpose-built office complexes in Kuala Lumpur City) and 600 questionnaires were sent selectively to the tenants of these office buildings with a 25% response rate. In the case of the shopping complexes, 11 shopping complexes were selected (representing 79% of shopping complexes in Kuala Lumpur City); a 26% response rate was achieved.

The means of tenants' opinions for each individual result from the TSPS were combined with the valuers' point scores producing a set of point scores (on the core valuers' belief combined and complemented by tenants' view) for each second level rental value-laden sub-attributes. This approach agreed with the valuers served to complement their opinions providing a composite point score. The composite score of opinions were included in a comparison format i.e. a form containing the main attributes, first-level sub-attributes and second level sub-attributes and the point-scores for each class of situation. The format enabled a structured inspection in terms of checklist that will guide the development of a 'reasoned comparison' between the properties which forms the basis of opinion of the valuers. An example of the format for a purpose-built office complex in terms of the main attributes; first-level sub-attributes ; second level sub-attributes; the different class situations and the respective point scores is illustrated in Table 5.3.

The inclusion of tenants' views on the degree of importance of certain rental value laden factors to complement opinions of experts is unique to this research for several reasons. First, as was discussed above, the general degree of importance of the factors can be combined with the valuers' consensus point scores to arrive at an overall point score for each of the class situations of the second level sub-attributes. Secondly, it highlighted the appreciation by the valuers of the importance of obtaining a formally elicited first-hand knowledge of the market (on the degree of importance of certain rental value-laden factors) to complement and aid their belief of the market (which was also in line with the view of the property managers). Thirdly, the tenants' opinion survey may provide additional rental value-laden factors to complement previous knowledge elicitation. For example, in the case of the purpose-built offices additional factors cited by the tenants included (1) proximity to airports, (2) standard of management, (3) concept of office suites (a concept where certain tenants have an exclusive right to the use of certain facilities within a purpose-built office complex), and (4) a user that may bring in large crowds to an office complex that may cause inconvenience to other office users (e.g. stock broker).

Table 5.3
Example of purpose-built office complex main attributes, first level sub-attributes; second level sub-attributes; class situations and the point scores

Main Attributes	1st Level Sub-Attributes	2nd Level Sub-Attributes	Class Situations	Valuers' Score (V)	Mean Tenant's Opinion (T)	Overall V*T
Location	Accessibility	Area - Core Distance	Within Core	9.200	0.707	6.508
			Up to 1 Km	7.200	0.707	5.093
			More than 1 Km	3.800	0.707	2.668
		Bus Stop Distance	Within 50m	10.000	0.650	6.500
			50m - 100m	7.800	0.650	5.031
			100m - 150m	5.600	0.650	3.612
			More than 150m	3.800	0.650	2.451

Stage 4 : Inspection of properties

The fourth stage in the process of constructing the model was to conduct the inspection of properties based on the attributes and sub-attributes that had been agreed by the valuers. Ninety two purpose-built office complexes and 14 shopping complexes throughout the Kuala Lumpur City were inspected and the point scores for each individual second level sub-factors were noted. Certain aspects such as a corner lot without any access advantage and the multiple usage of a purpose-built office complex in terms of shopping use of the ground floor were noted and brought back to the valuers' for further discussions.

Stage 5 : Finding weightings of main factors

The fifth stage of the process involved the compilation of rentals of 'standard lot' for the purpose-built office complexes and shopping complexes. The objective was to find the relative importance of the main attributes i.e. location and building (in terms of the weighting of each) for the purpose-built office complexes and the relative importance of the main attributes location, building and status of complex (in terms of the weighting of each) for the shopping complexes. Several steps were involved;

1   Calculation of maximum score for each main attribute.

The maximum score for the each main attribute was derived from the maximum sum of scores of all first-level sub-attributes. The sum of the scores of all first-level attributes came from the maximum sum of scores of all second level attributes. In the case of office complexes, the maximum scores of location and building were found to be 87 and 170 respectively. For shopping complexes, the maximum scores of location, building and status were 96, 254 and 54 respectively.

2   Calculation of proportion to maximum score for each main attribute of each individual property.

This was achieved by dividing the score for each main attribute of individual property (obtained from inspection in the stage four) with the maximum score for each attribute (as derived from step 1 above) and expressing them in terms of percentage. Two separate main lists (each for office and shopping properties) of all the proportion to maximum score for each main attribute of each individual property were compiled. The main list of the office properties was further divided into several sub-lists according to the area cores in which the properties were located.

3   Simple regression of rentals against the proportion to maximum score for each main attribute.

Simple regressions of the rentals of each individual property against proportion to maximum score for each main attribute of each individual property (based on the lists from step 2) were then undertaken. For the proposed 1997 revaluation exercise, the current rentals at the time when the research was undertaken was mid to late 1995. Rental evidence were searched from the property review section in the media at that time. Rental evidence of standard office space of fifty four different purpose-built office

117

complexes were collected. In the case of the shopping complexes, rental evidence of ground, first, second and third floors of 12 different shopping complexes within the Kuala Lumpur City were collected. From the regressions, the coefficients of each main attribute and (and thus regression equations) were obtained for the office complexes and shopping complexes. As the rental value was generally considered by the valuers as a function of the main attributes, the total weightings of the main attributes should equal one.

4   Finding the hypothetical maximum rent.

Using the coefficients of the main attributes, two maximum hypothetical rents each for a hypothetical office complex and a hypothetical shopping complex having the maximum scores (100%) for the main attributes were predicted. From this exercise, the hypothetical maximum rent of all the different divisions of the office complex (based on the different area cores) and the shopping complex were predicted.

5   Expressing each property's rent in terms of rent proportionate to hypothetical maximum rent.

This was achieved by dividing the rent of each property with the hypothetical maximum rent and then expressing them in percentage terms.

6   Finding the weightings of main attributes.

This was achieved using simple regressions of rents proportionate to hypothetical maximum rent against the respective proportion to maximum score of the main attributes for each individual property. All analysis of data was carried out using the Minitab statistical software package. An example of the summary of data of purpose-built office complexes in the Golden Triangle - Sultan Ismail Road core which were utilized in finding the weightings of Land and Building is indicated by Table 5.4.

In the case of the purpose-built office complexes as in the example provided by Table 5.4, the regression was undertaken between columns (4) and (5) as independent variables and column (7) as a dependent variable. For example, in the case of the Golden Triangle - Sultan Ismail Road core, the relative weightings of main attributes location and building for (as in Table 5.4) were found to be of 0.375 and 0.625 respectively. A summary of the weightings of the main attributes the purpose-built office complexes and shopping complexes for the different valuers' determined sub-locations are provided in Table 5.5 and Table 5.6 respectively.

Table 5.4
Example of data utilized in finding weightings of land and building

Building	Location Score (Max Score = 87)	Building Score (Max Score = 170)	Location Proportionate (%) to Max Score	Building Proportionate (%) to Max Score	Rent Max Hypothetical Rent = 6.6	Rent Proportionate (%) to Max Hypothetical Rent
(1)	(2)	(3)	(4)	(5)	(6)	(7)
KLIH	70	80	80.4598	47.0588	3.80	57.6273
Genesis	66	143	75.8621	84.1176	5.50	83.4079
AMMB	72	139	82.7586	81.7647	5.50	83.4079
S H Chan	69	106	79.3103	62.3529	4.10	62.1768
HLA	74	98	85.0575	57.6471	4.50	68.2428
G Hill	70	148	80.4598	87.0588	5.70	86.4409
Boustead	71	117	81.6092	68.8235	5.00	75.8254
W Bstead	71	69	81.6092	40.5882	3.70	46.1108
Kewanga	68	93	78.1609	54.7059	4.50	68.2428
Aetna	68	127	78.1609	74.7059	4.80	72.7923
L F Yong	67	87	77.0115	51.1765	3.90	59.1438
W Stephen	66	75	75.8621	44.1176	4.00	60.6603
Genting	75	136	86.2069	80.0000	5.50	83.4079
SPK	71	94	81.6092	55.2941	4.00	60.6603
Haw Par	70	97	80.4598	57.0588	4.50	68.2428
UBN	80	136	91.9540	80.0000	5.80	87.9574
Atrium	68	81	78.1609	47.6471	4.00	60.6603
M Sabre	69	119	79.3103	70.0000	4.50	68.2428
SMK	70	76	80.4598	44.7059	3.50	53.0778
IMS	72	61	82.7586	35.8824	3.80	57.6273
Nusantara	71	74	81.6092	43.5294	3.90	59.1438
Mui Plaza	76	106	87.3563	62.3529	4.50	68.2428

Table 5.5
Weightings of location and building (purpose-built office complexes)

Location	Number of Properties	Location Weighting	Building Weighting	Total Weighting
Sultan Ismail Road Core	22	0.375	0.625	1.000
Ampang Road Core	11	0.354	0.646	1.000
Raja Laut Road Core	4	0.535	0.465	1.000
City Centre Road Core	13	0.462	0.538	1.000
Fringe Areas	4	0.225	0.775	1.000
Total	54			

Table 5.6
Weightings of location, building and status (shopping complexes)

Floor Reference	Number of Rental Evidences	Location Weighting	Building Weighting	Status Weighting	Total Weighting
Ground	6	0.378	0.435	0.187	1.000
First & Second	12	0.340	0.376	0.284	1.000
Third	8	0.272	0.316	0.412	1.000

The weightings were used to predict rental per square foot of other office buildings in the same geographical area. For example, in the case of the Golden Triangle-Sultan Ismail Road core, the rental per square foot for the standard office space in another building namely Bangunan Yayasan Selangor with Location score of 73 and Building score of 74, the rental could be predicted as follows.

Proportionate Location Score: as a Percentage to Maximum Possible Location Score of 100% (i.e. 87)

$$73/87 \times 100 \quad = \quad 83.9080 \%$$

Proportionate Building Score: as a Percentage to Maximum Possible Building Score of 100% (i.e. 170)

$$74/170 \times 100 = 43.5294\,\%$$

Proportionate Predicted Rental Per Square Foot Score: as a Percentage to Maximum Possible 'Hypothetical' Rent of 100% (i.e. 6.60)

$$(0.839080 \times 0.375) + (0.435294 \times 0.625) = 0.314655 + 0.272059$$

$$= 0.586714$$

$$= 58.6714\,\%$$

Predicted Rental Per Square Foot = 6.60 x (0.586714) = MR 3.87 per square foot.

(Note : MR stands for Malaysian Ringgit)

The data for the shopping complexes were analysed as a whole for Kuala Lumpur City (in accordance with valuers' market knowledge) using the same procedure as with the purpose-built office complexes with an addition of main attribute Status of Complex besides the location and building.

In the case of the purpose-built office complex Figure 5.3 provides an illustration of the prediction model. Unlike detailed multiple regression analysis (MRA), which attempts to find the coefficients of a large number of independent variables, only the weighting of the main factors were considered. The simplistic nature of the model, nevertheless provided an objective, easily understood comparison between properties in the forms of point scores of each individual main attributes at the broad level of explanation with the possibility of viewing the detailed scores of each individual first level sub-attributes and second level sub-attributes.

The prototype and evaluation

Rapid prototyping (i.e. building the prototype as soon as the knowledge elicitation process starts) has not been adopted in this research framework due to the size of the knowledge base and the number of experts involved. Nevertheless, a modest prototype has been developed at a stage of the project when it was felt that the knowledge was adequate enough to stand as a platform for discussion among experts to develop further the knowledge-base.

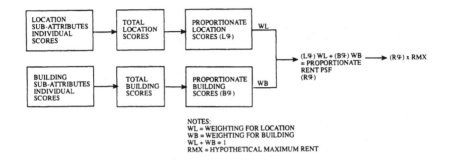

Figure 5.3 Rental value prediction model for office complexes

The prototype basically is divided into four modules i.e.:

    Module 1 : Purpose-Built Office Complex
    Module 2 : Shopping Complex
    Module 3 : Shop-house/Office/Flat
    Module 4 : Factories

Naturally, each module embodies the specific knowledge-base of the particular type of properties. The purpose-built office complex module contains a series of 'forms' or 'screen displays' embodying the knowledge of the experts integrated with the structured comparison format based on locational and building attributes (with both first level attributes and second level sub-attributes incorporated).

The individual scores of the second-level sub-attributes to location (to arrive at the total score of the main attribute location) and the individual scores of sub-attributes to building will also be added up (to arrive at the total score of the main attribute building). The proportionate scores of location and building (i.e. proportionate to the respective maximum score of location and building) will be multiplied by their respective proportionate weightings (i.e. proportionate to the maximum scores attainable) to arrive at an opinion of rental per square foot for the standard lot.

The class of the purpose-built office complex is (based on expertise of valuers and gauged objectively against the point scores) decided by the system and represented in the categories of 'Super', 'Class A', 'Class B', and 'Class C'. An option is also available for viewing the other purpose-built office complexes,

122

used as comparables and their respective location score, the building score (and how much they differ with subject properties scores) and their respective predicted rentals.

During evaluation, there were valuers who expressed the need for the system to be able to provide information (if any) about the actual rents (average rents) of the subject property and comparable properties. The actual rents could be provided together with the predicted rents of the subject property and the comparable properties and their respective location and building scores. The system could provide options to the user whether to adopt the actual rental or the predicted rental to the user. Which ever option is chosen, the practice should be consistent e.g. if predicted rent is chosen, all properties should be valued based on predicted rents and vice versa.

Providing actual rents alongside the predicted rents of the subject property and comparable properties and their respective location and building scores would be useful to the valuer in viewing the difference between actual rents and predicted rents and to provide checks if the difference is very large. The second part of the module contains the detailed accepted knowledge of the experts which comprise the valuation of individual accommodation in the office complex. Such an exercise is supported with the heuristic of valuers to expect the practical situation of 'lack of suitable rental data' in valuations especially for the more specialized accommodations such as the penthouse, sports club, swimming pool and even specialized storage rooms.

Module 2 for the valuation of shopping complexes has a similar format as module 1. It contains the knowledge-base relating for example to the position of the individual shop lots, the sensitivity of the rentals to size and the layout of the complex. In most cases, heuristics are adopted, complemented where possible, with intelligent cross-sectional analysis (analysis of the difference in rentals of two retail spaces, both with the same characteristics except for one feature, the influence of the one feature being reflected in the rental difference). The ultimate intention is to have an intelligent means of interfacing with a database (containing 'suitable' rentals of different accommodations within the office complexes) where an intelligent cross-sectional analysis could be undertaken to provide the percentage difference between different accommodation (as decided by the valuers). This will be supported with valuers' heuristics especially in cases where there is a lack of suitable rental evidence - the flexibility is inherently built into the system.

Module 3 for the valuation of shop-house/office/flat contains a section analysing the locational situation of the shop-house in terms of the general road along which the property is located and an analysis of the position of the shop-house/office/flat in terms of traffic flow, corner position and public transport. In accordance with the practice of the valuers, where rental evidence relating to the subject property and comparable properties in the immediate vicinity are scarce, appropriate heuristically assigned adjustment will be made in relation to other comparables located farther away. The second section comprises questions relating to the internal valuation of the shop-house e.g. zoning (where applicable) and valuation between the different floors incorporating rules relating to the legal aspects namely 'rebus sic stantibus'. Heuristics were applied where actual or comparable evidence is not available.

Module 4 consists of a knowledge-base of industrial properties. This has been further subdivided into sub-modules of different types of factories. The rules for location in each is rather broad reflecting the less sensitive nature of factories' rentals to different positions. Rules on the facilities of flatted factories (incorporating more of the planning and building regulation guided by valuers' knowledge) however are quite detailed. The second part of each sub-module comprises valuations of accommodation within factories (especially detached factories) incorporating production space, office/administration building(s), canteen and outbuildings. Heuristical judgment is inherent in the valuation of factories reflecting very experienced specialized valuers' knowledge for this type of property. For example, in making adjustment for size, a sliding scale in the form of percentage deduction with increasing size of the factory space is embodied in the prototype. The knowledge-base for the valuation of plant and machinery occupy a very special area of the module embodying the knowledge of the valuer from the only local authority practising this specialized valuation in Malaysia.

Objective testing of shopping complexes and office complexes modules

The research has also incorporated static evaluation in terms of testing accuracy of the 'opinion' of the system using the structured comparison model both for purpose-built office complexes and shopping complexes against the valuation of a suitably experienced core valuer. Based on a discussion with the core valuer, twenty one different purpose-built office complexes in various locations and nine shopping complexes also in various locations within the Kuala Lumpur city were selected for the testing of the model. The valuer was given two sets of rental evidence - one set consisted of rental evidence of purpose-built office complexes and the other set of shopping complexes. The rental evidence was also used for the construction of the structured comparison model.

The results of the testing of the model as compared to the core valuer's actual valuations are summarized in Tables 5.7 and 5.8.

For the purpose-built office complexes, the test showed a rental per square foot difference of within 10% compared to the core valuer's valuation for twenty of the properties. There was a difference of 12.75% for LUTH Building with the prediction falling outside the 90% confidence interval. A discussion with the valuer and analysis of the situation revealed that LUTH was valued lower by the valuer (despite its good building quality as reflected by the building score) as the building was mainly let to government bodies who were paying a lower rent than what the market was expected to pay for such a property. Rules relating to type of majority of tenants were incorporated to enable the system to make adjustment for type of tenants in making its prediction.

As a whole, the valuers agreed that such a model would be useful in providing reasoned justification for a particular valuation. The scores provided a clearer structured explanation. Moreover, the detailed point scores of each individual sub-attribute to both the location and building could be viewed through the system and compared with other comparable properties. This may provide an easily understandable explanation which may be useful in objection cases. It was found that the valuation by the valuer was rather generalistic taking into account location and building factors in general terms. Valuers however agreed the generality of how they perceived the properties but seemed to agree the usefulness of a system that could provide a structured and in-depth account of the valuation which was provided by the system. As can be seen in Table 5.7, the difference in rent between different properties as predicted by the system was more refined reflecting the detailed factors that were considered in the system. For example, SMK, Nusantara and Aik Hua which were all rather similar buildings in a same locality were valued at MR 3.50 per square foot by the core valuer. The system valued the buildings at MR 3.83, MR 3.81 and MR 3.77 respectively based on an overall predicted rent proportionate to maximum hypothetical rent.

Notwithstanding the importance of having an in-depth comparison between the properties, the valuers agreed that the system could also provide an option to value property in broad terms where if the point scores fall within a certain range the system could automatically assign a common rent per square foot for the properties. For example, in the case of SMK, Nusantara and Aik Hua, the overall predicted rents proportionate to maximum hypothetical rent were all within the 55 % to 60% range and it was agreed by the valuers that a rule could be developed so that the system could automatically provide a common predicted rent per square foot based on the average of each predicted rents i.e. MR 3.80 per square foot in this case. In other words, an element of flexibility in terms of choice of the degree of detail in the valuation could be built into the system in line with the valuers' expertise and when required by the valuer.

In the case of the shopping complexes, eight out of the nine properties tested indicated a rental per square foot prediction of within 10% of the core valuer's actual valuation. Only one property i.e. Ychn P. showed a difference of 10.5%. The case was discussed with the valuers and it was found again that the building

Table 5.7
Purpose-built office complex - results of computerized model testing against valuer's opinion (rent of standard office space)

Building	Loc Score (Max Score = 87)	Bldg Score (Max Score = 170)	Loc (%) to Max Score	Bldg (%) to Max Score	Rent (%) to Max Hypo Rent	Predict Rent psf (MR)	Valuer's Opinion on Rent psf (MR)	Diff. (%)	Conf Leve (%)
S Ismail Rd									
SPK	71.0	97	81.6092	55.2941	65.0000	4.29	4.00	7.25	90
SMK	70.0	76	80.4598	44.7059	58.0303	3.83	3.50	9.43	90
Nusantara	71.0	74	81.6092	43.5294	57.7273	3.81	3.50	8.86	90
Aik Hua	54.0	92	62.0690	54.1176	57.1212	3.77	3.50	7.71	90
Ampang Rd									
Getah Asli 2	62.0	103	71.2644	60.5882	64.7154	3.98	3.80	4.74	90
S Dredging	68.0	108	78.1609	63.5294	68.9431	4.24	4.00	6.00	90
MCA	70.0	103	80.4598	60.5882	67.9675	4.18	3.80	10.00	90
LUTH	58.0	30	66.6667	76.4706	73.3333	4.51	4.00	12.75	>90*
RHB	54.0	129	62.0690	75.8824	71.3821	4.39	4.50	-2.44	95
R Laut Rd									
Bumi Raya	75.0	84	86.2069	49.4118	63.0252	3.75	3.50	7.14	95
C & Carriage	65.0	124	74.7126	72.9412	67.5630	4.02	4.00	0.50	95
PKNS	75.0	84	86.2069	49.4118	63.1933	3.76	3.50	7.43	95
City Centre									
Public Bank	62.5	96	71.8391	56.4706	63.9344	3.90	4.00	-2.50	95
UMBC	58.5	103	67.2414	60.5882	63.9344	3.90	4.00	-2.50	95
KOP	55.5	69	63.7931	40.5882	51.6393	3.15	3.00	5.00	90
TSMB	58.5	98	67.2414	57.6471	62.4590	3.81	3.50	8.86	95
Bangkok B	62.0	71	71.2644	41.7647	50.8197	3.10	3.00	3.33	90
B D Zainai	62.0	90	71.2644	52.9412	61.6393	3.76	4.00	-6.00	
Fringe Area									
IGB Plaza	53.0	89	60.9195	52.3529	54.5098	2.78	3.00	-7.33	95
Perkim	59.0	81	67.8161	47.6471	50.5882	2.58	2.50	3.20	95
Pengkalan	51.0	106	58.6207	62.3529	61.7647	3.15	3.00	5.00	95

126

Table 5.8

Shopping complex - results of computerized model testing against valuer's opinion (rent of standard ground floor shop space)

Building	Loc Score (Max Score = 96)	Bldg Score (Max Score = 254)	Status (Max Score = 54)	Loc (%) to Max Score	Bldg (%) to Max Score	Status (%) to Max Score	Rent (%) to Max Hypo Rent (Max Hypo Rent = 26.18)	Predicted Rent psf (MR)	Valuer's Opinion Rent psf (MR)	Diff.	Conf. Level %
Weld	86	169	25.6	89.5833	66.5354	47.4074	70.6646	18.50	20.00	-7.50	95
Amp Pk	76	155	37.2	79.1667	61.0236	68.8889	68.2200	17.86	18.00	-0.78	95
City Sq	78	186	38.0	81.2500	73.2283	70.3704	74.4079	19.48	20.00	-2.60	95
Ychn P	81	145	36.4	84.3750	57.0866	67.4074	68.3728	17.90	20.00	-10.50	95
Sogo	86	185	42.4	89.5833	72.8346	78.5185	78.8770	20.65	20.00	3.25	95
Mall	76	200	40.6	79.1667	78.7402	75.1852	76.8144	20.11	20.00	0.55	95
Pertama	91	128	17.2	94.7917	50.3937	31.8519	62.9106	16.47	15.00	9.80	95
Campbl	77	119	12.6	80.2083	46.8504	23.3333	54.3545	14.23	13.00	9.46	95
Lot 10	85	190	47.8	88.5417	74.8031	88.5185	81.1306	21.24	20.00	6.20	95

aspect considered by the valuer seemed to be rather indiscriminate. For example the actual interior design in terms of lighting and decoration tended to be considered as the same as another nearby shopping complex (which was valued by the valuer at the same rent per square foot with Ychn P.) when in actual fact the detailed design aspects of the latter differed from the former.

As in the case with the purpose-built office complexes, a rule also could be developed in valuing the shopping complexes to give an option to the user to consider detailed scores in terms of certain experts determined ranges so that if the predicted rent proportionate to the maximum hypothetical rent falls within a certain range, the system could automatically assign a common predicted rent per square foot to the properties.

Conclusions

The research has shown that an expert system for the mass appraisal valuation of commercial properties for rating purposes in Malaysia can be developed from knowledge of several experts. It follows that where similar methodology exists, it should be possible to build similar mass appraisal systems for many other types of properties, for other purposes not only in Malaysia but also in other countries. Based on the research into eliciting knowledge from a number of experts in order to develop the system undertaken so far, several advantages can be highlighted.

•	In general it allows the process to overcome the problem of experts inaccessibility and hence allows better utilization of time.

•	Since the knowledge involved is diverse, even within the same local context, eliciting knowledge from different core valuers separately, can explore advantages in terms of generating multiple lines of reasoning and different strategic models of expertise.

•	Involvement of complementary valuers and specialists in the research can be useful in providing certain subsets of knowledge. (1) Valuers from other local authorities with different backgrounds of local experience can provide different contextual knowledge allowing for the possibility of the inclusion of aspects that might be overlooked by the core valuers and vice versa. In addition, it offers opportunities for eliciting technical and specialized knowledge such as knowledge to value plant and machinery. This is important as the system is intended to be applicable to most local authorities in Malaysia each with similarities and differences in the nature of commercial and industrial properties. (2) A private valuer can contribute market knowledge including technical rental forecasting knowledge especially in situations when some elements of forecasting are needed in the rating valuation process. Exploration of consensus group opinion of private valuers through the Delphi method may add a wider dimension of market knowledge to the valuation process. (3) An academic can provide additional guidance on legal aspects of rating valuation knowledge. (4) Knowledge elicitation from other specialized but related fields offered supportive specialized technical knowledge which can supplement the knowledge provided by the valuers. This adds depth to the knowledge elicited from the core valuers.

• Eliciting knowledge from several core valuers was useful in providing opportunities for comprehensively probing aspects in which heuristics could be more confidently applied especially when rental evidence related to these aspects is scarce.

• Eliciting knowledge from several experts has to a certain extent enabled the development of a comparison model for the valuation of purpose-built office complexes and shopping complexes. This is in terms of providing comprehensive knowledge structure and grouped opinions on the degree of importance of different classes of situations of the key elements in the knowledge which can be 'related' against rental evidence to provide weightings for location and building. The weightings could be useful for making rental predictions.

However, the model has introduced elements of rigidity; inability to work with limited data and inflexibility to accommodate new developments in the market. Nevertheless, the elicitation of point scores in the model may (subject to further research) complement experts' heuristics in selecting comparables and in making adjustments in the comparison process.

Prototyping was useful in evaluating, validating and refining the knowledge-base and to provide objective testing of the system. In addition, it also provides a means of further refining the knowledge-base in the system and allowing for an element of built-in flexibility. This has been exemplified by the suggestion by the valuers to provide a broad range of scores within a comparison model to allow for broader comparison between the properties.

The research has also found that inclusion of different types of properties has been useful in providing comparison between the different reasoning strategies adopted by the valuers in valuing the different types of properties. This has been particularly evident between the valuation of more standard properties (in terms of the nature of the building) e.g. shop-houses and standard factories and more complex properties e.g. purpose-built office complexes and shopping complexes. The former could be confidently valued by the valuers based on some heuristically assigned 'multiplier' to account for their different locations whilst the latter would necessitate a structured breakdown of factors and analysis of the factors in terms of scaled opinions.

References

Chow, L.K., Saad, F., and Teo, L.L., (1988), *Towards Better Performance and Greater Efficiency Among Valuation Officers*, Symposium Pertama Pegawai-Pegawai Penilaian, INSPEN.

Husin, A., (1993), T*he Measurement of Location - A Case Study of Eighteen Housing Schemes*, APRES Conference, Langkawi, Malaysia.

Jenkins, D.H. (1992), *The Use of Expert Systems in the Land Strategy of Cardiff City Council*, MPhil Dissertation (CNAA).

Jensen, D.L. and Wadsworth, W.M. (1990), 'Artificial Intelligence in Computer-Assisted Mass Appraisal; Comments on Jensen', *Property Tax Journal,* vol. 9 no. 1, pp. 5 -26.

Low, K.T. (1986), *Privatising the Rating Revaluation Exercise*, Seminar Kebangsaan Kadaran Kedua, July.

Nawawi, A.H. and Gronow, S.A. (1991a), 'Expert Systems in Rating Valuation', *Journal of the Society of Surveying Technicians*, vol. 18 no. 6.

Nawawi, A.H. and Gronow, S.A. (1991b), 'Valuation Strategies: Simplification of Valuation Beyond Recognition Using Expert Systems', *Journal of the Institute of Revenues, Rating and Valuation*, September.

Nawawi, A.H. and Gronow, S.A. (1992), *Rating Valuation of Commercial Properties in Malaysia - A Case for an Expert System*, paper presented in CPD Talk on Information Technology in Property (Module on The Horizon), Institut Penilaian Negara (INSPEN).

Nawawi, A.H., Gronow, S.A. and Hizam, R.B. (1993), 'Role of An Expert System in Rating Valuation of Commercial Properties in Malaysia', *Journal of the Institute of Surveyors*, Malaysia.

Nawawi, A.H., Gronow, S.A. and Hizam, R.B. (1994), 'Potential Application of an Expert System in the Valuation of Commercial Properties for Rating Purposes in Malaysia', *Journal of Urban Design*, Mara Institute of Technology, Malaysia.

Scott, I.P. (1988), A *Knowledge-Based Approach to the Computer Assisted Mortgage Valuation of Residential Property*, PhD Thesis (CNAA).

Scott, I.P. and Gronow, S.A. (1987), 'Expert Systems for Rating Valuation', *Rating and Valuation*, June 1987.

Wiltshaw, D.G. (1991), 'Econometrics, Linear Programming and Valuation', *Journal of Property Research*, vol. 8.

6 Computer assisted mass appraisal of farm land in British Columbia

A. Pearce

Profile

British Columbia, the western most province of Canada, is bordered by the Pacific Ocean to the west, the province of Alberta to the east, the Yukon Territory to the north and the United States to the south. The province is nearly four times the size of Great Britain and larger than any American state except Alaska. Mountainous topography with substantial areas of lowland and plateau country characterize the approximately ninety-five million hectares of the province of British Columbia. In 1994, the population of British Columbia was 3.6 million people and agriculture was the province's third largest resource industry behind forestry and mining.

Table 6.1
British Columbia primary resource industries

Resource Sector	1993 Gross Receipts
Forestry	$13.8 billion
Mining	$ 2.3 billion
Agriculture	$ 1.5 billion

Source: *Ministry of Finance and Corporate Relations, 1994 British Columbia Financial and Economic Review, (Province of British Columbia, 1994), p.86.*

British Columbia farm land

British Columbia Assessment (BCA) values 1.5 million properties annually, including 19,000 farms, many of which comprise more than one land parcel. There are 58,000 individual parcels officially classified as farm land by British Columbia Assessment, but many of these are hobby or lifestyle farms as opposed to commercial operations. The total area of land classified as farm is almost six million acres, 2.5 % of the total land area of British Columbia.

Grouped into eight agricultural regions (see Figure 6.1), BC.'s predominantly family owned and operated farms produce and market over two hundred agricultural commodities and eighty fisheries commodities both locally and globally. BC.'s large geographic area, including a variety of topographic, climatic and geological features, has contributed to the diversity of its agriculture.

Urban development pressure on rural land in the 1970s led to the development of British Columbia's most important provincial agricultural policy, the establishment of an Agriculture Land Reserve. Created in December 1972, the Agricultural Land Commission Act froze land with high agricultural capability and began a process by which most of the province's land with agricultural potential was designated as Agricultural Land Reserve. Developed as a result of diminishing agricultural land resources in areas of high urban development, the Reserve was intended to preserve land having high capability for agriculture for future agricultural use. Land uses permitted within the Agricultural Land Reserve are limited to agriculture or agriculturally compatible uses (i.e. agricultural storage, packing, grading facilities etc.).

British Columbia Assessment

British Columbia Assessment was created by Act of the provincial legislature in 1974. It evolved from a need for uniformity and consistency in appraisals for ad valorem property taxation. As a Crown Corporation, the mandate of BC. Assessment is to classify and value uniformly all real property in the province for taxation purposes. Its principal clients are municipalities, local taxing jurisdictions and the province who use the assessment roll as a base for levying property taxes to finance local services and to a lesser extent education.

Prior to BC Assessment's founding, property was assessed each year by the various taxing authorities and, although the law required that assessments be at market value, this was not uniformly the case. In the mid-1960s to early 1970s, real estate prices in the province rose swiftly which led to the introduction of legislative amendments to limit annual assessment increases. These limitations resulted in wide variations in the relationship of assessed values to market value, both for individual properties and between tax jurisdictions.

Figure 6.1 British Columbia agricultural regions

1	Vancouver Island/Coast:	aquaculture, dairy, hogs, poultry, vegetables, berries, kiwi.
2	Mainland/Southwest:	dairy, poultry, hogs, vegetables, berries, greenhouse(flowers).
3	Thompson/Okanagan:	orchards, vineyards, cattle, hogs, forage.
4	Kootenay:	orchards, honey, vegetables, cattle.
5	Cariboo:	cattle, forage.
6	North Coast:	cattle, commercial fisheries.
7	Nechako:	forage.
8	Peace River:	grain ,oilseeds ,honey ,cattle, game (reindeer, bison, fallow deer).

BC Assessment was established as an independent body, separate from the various taxing authorities, which would provide equitable market value property assessments throughout the province.

BC Assessment is organized into two operational sections:

1   **Valuation Services** - geographically divided into 26 local community offices. The primary functions of Valuation Services are to inspect and value all properties and to accurately compile all information necessary to prepare the assessment rolls.

2   **Support Services** - encompasses five head office divisions: Computer Services, Financial Services, Human Resources, Policy, Audit and Legal Services and Technical Services. These divisions provide expertise and services necessary to produce the assessment rolls.

Based on a requirements study of the information systems needed to fulfil its mandate, BC Assessment commenced construction of the 'Computer Assisted Property Assessment System' (CAPAS) in early 1980. CAPAS operates on an on-line interactive basis, allowing direct retrieval or update of information directly. Principal benefits of the system are increased productivity, and a fully documented, controlled, and integrated property database which is easily maintained, readily accessible, and truly responsive to the needs of BC Assessment.

Computer assisted property assessment system (CAPAS)

BC Assessment uses a large IBM mainframe accessed province-wide through terminals and personal computers with mainframe connection. All valuation offices access the central mainframe computer via a dedicated high-speed teleprocessing network. As more personal computers and pen-based computers are installed in the local offices, the mainframe will fulfil largely a data warehouse role and more processing will take place locally. CAPAS currently consists of three major categories of systems:

Data Maintenance System The Data Maintenance System allows for the input of data required to produce the assessment rolls and notices (i.e. owner names, addresses). A major source of property information is the Land Titles Office. This office holds the official title of each property in the province against which all interests in property are registered. This provincial centralized land title registry is the major source of three types of information regarding real property transactions:

134

1   The name and address of assessed owners for assessment and tax notice mailing.
2   Sales information for use in property valuation.
3   Copies of subdivision plans for basic data entry.

Property ownership, legal descriptions, survey plans and street addresses are obtained from the Land Titles Office and entered onto the database. Property sales information is used for the direct sales comparison approach in the valuation of properties in their highest and best use.

Statutory System The Statutory System enables BC Assessment to fulfil its statutory obligations by producing all assessment rolls as well as their corresponding value summary reports. It also produces reports for various taxing jurisdictions to assist in determining their levies and auditing the data.

Appraisal Assist Systems Nine computer subsystems comprise the Appraisal Assist Systems which assist the appraiser in the valuation of the nine classifications of real property in BC. The nine subsystems include:

Land Calculation: used to record land inventory and land rates.

Residential Improvement: captures the inventory from field cards and calculates manual replacement and replacement cost new less depreciation costs for residential buildings.

Sales: used to capture and adjust sales data, to maintain sales listing information and opinions of value and to analyse assessment-to-sale ratios.

Commercial: captures inventory and income data to calculate property values using the Cost, Income and Direct Comparison Approaches.

Ad Valorem: captures data for Ad Valorem structure (grain elevators etc) and provides functions for factoring and depreciation.

Timber: maintains data for valuing unmanaged and managed forest land.

Major Industrial Properties:	captures building data of major industrial properties for calculating values.
Servicing:	captures data which will flag the property as requiring an appraisal inspection.
Commissioner's Rate Structure:	captures data from continuous structures (railway, pipelines etc.) subject to Commissioner's rates.

Valuation

The market value of each property is estimated as of 1 July each year. The annual assessment roll is completed on 31 December at which time assessment notices are mailed to property owners and the assessment rolls are mailed to taxing jurisdictions throughout the province. From January to 15 March, the Court of Revision conducts assessment appeal hearings. The authenticated roll, reflecting the changes resulting from the Court of Revision, is completed and mailed to taxing jurisdictions on 31 March. From this tax base the taxing jurisdictions determine their tax rates and mail their tax notices in June of each year.

Classification

BC Assessment uses nine different property types to classify land according to use. Each taxing jurisdiction annually determines a different tax rate for each property type. They include:

Class 1   Residential (Includes farm outbuildings and residences)

Class 2   Utilities

Class 3   Unmanaged Forest Land

Class 4   Major Industry

Class 5   Light Industry

Class 6   Business and Other

Class 7   Managed Forest Land

Class 8   Recreational

Class 9   Farm Land

History of the farm assessment system

Prior to 1974, each assessing jurisdiction set its own standards for the appraisal and taxation of farm land. Rural areas were assessed by the province as small taxing jurisdictions could not afford qualified assessors. Both the approaches to valuation and the criteria for farm classification varied between jurisdictions. In particular, the level of required agricultural activity to be eligible for the taxation benefits of farm classification differed between assessing jurisdictions. The tax benefits include preferential assessments and tax rates that result in lower property taxes, exemptions from provincial sales tax on farm supplies and a reduction in tax on gas used to fuel farm machinery.

Since 1974, the classification criteria and valuation methodology of farm land has been standardized by BC Assessment province wide. Standards for the classification of land as farm regulate the uniformity in application of farm eligibility criteria throughout the province. Farm land valuation schedules set by the Assessment Commissioner regulate the process of farm land valuation province wide.

In 1983, the province and municipalities were given the authority to set different tax rates for each of the nine property classes on the property's assessed value. Assessed values are uniformly based at market value for all properties. The tax rates on properties classified as 'farm' are generally the lowest of all nine classes. However, in municipalities with large numbers of 'hobby' farms, the farm tax rates tend to be set higher than the 'residential' rates to partially offset preferential assessment and exemptions which apply to 'farm' land.

Preferential assessment

In British Columbia and most other North American jurisdictions, farm land receives preferential assessment if use of the land meets certain standards. The underlying reasons for preferential assessment for farms are generally the same:

1   Farming requires the use of larger proportions of land than other activities. Assessment and taxation of farm land on the same basis as land used for other purposes could result in farmers paying a disproportionate share of taxes.

2   The level of services provided to farmers from property taxes tend to be lower than services provided to other land owners.

3   Farm land and improvements are essential ingredients to food production. Philosophically there is a desire for taxes to be kept as low as possible to minimize the basic cost of primary food production.

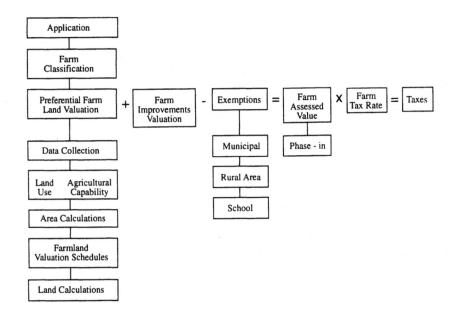

Figure 6.2 Farm assessment and taxation

The objectives of the farm assessment system are:

1   To implement a consistent approach to farm land classification and valuation throughout the province.

2   To support the family farm in all of its commercial endeavours.

3   To contribute to the preservation of farm land.

These objectives are achieved through the adherence to provincial standards for farm classification and a preferential method of valuation for these parcels. The standards for the classification of land as farm specify the conditions that must be met if land is to be assessed as a farm for property tax purposes.

Most of the nine property classes use the theory of Highest and Best Use to derive the market value for each property, but farm land is an exception, being valued at its actual value for farm purposes without regard to its value for any other purpose. This use value is generally lower than market value because it does not reflect the competing forces of urban growth or recreational farmers. The difference in values is particularly significant on the urban/rural fringe where pressure to develop rural land is significant.

The use valuation of BC farm land, combined with relatively low tax rates and numerous exemptions, give significant tax advantages to farmers near the urban fringe where land values tend to be high. This is particularly true for small acreages where market values are much greater than their value in farm use. Together with the Provincial Agricultural Land Reserve, the farm assessment and tax system contributes to preserving agricultural land by enabling owners to hold land in its lowest cost use.

Classification

Land may be classified farm if it meets certain criteria based on size and agricultural capability. The standards for the classification of land as farm were designed to be simple, objective, equitable, attainable with reasonable farming effort and consistent with most existing British Columbia agricultural and taxation policies.

For assessment purposes, most property types are automatically classified according to use, but to be classified as farm, the owner must explicitly apply for classification. This is in part due to the substantial property tax benefits associated with having land classified as farm. However more practically, the assessor requires information regarding the agricultural production that will be sold to meet the minimum income requirement for farm classification.

The property owner makes application using one of two forms. The first form is used when a farm has met the income requirement in one of the past two years or is capable of meeting it in the coming year. The second form is used when a property is being developed as a farm and the required income from the sale of agricultural products is not anticipated for up to five years. This developing farm is 'flagged' on the database for annual inspection once farm classification has been granted to check that the property owner is complying with his commitment to develop the property into a farm. The income requirement must be met within five years or the property is declassified.

The income requirement for property to be classified farm varies with parcel size. Table 6.2 outlines the income requirement from the sale of agricultural products for parcels of various sizes. The following is a sample income requirement calculation for a property greater than 10 acres:

Farm Income Calculation for a 100 acre property:

First 10 Acres	$2,500
Farm Value of Remaining 90 Acres= $36,100	
5% x 36,100 =	<u>1,805</u>
Total Farm Income Requirement	**$4,305**

Table 6.2
Farm classification income requirements

Parcel Size	Income Requirement
< 2 acres	Greater part of farmer's livelihood from the sale of agricultural products.
2-10 acres	$2,500.
>10 acres	$2,500 + 5% of the farm value of the remaining area of the farm.

The income must be received from the sale of primary agricultural products raised on the property. A list of acceptable farm products is included in the standards as a guide to property owners.

> **Primary Agricultural Production** - livestock raising, poultry raising, egg production, dairying, horticulture, apiculture, aquaculture, fur farming, plantation culture of Christmas trees, seed production, sod farming, forest seed orchards, wool production and includes the growing or raising of an agricultural crop for food for human or animal consumption.

A farm may be composed of a single parcel or a group of parcels and may be entirely owned or leased. Details of a lease agreement must be submitted with the farm application to BC Assessment by the owner in order to qualify for farm classification. Administratively, to determine classification eligibility, each parcel within a farm operation is given a common farm unit number on the database by the BC Assessment appraiser. This enables the appraiser to identify all of the properties being farmed by an owner or lessee as a single farm unit. Farm properties may be declassified if:

1   The land ceases to be used for farming purposes, or
2   The land fails to meet the farm income requirement.

A property which no longer qualifies for farm classification is generally reclassified as residential and valued at market value in its highest and best use.

Farm land valuation schedules

The principal mechanism for implementing preferential tax treatment is preferential assessment or assessment of the land on the basis of its value as a farm without regard to its possible value for other uses. Land which qualifies to be classified as farm land is valued as a farm even though it may have a higher value for other purposes. Farm land valuation schedules are developed to simplify the farm land valuation process.

There are 87 farm land valuation schedules in BC. which vary by geographic location. New schedules are created in areas where the land use and agricultural capability differ sufficiently to affect farm land values. In addition to these regular schedules, special schedules are used for valuing certain farm operations such as aquaculture, orchards/vineyards, grains/oilseeds and cattle ranches. Since schedules were put in place almost 20 years ago, very little change annually has been required because the demand for farm properties has not increased significantly over this period.

Table 6.3 is a sample of a regular farm land valuation schedule that is composed of a number of rates which reflect the farm value per acre of land for each different agricultural capability and use. Unlike in a market value system where the value/acre generally declines relative to increasing parcel size, under a value in use system a large parcel will be valued at the same rate as a small parcel. This is so because each acre of farm land should produce the same income from agricultural production regardless of the total parcel size. Therefore, farm value rates are not adjusted for size. This has created an increased benefit to small parcels, whose value/acre may be substantially larger under a market value system than under a value in use system.

The income approach to valuation was used to determine the farm land rates by capitalizing farm land rental rates or net farm incomes to produce a rate per unit (acres). A sample calculation follows:

Cultivated land Valuation:

Hay Crop yield: 4 ton / acre
Annual Income: $80 / ton x 4 ton / acre = $320 / acre
Expenses: $170 / acre

141

Net Return: $150 / acre per year
Capitalization Rate: 7%
Value of Cultivatable Class 1 Land: $150 = $2,140 per acre
                                    0.07

Adjustments to some scheduled farm values are permitted to account for distance to the market, schools, water availability, electricity and road access. Sample adjustments to schedule values are:

Utilities   Roads

Electricity   0%   Paved   +5%
No Electricity   -5%   Gravel   0%
                                    Dirt   -5%

                                    No Access   -10%

Table 6.3
Farm land valuation schedule

Land Use	1		2		3		4		5	
Land Capability	Cultivated $	Rate Code	Irrigated Special Crop	Rate Code	Rough Cleared	Rate Code	Permanent Pasture	Rate Code	Unimproved	Rate Code
1	2,140	9011	2,640	9021	1,160	9031			550	9051
2	1,760	9012	2,200	9022	970	9032			455	9052
3	1,410	9013	1,760	9023	775	9033			365	9053
4	990	9014	1,240	9024			545	9044	260	9054
5	820	9015	1,025	9025			410	9045	215	9055
6									15	9056
7									15	9057
8 Farmstead	1,760									

The cattle ranch schedule includes rates for valuing rangelands which are based on the elevation and condition of the property. Most of the estimated 10 million hectares of rangelands is leased from the Crown with the occupier (lessee) responsible for paying property taxes. The availability of Crown rangeland for a low lease fee enables British Columbian ranchers to be more competitive with producers in other regions.

Farm land schedule rates are audited against actual farm sales to ensure that these rates do not exceed market values. The appropriate farm land rates are selected for a parcel according to land use and agricultural capability.

Land use

Using a combination of air photograph interpretation and on-site inspections, the property is divided into areas which are classified according to land use. For the majority of the province the farm land use classifications are:

Cultivatable
Irrigated Crop / Special Crop
Rough Cleared / Rough Pasture
Permanent Pasture
Unimproved
Farmstead

Unlike the regular farm land valuation schedules whose rates are based on use and agricultural capability, the special schedules including cattle ranchlands, foreshore leases used for aquaculture and orchard/vineyards have rates based on other factors. For example, the Orchard/Vineyard Schedule categorizes land according to topography, soil type and frost risk (slight, moderate, high).

Variations in rates between land uses should reflect the relative costs of improving the land from category to category. For example, the cost to develop unimproved land into pasture land would include tree and stump removal, root raking, ploughing and seeding costs. This cost is reflected in the difference in rates between these two land uses. The highest valued land is irrigated land or land planted to a special crop (perennial) and the lowest valued land is unimproved land.

Land capability for agriculture

For farm land assessment, the consideration of soil and climate is important for the simple reason that one piece of land can be economically several times more productive than another. For this reason alone the quality of land should form the logical foundation for equitable land assessment. Mapping which indicates the agricultural capability of land, taking into account soil and climatic features, was produced for the province in the 1960s and is most important for the farm assessment process.

The Canada Land Inventory system rates the agricultural capability of land according to limitations that would restrict the range of crops grown on it. Lands are grouped into seven classes according to their potentialities and limitations for agricultural use depending on inherent soil and climatic characteristics. Agriculture capability classifications take into account the range of crops possible, and not productivity (i.e. yield/acre). The seven agricultural capability classes are:

Class 1 -   land in this class has no significant limitations in use for crops.

Class 2 -   land in this class has moderate limitations that restrict the range of crops or require special conservation practices.

Class 3 -   land in this class has moderately severe limitations that restrict the range of crops or require special conservation practices.

Class 4 -   land in this class has severe limitations that restrict the range of crops or require special conservation practices, or both.

Class 5 -   land in this class has very severe limitations that restrict their capability to produce perennial forage crops, and improvement practices are feasible.

Class 6 -   land in this class is capable only of producing perennial forage crops, and improvement practices are not feasible. Provide some sustained grazing for farm animals.

Class 7 -   land in this class has no capability for arable culture or permanent pasture. Includes rockland, bodies of water and other non-soil areas.

For each Class, associated subclasses indicate the type of limitation to agriculture use for land in that Class. No more than two subclasses are noted for each class of soil as denoted by a small consonant subscript on the maps. Subclasses include:

(c)	Adverse Climate	(d)	Undesirable soil structure and/or low permeability
(e)	Erosion	(f)	Low Fertility
(m)	Moisture limitation	(n)	Salinity
(p)	Stoniness	(r)	Consolidated bedrock
(s)	Adverse soil characteristics	(t)	Topography
(w)	Excess water	(x)	Cumulative minor adverse characteristics

Canada Land Inventory maps are available which indicate land capability for agriculture of properties in British Columbia at a scale of 1:50,000. These maps were developed from aerial photographs with site inspections by soil specialists. Farm parcels can be located on the appropriate map and the Class determined for each farm land component. An example of a parcel classification is as follows:

$$3^7_m - 5^3_t$$

This CLI rating indicates that the land within these delineations is 70% Class 3 land with a moisture limitation and 30% Class 5 land with a topographical limitation.

Table 6.4 is an example of how an appraiser would identify two farm land components of cultivated land with the above-mentioned CLI rating.

Table 6.4
Canada land inventory components

32 Acres of Cultivatable Land:			
1	32 acres x 0.70	=	22.4 acres CLI 3
2	32 acres x 0.30	=	9.6 acres CLI 5
			32.0 acres

The rate codes from the appropriate farm land valuation schedule would be selected to value each of the two components of cultivatable land.

Data collection

Once the land has been classified as farm, data must be collected to assist in the valuation of the property. Data used to value farm properties is collected through the application form, a field inspection and from other sources such as maps, aerial photographs and building permits. Details of the farm land, farm outbuildings and the farm residence are collected and entered onto CAPAS for use in valuation.

Each property in the province can be identified on the database by it's individual folio number. The folio number indicates the *area* and *jurisdiction* in which the property is located and a unique numerical identification for the property. The *area* represents a large geographic region which is serviced by one of BC Assessment's 26 Area offices. The *jurisdiction* identifies the taxing jurisdiction, whether a municipality or rural area.

Area	Jurisdiction	Individual Property
01	**- 234**	**- 04503.000**

The property classification is recorded using a property class code (01-09).

Residential Class	**01**
Farm Class	**09**

An actual use code is assigned to each farm property to identify the agricultural product that is being produced. For example, actual use code 110 would identify the property as being used to grow grains or oilseeds.

During the inspection of land, appraisers collect specific property inventory that may influence the final calculation of value. To record these characteristics, a farm property record was designed for ease of inventory and data collection. Property characteristics which are identified on a farm property record and input as variables on the database include:

General Property Specifics

Folio Number
Owner Name and Address
Legal Description of Property

Farm Specifics

Actual Use:	identifies the type of farm (i.e. dairy, beef, grain)
Farm Unit:	identifies the parcel as operated as part of a farm unit.
ALR code:	identifies land located in the Agricultural Land Reserve. Coded if the property is located in the ALR. Blank if the property is not in the ALR.
Lot Size:	dimensions (acres).
Air Photo:	most recent air photograph which covers the property.
Location:	identifies the cadastral map on which the property is located.
Services:	indicates water, access, electricity (for purposes of adjustments to value).
Topography:	indicates slope for purposes of orchard/vineyard valuation.
Frost:	indicates degree of frost risk for purposes of orchard/vineyard valuation.
Distance To:	nearest market, town, grain elevator (for purposes of adjustments).

Farm Land Components

Component: each parcel may be divided into components for purposes of applying farm land valuation schedules (up to 99 components). The components identify a area of land of a specific CLI class and land use.

Land Use: is the physical inventory of the land identifying the land utility necessary for application of farm land valuation schedules (cultivatable, pasture).

Soil: soil type recorded from soil maps or site inspection.

Capability: normally identified from CLI maps and is required for application of farm land valuation schedules.

Acreage: area of each component in the parcel.

Rate Type: this code relates to the unit of comparison on the schedule (acres).

Rate Code: identifies the appropriate rate from the farm land valuation schedules. Farm rate codes are numbered from 8000 - 9999.

Rate: identifies the actual value per acre of the corresponding rate code.

Value: value of the component determined by multiplying the component acreage by the rate.

Adjustments: adjustments for services and distance to market as allowed by the farm land valuation schedules.

Final Value: sum of all farm land components. This is the value of farm land.

At the bottom of the farm property record, the appraiser indicates the date that the property was inspected, his name and a code which identifies the purpose of the inspection. The reverse side of the farm property record provides an area to record characteristics of improvements such as residences or farm outbuildings.

Appraisers may annually collect farm income data from property's flagged (selected) on the database as marginal by identifying what threshold level of farm income is considered marginal. Where the income requirement for a property is $2,500, an appraiser may choose to flag all those properties classified farm where less than $4,000 of income from sales of agricultural products is declared on their application form. The property owner is required to detail farm production and income in order to continue to qualify the property for farm classification.

Land calculation system

The *land calculation system* provides the CAPAS facility to capture land inventory and rates. This system is an automated tool to assist in the calculation of land values based on market-derived information which is entered into the system in the form of farm land valuation schedules.

The land calculations are determined by retrieving the appropriate farm rates from the land tables (farm land valuation schedules) and calculating the actual values from the recorded land inventory. This will result in working values for the farm land as illustrated in Figure 6.3. These working values will eventually be transferred to the property information database to be reproduced on an assessment roll as assessed values.

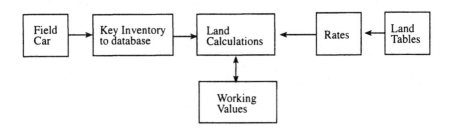

Figure 6.3 Farm land valuation schedules

The land calculation system calculates a total value for each folio on the system. In order to update the property database with the calculated land values, a value transfer must occur. A value transfer is an on request computer routine which will take the calculated values from the land calculation system, updates them onto the property database, and replaces the existing values. The land values are transferred to the property database for reproduction onto assessment notices and rolls.

The land calculation system used to generate values for farm land is applicable once the property has been classified as Class 9 - Farm. Farm land is divided into components which represent areas of land that are categorized by land use and agricultural capability. Each component has a corresponding rate code and rate (value/acre). The component dimensions should sum to the total farm land area (usually corresponds to the parcel land dimensions except if a portion of the property is classified as an alternative use). Actual values of up to 99 components per parcel are summed to determine the total actual value of farm land.

Annual updating of farm land schedule rates and inventories occurs, then calculations of land value are performed automatically by the land calculation system.

Rate Amount x Component Dimensions = Assessed Value

The four standard units of comparison used to calculate a value are area rate, standard lot, square measure or frontage rate. Farm land is valued by area and is recorded in acres. The 4-digit rate codes found on the schedules are numeric codes that represent a rate amount for a component in a specified area. It is used to identify a group of components of similar value characteristics. Farms are identified by:

8000 - 8999 farm - non-soil oriented uses
9000 - 9999 farm - soil-oriented uses

The first 2 digits identify the appropriate farm land valuation schedule. The third digit identifies the land use (i.e. cultivated, unimproved etc.). The fourth digit identifies land capability (i.e. CLI 1 - 7). The non-soil oriented uses include aquaculture, orchard/vineyards and cattle ranches. These special schedules do not use agriculture capability (CLI) as a factor influencing land values.

Properties classified farm may revert to residential classification if the property fails to annually meet the criteria established in the farm standards. The appraiser has the option of creating a single component which reflects the market value of the entire parcel and suppressing it while the property is classified as farm. If this component is flagged to be suppressed, any value for this component will not be passed on to the assessment roll. The flag can be released if the property reverts to residential classification and the previous suppressed market value can become the new assessed value.

Exemptions reduce the farm land and building values from the total assessed value. Exempt tax codes are entered by component and are used to identify the exemptions which must be applied to each particular component.

The sales system is used to audit farm land valuation schedule rates. Occasionally, appraisers examine large farm sales retrieved from the sales system to determine if schedule values are consistent with farm sales in a particular jurisdiction by comparing the rates to the sale value/acre. If farm land market values decline relative to the schedule values, the rates are adjusted downwards by the Assessment Commissioner. With parameters selected to target the sales appropriate for comparison, a farm sales report is generated for the area to assist in analysis. Parameters typically used to select sales are geographic area, size, vacancy and land use. To target sales of a particular type of farm, actual use and manual class variables (identifies farm outbuildings) may be specified. For example, to report sales of dairy farms, select the actual use code for dairy farms, 160-161, and manual class code 4202 for milking parlours. Sales of larger parcels of farm land are targeted to better represent value in farm use as smaller parcels are often sold to non-farmers. Alternatively, the appraiser may use the income approach to verify farm land values where pure farm land sales transactions are scarce.

Assessed value to sales value ratios are also used to determine whether farm land rates are a reasonable estimate of farm land values. The difficulty in determining the value of farm land through sales comparison is that in many areas of the province, the urban influence has distorted the value of land from its value as farm land. It is not unusual for a farm sales value ratio to equal less than 0.3. This indicates that the value of farm land as calculated using the farm land rates is 30% of it selling price. These sales obviously reflect other factors than farm value.

The servicing system flags properties requiring inspection. A flag is used to mark a folio on the database for inspection for one of a variety of reasons. There are three types of farm flags which may be captured on CAPAS:

1   Marginal Farms
2   Farm Leases
3   Developing Farms

Farm properties may be flagged if they are considered 'marginal'. Leased farm properties are flagged, so that the appraiser can ensure that he has a copy of a current lease in order to continue to qualify for farm classification. Developing farms are flagged to be inspected annually to ensure that the owners are progressing in their plan to develop the property into a farm within five years.

Valuation of farm improvements

The residential improvement system is used to value residences and farm outbuildings using the cost approach to valuation. The residential improvement system provides the facilities to apply cost rates to residential inventory to yield Manual Replacement Costs (MRC) of farm buildings and the farmer's dwelling. The MRC is adjusted by the application of cost and market factors, relating the manual costs to local conditions, to yield a Replacement Cost New. This value is depreciated to yield a market adjusted Replacement Cost New Less Depreciation. It is beyond the scope of this chapter to review the residential improvement system in its entirety and so a general overview of the valuation of farm outbuildings is provided.

Manual class codes identify the structural characteristics of the improvements of a property. They are used to facilitate the grouping of specific structural and/ or architectural characteristics for administrative, valuation and statistical purposes. Individual farm outbuildings can be identified by their manual class code. For example, a milk parlour of average quality has manual class code 4204.

CAPAS stores inventory for farm outbuildings based on manual class. The inventory of a milk parlour might be:

Outbuilding 1

Outbldg Area	5600 SF
Outbldg Use	Milk Parlour
Manual Class	4204
Cost Year	75
Effective Year	80
Depreciation Rate	2.00 %
Present Value	56,400

BC Assessment developed a farm building cost manual for use by field appraisal staff in estimating farm building values. The Replacement Cost New of farm buildings is manually calculated and the result entered into the database. The depreciation tables and local cost multipliers are coded on the database and are applied to the Replacement Cost New automatically according to the building's manual class code. The resulting Replacement Cost New Less Depreciation values are recorded as the farm building and residence assessed values on the database to which farm exemptions are applied.

Farm phase-in

Farm land assessed values are phased in over a number of years to lessen the impact of assessment increases in any given year. The intent of the phase-in is to buffer the farmer from large tax increases as a result of a large increase in land assessment in any one year. It also has the effect of shielding farmers from increases due to changes in inventory, i.e. clearing land. An assessment on farm land is phased-in if the current assessed value before exemptions exceeds the assessed value for the preceding year before exemptions by more than 10%. CAPAS automatically makes this calculation as shown in Table 6.5.

Table 6.5
Farm phase - in

Assessed value in preceding year:		$50,000
Assessed value in current year:		$60,000
Phase-in Calculation $50,000 x 110% =	$55,000	
(60,000 - 55,000) x 25% =	1,250	
Phased-in Value in Current Year:		$56,250

Farm exemptions from taxation

Several exemptions from taxation exist that further reduce the property tax burden to farmers. Farm improvements and land are coded to ensure that they receive the appropriate exemptions during the final calculation of taxable values. The taxable values are used by the taxing jurisdictions to determine the tax base upon which taxes are actually levied.

Assessed Value - Exemptions = Taxable Value

Farm exemptions can be categorized into three groups: Municipal, Rural Area and School. In the province of British Columbia, there are three taxes levied to property owners. Municipal taxes are levied to property owners for services provided by municipalities. Taxes are levied by the provincial government to property owners in rural (non-municipal) areas for services provided. And finally, School taxes are levied on all properties (both municipal and rural areas) to support the public school system.

Municipal Farm Exemption Farm outbuildings on property classified farm located in a municipality are exempt up to $50,000 of their assessed value for the purpose of municipal taxation. The farmer's residence is fully taxable.

Rural Area Farm Exemption Farm outbuildings and the farmer's residence are exempt from taxation for the purpose of rural taxation.

School farm exemption

- Farm outbuildings are exempt up to $50,000 of their assessed value for the purpose of School taxation in both rural and municipal areas.

- Land within the Agricultural Land Reserve is exempt up to 50% of the assessed land value for the purposes of School taxation. This applies to:

  1   Land classified as farm.
  2   Land used for residential purposes.
  3   Vacant and unused land.

Exemption (b) was created in an attempt to recognize the restrictions of use imposed on a property within the Agricultural Land Reserve.

Other Farm Exemptions The following items found on farm land are exempted from assessment and taxation:

- fruit trees
- manure storage facilities
- machinery and equipment

Exempt tax codes indicate if a land component or improvement is fully or partially taxable and which exemption is applicable (ALR, rural outbuildings etc.).

Court of Revision and Assessment Appeal Board

The Court of Revision is the first level of appeal for a property owner who is dissatisfied with their property classification or valuation. CAPAS provides for the automated logging and scheduling of appeals. Courts of Revision are appointed members of a local community who hear appeals on assessments of land and improvements in taxing jurisdictions throughout the province. Special Courts of Revision may be appointed, comprised of persons experienced in agriculture, to hear complaints with respect to the classification of land as a farm.

Most farm property owners appeal the property classification as opposed to the valuation as the farm land rates are not appealable. Owners of properties that are refused farm classification may appeal to the Court of Revision. The Assessment Appeal Board is the level of appeal for a property owner who is dissatisfied with the Court of Revision decision. It is the highest 'fact finding' tribunal. Members of the Appeal Board are generally professionals with some experience in the legal or appraisal professions. Appeals from decisions of the Assessment Appeal Board may be on points of law only to the Supreme Court of British Columbia.

Taxation of farm land

An essential relationship exists between the assessment areas and the taxing jurisdictions since the prime objective of BC Assessment is to provide value information for the purpose of taxation. BC Assessment provides property information to the taxing jurisdictions annually in the form of assessment rolls.

Taxable Assessed Value x Tax Rate = Gross Taxes

Provincial, municipal and local governments determine the tax rates for the nine classes of property which will generate the funds necessary to meet budgetary requirements for services to citizens of the province.

Residential homeowner rebate

Residential homeowners are rebated a portion of their taxes annually by the provincial government. This is called the Home Owner's Grant and is available to owners residing in their homes, including farmers, with properties valued up to $475,000.

Case study - dairy farm

This is a case study of a dairy farm assessed and taxed within British Columbia. The actual farm is comprised of several parcels. This example will go through the valuation of the home parcel on which exist the farmer's residence and several farm outbuildings. A description of the valuation process precedes the example.

Area	Jurisdiction	Neighbourhood	Roll Number	Actual Use	Farm Unit No.
01	332	620	03039.000	160	6073

6469 West Saanich Road
Lot 1, Plan 25609, Section 8, Range 1W, North Saanich Land District
Windy Farms Ltd.

Identification

This is a replication of the data collected and used by CAPAS to calculate actual values of a farm folio. This particular property is identified by the *area* (Capital), *jurisdiction* (North Saanich), *neighbourhood* (Ardmore) and roll number (identifies this particular property). Actual Use code 160 identifies this parcel as part of a Dairy farm. The Farm Unit Number (6073) identifies this parcel as belonging to a larger farm unit comprised of several properties operated by the same farmer. The property address, owner name and legal description are provided as further identification to the location and ownership of the property.

Improvement valuation

	LCM	Replac. Cost New	Eff Yr	Deprec Tbl	Deprec	RCNLD Value	Market Value
MB	1.284	236,314	67	U710	PHY 21.5	185,506	185,506
CP	1.284	18,298	67	U710	PHY 21.5	14,364	14,364
PL	1.284	45,959	69	U710	PHY 21.5	36,078	36,078
					RCNLD	00	01

Improvement value calculation

Residential improvements The residential improvements appear next on the field card. MB (mainbuilding), CP (carport) , PL (pool) identify the type of improvement. LCM is the local cost multiplier used to adjust values to reflect local costs. The replacement cost new for each structure is calculated. The effective year (Eff Yr) is used to determine the depreciation (Deprec) from the appropriate depreciation table (Deprec Tbl). The depreciation is subtracted from the replacement cost new for each structure to determine the replacement cost new less depreciation (RCNLD) value or market value. Code 00 is an exempt tax code that identifies the residential improvements as fully taxable. Code 01 is the property class code which identifies these improvements as residential.

Farm improvements

```
OB   2.544  143,716  80    Rate  2.00          103,476    103,476
Man Class 4204  Outbuilding 1    Tot   28.00

OB   2.544  406,435  80    Rate  2.00          292,633    292,633
Man Class 4203  Outbuilding 2    Tot   28.00

OB   2.544  50,880   80    Rate  0.10           50,168     50,168
Man Class8001   Outbuilding 3    Tot   1.40

OB   2.544  91,330   87    Rate  2.00           78,544     78,544
Man Class 4202  Outbuilding 4    Tot   14.00

OB   2.544  40,808   83    Rate  1.50           34,075     34,075
Man Class 4215  Outbuilding 5    Tot   16.50

OB   2.544  18,302   80    Rate  2.00           13,177     13,777
Man Class 4206  Outbuilding 6    Tot   28.00

                                 RCNLD   21  10
```

Farm outbuilding value calculation The valuation of farm outbuildings is similar to that of residential improvements. The Man Class identifies the type of farm structure.

Man Class	Structure Type
4202	Maternity Pen/Calving Barn
4203	Good Quality Barn
4204	Milking Parlour
4206	Manure Storage
4215	Good Quality Machine Shed
8001	Bunker silo

Code 21 is an exempt tax code that identifies these improvements as farm buildings eligible for exemptions under the Municipal and School Acts. Code 10 is a property tax code which identifies these improvements as farm outbuildings.

Land value calculation

CP	Code	Amount	Dimension	ET	PC	Component
01	N-0340	125,000	40.000 A	00	09	588,815

Suppress Value Transfer

CP	Code	Amount	Dimension	ET	PC	Component
10	A-9018	1,760	1.780 A	20	09	3,132
11	A-9021	2,640	17.440 A	20	09	46,041
12	A-9022	2,200	30.880 A	20	09	67,936

Total 117,109
say 117,000

Land value calculation Land is valued by components (CP). Component number 01 is the market value of the property as if classified residential. This value is suppressed as long as the property remains classified farm. Components 10-12 are the farm components. The Code identifies the appropriate rate to use from the farm land valuation schedules. The Amount is the rate amount taken directly from the farm land valuation schedule which corresponds to the identified rate code. The Dimension is the area of land which will be multiplied by the rate code. The rate code identifies the land use and agricultural capability. The exempt tax code (20) identifies this component as farm land that will receive the ALR exemption under the School Act. This component is in property class (PC) 09 which identifies it as farm land. The dimension multiplied by the rate code amount will determine the Component value. The sum of all of the component values will result in the farm land value for this property.

Roll Value

ET	PC	Land	ET	PC	Improvement
20	09	$117,000	00	01	$235,900
			21	10	$572,600
Total Roll Value					$925,500

Total roll values These values are the total assessed values for a single property which will be transferred to the property information database for use on the assessment roll.

Assessment notice The values on the assessment notice mailed to each property owner will appear like this:

	VALUE	**CLASS**
Land	$117,000	Farm
Buildings	$235,900	Residential
Farm Outbuildings	$572,600	Residential
Assessed Value	**$925,500**	

Tax Base	Municipal	School & Other
	$925,500	$925,500
Less Exemptions	-50,000	-108,500
Taxable Value	**$875,500**	**$817,000**

Taxes Information on the tax notice will appear like this:

Municipal Taxes	**Taxable Value**	**Tax Rate (per '000)**	**Taxes**
Land	117,000/1,000 x 1.50 =		$ 175.50
Residence	235,900/1,000 x 1.20 =		283.08
Farm Outbuildings	522,600/1,000 x 1.20 =		627.12

School & Other Taxes

Land	58,500/1,000 x 8.50 =		497.25
Residence	235,900/1,000 x 5.00 =		1,179.50
Farm Outbuildings	522,600/1,000 x 5.00 =		2,613.00
		Gross Taxes:	**5,375.45**
		-Homeowner's Grant:	**- 470.00**
		Net Taxes:	**$4,905.45**

Strengths of farm assessment system

The strengths of BC Assessment's farm assessment system are:

1   Simplicity

The farm land valuation schedules developed 20 years ago are applied simply to determine farm land values and assist in the mass appraisal of 60,000 parcels annually. As farm incomes and therefore farm land values have not changed significantly over this time, relatively few adjustments to the schedule rates have been necessary.

2   Lack of sales data

As farms do not transfer as frequently as residential or other types of properties, this system of valuation does not require a lot of appraisal time analysing scarce pure farm sales data. The system of applying scheduled rates derived from farm income analysis produces a proxy of farm value.

3   Farm property database

BC Assessment has the most up to date, definitive database of farm property information in British Columbia as field appraisers physically inspect and inventory each farm in the province. This information is extremely valuable in developing agricultural policy and measuring impacts to farms from changes in government policy.

Limitations of the farm assessment system

The limitations of BC Assessment's farm assessment system are:

1   Equity

Due to the difference in exemptions, the taxable farm land value varies between rural and municipal areas which results in an inequity of taxes between farms of the same value in rural and municipal areas.

2   Cost

Although the valuation process is simple, farm land takes a disproportionately large time investment to monitor marginal farms to ensure that they are continuing to meet the criteria to sustain farm classification on their property. Farm land generates a small amount of revenue for taxing jurisdictions compared to other property types, however it takes a large amount of the staff time to process applications, inventory and field check farm land.

3   Classification system

Approximately one-third of the farm units in British Columbia produce 95% of the provincial farm output and yet all farms enjoy the benefits of preferential assessment. Property tax benefits are shifting from the commercial farm to non-commercial owners of rural estates, hobby farms and properties held for urban development. These properties are only farming enough to meet the low level of required income ($2,500) to sustain farm tax classification status and, although not contributing significantly to the agricultural economy, are receiving significant benefits.

Proposed farm assessment and taxation system

Due to the limitations of the current farm assessment and taxation system, there is some consideration of a system that would transfer the property tax burden from the farm land and farm outbuildings to the residence and an area of land associated with the residence. The farm land and farm buildings would be exempt from taxation. The home and homesite would be taxed at a residential rate. All exemptions would be removed. The objectives of this system would be to eliminate inequities between municipal and rural area farms and to target the taxation benefits to land and/or capital intensive farms.

New technology

GIS

BC Assessment is currently piloting a digital based Mapping Information System. The system is microcomputer based. A digitized provincial road map was purchased from the Ministry responsible for Transportation and Highways. Computer based mapping software was acquired which produced a computer generated base map with coding for particular properties from the CAPAS database. Individual assessment data is attached to the mapping system and can be used for sales analysis in neighbourhoods. In addition, survey plans and aerial photographs can be scanned and possibly stored on CD ROM files.

The farm applications of this technology are immense. Land use areas could be calculated from the aerial photographs using computer software. The CLI mapping has been digitized in several areas of the province. If these map layers could be superimposed within a GIS system, the appraiser could determine the area of farm components quickly and easily. The Agricultural Land Reserve boundaries could also be digitized to audit current coding.

Pen-based hand-held computers

Pen-based hand-held computers are currently installed in 6 assessment area offices. These computers can be taken into the field and inventory data collected, values calculated and verified on site. Once back in the office, the data can be downloaded into the mainframe. This will eliminate keying errors and save clerical time. The appraiser can also capture the building sketch electronically. This eliminates the need to keep a hard copy of each field property record.

Expanded actual use codes

A more expansive farm actual use coding system has been developed by the Ministry responsible for Agriculture, Fisheries and Food. This system is being considered for implementation by BC Assessment. This will enable appraisers to identify specific land uses within their areas (i.e. number of acres planted to raspberries, cauliflower, cranberries etc.). The current farm actual use codes are limited to eight general types of farms.

Farm outbuildings computerized

The valuation of farm outbuildings will be eventually computerized. Currently inventory is collected on the database, however assessment calculations are manually entered.

References

BC Assessment, (1992), *CAPAS Overview*, BC Assessment Authority.
BC Assessment, (1992), *Land Calculation System*, BC Assessment Authority.
BC Assessment, (1992), *Information Systems Plan*, BC Assessment Authority.
BC Assessment, (1993), *Mapping Information System Plan*, BC Assessment Authority.
Hughes, C., (1992), *Real Property Assessment*, UBC Real Estate Division.
Ministry of Finance and Corporate Relations, (1994), *1994 British Columbia*

Financial and Economic Review, 54th Ed., British Columbia.

Ministry of Finance and Corporate Relations and Ministry of Municipal Affairs, Recreation and Culture, (1991), *Property Tax Treatment of Agricultural and Forest Land in Canada: Implications for Land Use Policy*, British Columbia.

Runka, G.G., (1973), *Land Capability for Agriculture*, Kelowna: BC Dept. of Agriculture.

7 Mass appraisal of agricultural property in Sweden

A. Sundquist

Introduction

Real estate assessment and property taxation have deep roots in Sweden. As early as the 16th Century, King Gustaf Wasa introduced real property lists (land registers) which formed the basis for property taxation. In more recent years, general assessments of all real property have been carried out regularly, and during the last fifty years at five yearly intervals. Since 1988, general assessments have been carried out in six-year cycles with the assessment of different categories of real property every second year. In Sweden, real property assessment is regulated by a special Law, the Real Property Assessment Law of 1979 (FTL), used for the first time for the general assessment in 1981.

Besides the Real Property Assessment Law there are a few rules which are promulgated by the Government and The National Tax Board in Sweden (RSV). An outline of the main rules is presented in Figure 7.1.

Real property assessment means a general valuation of the real property units using a model with data normally provided by the owner. The assessed value is based on its value on the open market and represents 75 % of the market value during one specific year, known as the reference year. As well as the general assessment, a real property unit is subject to assessment if the property in question has been physically altered to the extent that it affects the assessed value. As well as the two kinds of assessments already mentioned, of which the general assessment is by far the most important, Sweden also has a system of changing the assessed value on an index linked basis. These recalculations of the assessed value will be carried out every year in close connection with the general assessment starting in 1996.

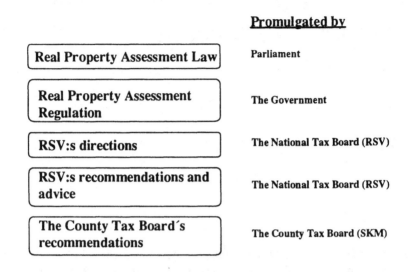

Real Property Assessment Law	Parliament
Real Property Assessment Regulation	The Government
RSV:s directions	The National Tax Board (RSV)
RSV:s recommendations and advice	The National Tax Board (RSV)
The County Tax Board´s recommendations	The County Tax Board (SKM)

Figure 7.1 Property tax rules and regulations

The purpose and use of the assessed value

The assessed value, which is 75 % of the market value during a particular year, is primarily used for taxation purposes. The assessed value forms the basis of the real property tax as well as some other taxes including inheritance and gift tax, the wealth tax and stamp duty, the latter being a tax which is levied in connection with the purchase or mortgage of real property. The assessed value also forms the basis of other types of charge, for example road maintenance charges and other instances where costs of common facilities are shared. The assessed value is also often used as a loan value and for general valuation purposes, for example in calculating price trends or in the use of 'P/A' figures (purchase price/assessed value) to estimate the value of a particular property.

In principle, all real property is liable to taxation and will have an assessed value. Exempt from liability to taxation are 'special units' (buildings for special purposes) such as military defence buildings, buildings used in connection with public transport, hospitals, schools, buildings used for leisure and sport, buildings of cultural interest, buildings for state, county or local authority administration, etc. FTL contains detailed rules on what type of property is to be exempt from liability to taxation. A great number of precedents have contributed to facilitate the problems of defining different types of real property.

At present (1996) property tax is 1.7% of the assessed value per year for homes for one or two families (small houses) and dwelling houses on agricultural units. For apartment blocks the property tax is 1.7 of the assessed value per year. For commercial areas (shops, offices etc.) the property tax is 1.0% and for industrial units including power plants the property tax is 0.5%. Agricultural units are exempted from property tax.

Currently (1996) the total property tax contributes about SEK 15 billion to the total state tax income which is in the region of SEK 370 billion. As well as the SEK 15 billion, a further SEK 4 billion is added to the state income from taxes and charges based on the assessed value.

Regularity of assessment

Swedish real property is divided into units. In principle, assessment covers all real property throughout Sweden. Assessment will also include property consisting of a building erected by someone other than the owner of the land, i.e. the building and the site having separate owners.

A differentiation is made between *general* and *special* assessment. General assessment is carried out according to the following schedule;

•   1988 and every following sixth year (1994, 2000 and so on) apartment blocks, commercial buildings, industrial units (including power plants, gravel pits and quarries) and special units.

•   1990 and every following sixth year (1996, 2002 and so on) dwelling houses for one or two families, including holiday homes.

•   1992 and every following sixth year (1998, 2004 and so on) agricultural units.

The new assessed value is known as the base value and is valid from 1st January of the year of assessment and the following six years. After that period there will be a new general assessment in which all relevant information concerning the real property and the market price levels will be examined. In between the general assessment years, special assessments are carried out. In this case, the base value which was determined as the result of the general assessment carried out earlier is adopted as from 1st January every year until a new general assessment is made, provided that the real property has not undergone any physical alterations. If the physical condition of the property has been altered

165

during the year to such an extent that the assessed value has changed by at least 20% or a minimum of SEK 25,000, a new assessment based on the principles and price levels of the last general assessment will be carried out. Otherwise the previous base value is retained.

From 1996, a 'recalculation' (index number) procedure will be introduced alongside the general and special assessments. By means of this the base values mentioned above will be recalculated every year by the application of an index number based on price trends and price levels of the particular type of real property and for a particular area (region, local authority, etc.). The purpose of the recalculation procedure is to allow the base values, which have remained unchanged during the six-year period, provided the property has not been subject to any physical changes, to gradually follow the price trends of the type of real property in question. This will eliminate the risk of substantial increases in price which can occur during the six-year period and provide for a more gradual adjustment to current price levels instead.

Object of assessment

The object of assessment is known as the assessment unit. Generally speaking, real property is identical with the assessment unit. However, in some cases it may consist of two or more assessment units because different parts are used for different purposes. For example, a real property unit which includes both a dwelling unit and a workshop where the same owner runs a business will normally be divided into two, or indeed several assessment units, depending on the use of the different parts. The reverse situation can also occur, for example, when two or more real properties together form a farm with one owner. In that situation, the real properties will together constitute one assessment unit, known as an agricultural unit. When it comes to a building erected on a rented site, the building will constitute one assessment unit and the site another assessment unit.

Organization

Matters concerning real property taxation are dealt with by a special government agency under the Ministry of Finance known as the National Tax Board (RSV). This body has the responsibility for the actual work of real property taxation. The National Land Survey of Sweden, which is a government agency under the Ministry of Environment, is responsible by law for a large part of the preparations which precede the work of actual taxation. Figure 7.2 is a representation of the organizational structure.

166

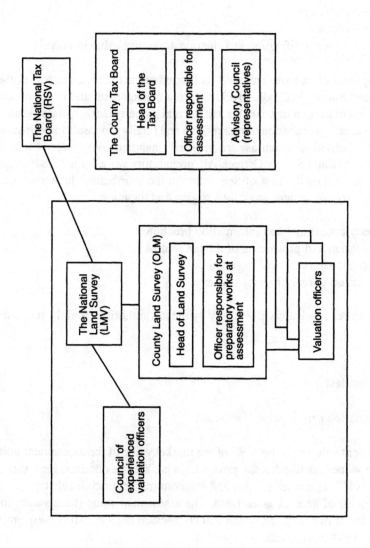

Figure 7.2 Organizational structure

Real property assessment consists of two independent parts, the preparatory work and the assessment work. The preparatory work includes:

- market analysis
- evaluation of the previous assessment
- construction (or overhaul) of the valuation models
- examination of market data
- the construction of tables
- computer support
- test valuations
- proposals for classification in valuation areas and valuation levels

The development of valuation methods is carried out at the headquarters of the National Land Survey in Gävle, in addition to a management and coordinating role for the rest of the country. Analysis of the real property market, classification of valuation areas, examination of market data and finally proposals for valuation levels in the individual counties, are primarily handled by personnel within regional or local Land Survey Offices. All preparatory work for the assessment must be completed on the first of September in the year before the assessment year. The actual assessment work then begins and includes:

- property tax returns and information brochures
- examination and processing of the tax returns
- formal decisions
- information to real property owners.

These procedures are dealt with entirely by the tax authorities mainly at county level.

Valuation models

General valuation principles and methods

The assessment value must be 75% of the market value of the assessment unit. The market value is defined as the price which is likely be obtained for the real property if sold on the open market and refers to market price levels two years prior to the year of general assessment. The assessment value (base value) for houses for one or two families, which will be assessed in 1996 will consequently be based on 1994 price levels.

The market value should, in the first instance, be determined according to prices achieved from property transactions in the area. The Assessment Law does permit valuation authorities to use the yield method of valuation, where the principle is to estimate the future income and expenses likely to be incurred in the use of the real property and, on the basis of this information, estimate the price that the average, intelligent buyer would be willing to pay. As a last resort, the Assessment Law permits the market value to be estimated on the basis of the cost of a new construction but taking into consideration depreciation due to age and use. In the majority of cases the market data approach is used to estimate the assessed value. The market data approach is used exclusively with regard to houses for one or two families. For apartment blocks and commercial buildings, the yield approach is used being based on the actual rent or an estimated rent, but with price levels supported by market data.

For the more unusual types of industrial property, the value is estimated on the cost of reconstructing the type of property in question, and takes into consideration depreciation due to age and use. Even in these cases there are elements of adaptation to market data. Valuation of electrical power plants is based on the production of electricity, the location of the power plant, etc., and as far as hydroelectric power schemes are concerned, on the possibility of regulating water flow. Valuation of gravel pit units is based on the production of gravel, stone, etc., as well as the income from the rights to quarry that particular kind of mineral. For agricultural units, the different parts are individually valued using different methods. Valuation of arable land, pasture and forest is partly based on yield calculations, but the final price is always based on market data. Farm buildings are valued according to the cost of construction less depreciation, but at the same time taking into consideration market trends. Farmhouses are valued using the prices from house sales in the surrounding countryside as a guide, with market price levels also being taken into consideration, as well as the value of the entire agricultural unit.

For all assessment units other than agricultural units, the land value and the building value are determined together to give the total assessed value (base value). Agricultural units are different in that they are given separate values for the site, farmhouse, farm buildings, agricultural land (arable land and pasture) and forestry land which includes both forest and barren land.

Arable land and pasture

According to the Real Property Assessment Law, arable land is land which is used or which is suitable for cultivation or pasture and which is suitable for ploughing.

169

The valuation model for arable land is as follows:

$$V = (S, Q, D)$$

where
V = assessed value
S = size
Q = quality
D = drainage

Size indicates the area of the arable land in hectares, while the quality covers a combination of the production capacity and the conditions of use of the arable land. The production capacity is determined in relation to the production capacity of normal land within the value area, while the conditions of use are determined by weighting the slope and field form of the arable land, its position in relation to other large, neighbouring arable land areas and to obstacles in use. The classification of arable land is carried out in five quality classes and is as follows:

Production capacity   **Conditions of use**

Class 1:
Much better (+ 30%<) than normal in the valuation area   Normal

Class 2:
Better (+10 - +30%) than normal in the valuation area   Normal

Class 3:
Normal for valuation area   Normal

Class 4:
Worse (-10 - -30%) than normal in the valuation area   Normal

Class 5:
Much worse (-30%<) than normal in the valuation area   Normal

If the conditions of use deviate from normal, the quality classes are adjusted one step upwards or downwards in the tables.

The drainage conditions are determined by considering the existing drainage, the condition of the main sewer and the need for the land to be drained.

Classification is carried out in three different classes:

- arable land which is satisfactorily drained by 'systematic underdrainage' carried out after 1970
- other arable land which is satisfactorily drained or self-draining
- arable land which is not satisfactorily drained.

There are tables based on both quality and drainage valuation factors for arable land, where the relative value of satisfactorily drained arable land of normal quality is always set to SEK 1,000 per hectare. The range of the absolute level values in the ratio tables varies, but a normal arable land valuation table appears in Table 7.1.

Table 7.1
Relative arable and pasture land values in the valuation level of SEK 10,000 - 18,000 per hectare

Arable land				Pasture land
Quality	Drainage			Quality
	1	2	3	
1	1,350	1,200	1,050	650
2	1,230	1,100	940	600
3	1,150	**1,000**	850	450
4	1,070	900	770	300
5	950	800	650	250

Table 7.1 contains relative hectare values, and is suitable for a certain level of the total value for normal arable land within the valuation area. The market value of normal arable land within the valuation area is determined on the basis of purchase price statistics. If the market value is determined at SEK 15,000 per hectare, the specified values will thus be multiplied by the level factor 15.

The relative values vary depending on the valuation level within the area. Table 7.1 shows the relation of 1,350 : 650 between the best and the worst arable land. The corresponding relation amounts to 1,600 : 400 in the country's poorest agricultural districts, while that in the country's best agricultural districts has fallen to 1,170 : 840. Sweden is an elongated country with a span of nearly 2,000 km, resulting in a variation in market value for normal arable land of between SEK 1,000 per hectare in the far north and SEK 50,000 per hectare in the far south, which is why six such relative tables are applied in the country at present. As shown in Table 7.1, there is also a fixed connection between arable land and pasture land in each table. According to the Real Property Assessment Law, pasture land is land used for or suitable for use as pasture land and unsuitable for ploughing. There is only one valuation factor to be determined for pasture land, namely that of quality. The value of pasture land is thus determined in accordance with the formula;

$$V = F(S_1 Q)$$

where
V = assessment value
S_1 = size
Q = quality

The valuation factor is divided into the following five classes:

Class 1:   Pasture land with a **better** yield and quality (+30%) than the average in the valuation area and **adjacent to** the agricultural centre

Class 2:   Pasture land with a **better** yield and quality (+30 %) than the average for the valuation area but **not adjacent to** the agricultural centre

Class 3:   Pasture land with a **normal** yield and quality for the valuation area

Class 4:   Pasture land with a **worse** (more than 30%) yield and quality than the average in the valuation area

Class 5:   Pasture land with a **worse** (more than 30 %) yield and quality than average and which can be expected to be used for the production of timber in the near future.

The relative pasture land valuations vary from SEK 650 per hectare for class 1 down to SEK 250 per hectare for class 5 in all relative tables. This means that the best value currently (1995) varies from SEK 650 per hectare in the far north to a SEK 30,000 per hectare in the country's best agricultural districts.

Forest and forestry wasteland

Forestry land is land which is suitable for timber production and which is not used to any large extent for other purposes. The land shall be seen as suitable for timber production if it can produce an average of at least one cubic metre of

172

timber per hectare per annum in accordance with the established methods of assessment. If the land lies next to forestry land but does not produce one cubic metre of timber per annum per hectare, it is classed as forestry wasteland.

The valuation of forestry land takes the following valuation factors into consideration:

- size, considering the area in hectares of the forestry land
- capacity concerning the timber-producing capacity in cubic metres per annum and hectare
- cost, which is determined regarding the most important cost and quality factors which influence the value of the timber production
- growing stock of conifers in cubic metres per hectare
- growing stock of beech and oak in cubic metres per hectare
- growing stock of other deciduous trees in cubic metres per hectare
- rough forestry percentage including that part of the timber stock which consists of wood with a diameter of at least 25 centimetres of bark at chest level.

The following five classes apply with regard to capacity:

A:	**very high** timber production capacity (worth)	
B:	**high**	"
C:	**average**	"
D:	**low**	"
E:	**very low**	"

Since timber production capacity of forestry land varies so markedly from North to South, the classes in question are significant, measured in cubic metres per annum per hectare, in various parts of the country. Classification is linked to groups of counties. Capacity class C can be used as an example, meaning that, on average, production capacity in certain determined geographical areas in the northern most part of Sweden means a timber production of 2 - 3 cubic metres of forestry per annum per hectare, while corresponding production in the most highly productive parts of southern-most Sweden is 7 - 10 cubic metres per annum per hectare, thus representing very significant differences.

Cost classification, which is also important within the same county groups is applied to the capacity valuation factor, which is determined with reference to cost and quality factors which influence the value of timber production. This covers firstly the distance to be transported, i.e. the distance for which the timber must be conveyed cross-country, but also the nature of the terrain. Secondly, felling costs also are an influence on the value in so far as the cost of felling spruce trees is regularly higher than that of the pine, which means that a significant number of spruce trees represent higher costs and therefore a higher cost class.

Nine cost classes are currently used, where;

Cost class 1: corresponding to a very low cost (30 % lower total costs than cost Class 5)

Cost class 5: average cost for the county group

Cost class 9: corresponding to a very high cost (30 % higher total costs than cost class 5).

The cost classes are determined on the basis of a number of 'indicator questions', which concern the cross-country transport distance, the nature of the terrain, the structure and quality of the growing stock, etc. The growing stock of coniferous wood, beech and oak and other deciduous trees is determined using normal forestry measurement methods. The larger forestry owners almost always have access to the management plans where the growing stock is regularly audited. A special audit of the growing stock of deciduous trees such as beech and oak and other deciduous trees only takes place in the four southern-most counties where beech and oak are grown to an appreciable extent. In other counties, the growing stock audit is divided into only coniferous and deciduous trees respectively.

The percentage of coarse forest is intended to reflect the particular benefits which regularly accompany the presence of coniferous trees and which lead to greater exploitation possibilities of a coarser and more valuable timber assortment, primarily saw timber, while poorer forests as a rule provide a considerably greater proportion of pulp wood during felling. The assessment value of forestry land with growing forest is determined in accordance with the formula:

$$V = F(VGSF, VGSC, VFBO, VFOT)$$

where
V = assessment value
VGSF = coniferous growing stock < 25 cm
VGSC = coniferous growing stock 25 cm or coarser
VFBO = growing stock of beech and oak
VFOT = growing stock of other deciduous trees

Since the composition of normal forest and growing stock varies substantially between different parts of the country, there are five different estimation functions

174

for the country as a whole used as a basis for determining the assessment value. The assessment value for normal forestry land varies from around SEK 2,000 per hectare in the northern most parts of the country to almost SEK 20,000 per hectare in the areas in Southern Sweden, where the forestry values are the highest. The valuation model described are used for all forestry units with a minimum of 20 hectares of forestry land. In order to bring about a desirable simplification of the assessment of smaller forestry land holdings, which constitutes a substantial part of all the country's forestry units, a 'simplified model' was introduced in 1992 for assessing agricultural units with forestry land of less than 20 hectares. The simplified model only takes into consideration the valuation factors of size, i.e. area in hectares and growing stock, which means a significant simplification in terms of declaration and later auditing and processing.

Forestry wasteland is assessed in accordance with a simple model, which takes into consideration the valuation factors of size, i.e. area in hectares, and quality. There are two classes for the valuation factor of quality:

Class 1: forestry wasteland with a growing stock of more than 40 cubic metres of forest per hectare

Class 2: other forestry wasteland.

The values applied to forestry wasteland vary in relation with the valuation level on forestry land from a minimum of SEK 30 per hectare for quality class 2 in the north to SEK 1,800 per hectare for quality class 1 in the southern parts of the country. This value is primarily derived from the value of the forestry wasteland for different types of hunting.

Farm buildings

The valuation models for farm buildings are based initially on the replacement costs for a corresponding building. The investment in farm buildings on the market value of an agricultural unit is, however, very limited, and the values of the farm buildings are therefore proportionally low. It is not only depreciation according to age and use which occurs at a rapid rate, but the market value of a newly-built farm building will, as a rule, fall substantially below the cost of replacement. This has been verified by the studies carried out by the Swedish property market for agricultural units.

The valuation model takes the following form:

$$V = F(C, S, A, Q)$$

where
V = assessment value
C = building category
S = size in square metre
A = age
Q = quality

The building category valuation factor involves the division of agricultural buildings and horticultural buildings into 15 or so different building categories, from different types of animal enclosure to engine rooms, grain silos and other storage buildings, such as greenhouses, etc. The size is as a rule measured in square metres of building space, and in some cases in cubic metres of storage volume.

The age is specified over one value year. The value year for buildings which have not been the object of renovation or extension is the same as the year of initial construction. Certain supplements are applicable to farm buildings which have been renovated or extended, which can then change the value year.

The quality valuation factor is divided into three classes:

Class 1: building of **good** design for modern production and in **good** condition

Class 2: building of an **acceptable** design for modern production and in **acceptable** condition

Class 3: building of an **unacceptable** design for modern production, in **poorer condition** and **other simpler** buildings.

On the basis of the above valuation factors, a collection of statistical tables has been designed to show relative assessment values for different types of building and different combinations of size and quality.

One example of an 'E table' for engine room, farm workshop and similar buildings with the value year 1960 or later is shown in Table 7.2.

The relative figures shown in Table 7.2 will be multiplied by a level factor which varies between 100 for the northern most parts of the country and 400 for the best agricultural districts in the country. This means that, for instance, a normal quality, i.e. quality class 2 (building with concrete or asphalt floor and ceiling height of 4.2 metres, etc.) engine room of 300 square metres in the country's best agricultural districts is given an assessment value of 400 x 160 = SEK 64,000. In the northern most parts of Sweden, where the lowest farm building values are situated, the same building is given an assessment value of 100 x 160 = SEK 16,000. In both cases, the assessed market value (i.e. the assessment value of 0.75) is far below the estimated cost of replacement. Studies of the property market for agricultural units show, however, that this is the case.

Table 7.2
E table engine room, farm workshop, etc., (building category no. 32)

Floor space of the building on the ground in square metres	Quality class 1	2	3
51 - 100	90	50	40
101 - 150	130	90	70
151 - 200	170	120	90
201 - 250	210	160	120
251 - 300	260	200	150
301 - 400	310	250	190
401 - 500	380	300	230
For each additional 100 or part 100	60	50	40

Dwellings

The dwelling on an agricultural unit is assessed in accordance with procedures used to assess single-family rural dwellings. The valuation factors used to decide the assessment value of housing and associated building site are:

for the building site

- size
- water and sewage systems
- special position

for the valuation of the building

- size
- age
- standard
- order of value

Size means the area of the building site and the housing area of the single-family dwelling. Special position means how close the site in question is situated to a beach frontage.

Order of value means the final order number of the housing in respect to the valuation of the building site in question. The most valuable building on the site is given an assessed value based on the three valuation factors of size, age and standard, but the value of other single-family dwellings on the same site, e.g. a pair of annexes connected to a main building, is reduced with regard to the fact that they cannot constitute independent units.

The assessed values of single-family dwellings vary considerably throughout the country. The values are determined using tables based on the different valuation factors. A level factor which is specific to every valuation area is included in the estimation function and determines the final assessment value. The divisions in the valuation areas follow the general division between single-family dwellings. However, only 10% of the country's 7,000 valuation areas for single-family dwellings relate to single-family dwellings on agricultural units.

Computer assistance in preparatory works

Market data and other information for valuation

LMV has access to a database of completed acquisitions of real property in the country for its work with general property assessment. The database, which covers the whole of Sweden, currently contains more than 700,000 acquisitions of properties since 1986. This database is continuously updated with the new purchases completed and where registration has been granted. The documentation is thus collected at the time of application for registration. Suspect transactions and other obviously non-commercial purchases are sorted out at the same time as the preparation of the application for registration, so that the database in principle only contains 'straightforward' acquisitions. Work bases are set up in which the data base is further examined and a more stringent removal of transactions judged to be unsuitable to form the basis of general property assessment can take place. Acquisitions where there is a clear common interest between purchaser and vendor, which was not known when the registration was granted may, therefore, be removed from the work base, while the official property price database is always unchanged once purchases have been entered into it.

On analysing the property market, the information submitted at the time of application for registration on date of purchase and purchase price, etc., are studied in depth together with the register information on the physical condition, i.e., position, size, age, standard, etc., of the property. This analysis is undertaken using ADBTAX. It should be mentioned that, for the general property assessment of single-family dwellings carried out in 1996, LMV has had access to regional prices for its analyses and for level setting, etc., which entailed some 126,000 completed purchases of single-family dwellings in the country between 1992 and 1994.

ADB support: general

At present, the assessed value is based on a general property tax return form, which is completed in connection with the general assessment. January 1st of the assessment year represents the 'date of condition'. Details of the physical condition of the property are linked to this date so that the details given in the property tax return form will refer to the physical condition of the property at the beginning of the assessment year. Information records from the previous general real estate assessment have been stored, and a gradual change-over to a register-based assessment is being carried out in Sweden. The aim is that in future all general real property assessment will be based on a register, the contents of which will be continuously updated. This will mean that the general property tax return forms can gradually be dispensed with.

There is a well developed CAMA system named ADBTAX for market analysis which allows, analysis of comparative purchases and what we call the test valuation, which has functions for sorting out irrelevant purchases, for the calculations of price trends and for confirming the final price level in a special area.

As opposed to former general property assessments, ADB support for AFT96 was given a broader formulation which also includes relevant map processing. During the autumn of 1993, a preliminary study was carried out concerning the possibilities of using digital technology in connection with setting up the 'standard value maps' for general property assessment. The preliminary study was followed up by a main study with the aim of finding suitable technology for the work in question. The main study established that the most suitable approach considering the availability of digital map databases was to work with a digital map database based on the topographical map on the scale of 1:50000 and then use the raster version of it.

In the case of the choice of geographical information system (GIS), three different systems were tested; the choice then fell to the Arc/Info, as now used, in combination with its specific tool ArcView.

The digital support for map processing helps to facilitate the whole work process from the preparatory work, through to the production of standard value maps, to the printing of the declaration forms, that is to say, we have achieved in Sweden a complete digital production line for map and property information relevant to property assessment.

In order to avoid some of the difficulties always associated with a 'technology change', it was decided until recently to keep apart the two main sections of

ADB support. These main sections are known as ADBTAX and GISTAX. The former contains the sections which were traditionally used during earlier general property assessments and were part of or rather constituted the ADB support at the stage of the preparatory work, while GISTAX contains the sections associated with the geographical information and map processing and which were formerly processed in a traditional way using paper maps.

The basic outline of the ADB support for the preparatory work AFT96 is as shown in Figure 7.3.

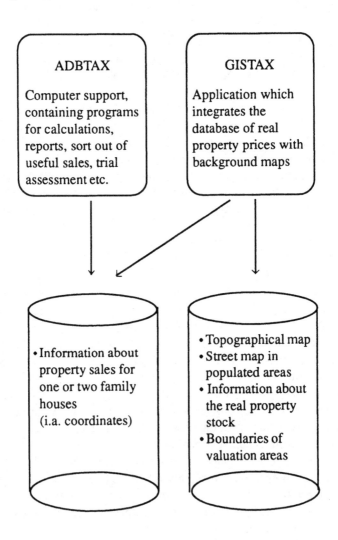

Figure 7.3 Data and GIS support

The ADB support is developed in a Windows environment. It is user-friendly and this aspect has been intentionally prioritised to a certain extent at the cost of the speed of the system, i.e. response times, etc. The fact that it is user-friendly means, among other things, that several functions are 'self-teaching'.

The valuation technician normally accesses ADBTAX and GISTAX using special 'icons'. A special login, whose functions include controlling and regulating the authority to work in the system, is required to get into ADBTAX. Anybody who logs onto ADBTAX can, in principle, read the whole of the AFT96 base. On the other hand, only the valuation technician responsible for a given local authority has the authority to change information. Authority in this case means, to be able to correct or change information on the purchases, delete purchases and change the valuation area divisions and the valuation area to which purchases belong. It is thus possible for the valuation technician to go outside of his local authority regarding the production of price trends, for example, or estimating A\P, since these stages in principle only involve 'reading' the AFT96 base without being able to go in and change any information. The authority routines are part of the security of ADBTAX. In addition to this, there are certain security routines built into the system, which means that 'backup' is taken at specified intervals.

ADBTAX (CAMA system)

ADBTAX is built up around the following six different principal functions:

- Purchases
- Recalculation figures
- Valuation area division
- Standard values
- Results
- Reports

'Purchases' involves working with the purchases in a special work database. The area which is relevant to the work is specified using the appropriate county or local authority code. The purchases are initially divided into two groups, purchases 'flagged for inspection' and 'other purchases'. The fact that the purchases will be inspected and removed if necessary is common to both groups. The difference between the groups is that the purchases in the 'flagged purchases' group have not satisfied a preliminary sorting out process, whereas the other purchases have. Remaining approved purchases and purchases that have been sorted out can be shown on the screen or in different kinds of lists. The valuation technician indicates in the database the reason or reasons used for sorting out a purchase and not allowing it to remain as a basis for continued estimation work.

181

Under 'Detailed information' are a number of entries of information about the purchase in question, including information on the purchaser and vendor, which can be a guide in determining any common interests. If at a later stage it shows that sorting out was not justified, it is possible to move the purchase over to the approved purchases by deleting the sorting out code.

The 'Recalculation figures' function is used to calculate price trends and recalculation figures for purchases from different years. The selection of properties can be made in a number of different ways. With the exception of geographical selection criteria, it is possible to select from type of property, size, age, standard, etc. Assessed market value, assessed property value, area of site, etc., can also be selected. It is thus possible, within a broad framework, to make a selection which is considered suitable for the price trend covered by the analysis. The selection of price trend can be stored for use at a later date. The price trend can either be calculated as a straight line or as a curve.

The 'A/P' function shows the number of purchases and average A/P (assessment value/purchase price) for a certain selection of purchases. The function is used to give the valuation technician a rapid picture of what effects a selection of level factors for a specific area has on the purchases which are the basis of setting the level in the area.

The 'Standard values' function processes the valuation areas and their standard valuation information, i.e., the level factors which regulate the assessment value. New valuation areas can be created here, and the standard valuation information associated with the area in question is specified here. When a valuation area contains far too few purchases, in order to be able to set the levels with certainty, several areas of a similar type, e.g. a county's community centres, can be joined and processed together if the valuation technician considers that the property market works in a similar way in the different areas. The areas which are to be processed together are also handled under this function. Such 'test valuation areas' are created by the community centres, for example, in sparsely-populated areas to ensure that the levels will be satisfactorily set.

There are a number of different result reports under 'Results' and 'Reports' where the valuation technician can analyse everything on screen as the work progresses or print it out to analyse at a later date by himself or in consultation with other valuation technicians in the county. The result reports are first and foremost intended for peoples' individual work, but can of course also be used for presentations to the tax authorities, reference groups, etc. A number of different selection options are presented on screen with regard to the way in which the calculated results are to be presented. Every one of the 'result types' gives a particular presentation of the calculated results, which in turn makes certain particular analyses of the outcome possible.

GISTAX (GIS system)

At the preparatory work for the general assessment of single- and two-family dwellings in 1996, the new GIS tool GISTAX was used for analysis of both purchases and the total stock of houses, for computer drawing of maps marking areas of different value, and finally to connect a separate real property with the corresponding valuation area and together with the value level attributed to the valuation area in question. GISTAX is a geographical information system, GIS, which has been developed in Arc/Info and ArcView and which is used both for the analyses of purchases and the real property stock, as well as for changing the boundaries of valuation areas.

As mentioned earlier, the country is divided into 'valuation areas', these are areas in which the real property market functions in practically the same way, and where the price setting and the level of the market value are uniform. Where single or two-family dwellings are concerned, the country is divided into more than 7,300 valuation areas, each one carefully defined on valuation maps. Changes to the real property market, both at local and regional level, take place on a regular basis and change the relations of values. New areas of single or two-family dwellings are built in various places, major routes are extended or relocated, the local authority water supply and sewage networks are also extended, etc., every condition affecting the market of single or two-family dwellings and contributing to the previous division of areas according to value having to be revised and in many cases changed. The examination task is dealt with by a large number of assessment technicians at the National Land Survey, and, naturally, with the assistance of the map. GISTAX is designed to facilitate the examination task and the subsequent map-work.

GISTAX uses different sets of map data. The base of GISTAX is a background map, essentially a map in raster format, whose contents primarily correspond to the topographical map with a scale of 1:50000. Since the degree of detail in many densely-populated areas is insufficient, this basic material has consequently been supplemented by a large-scale database, that is, digital maps of densely-populated areas and with similar accuracy of detail as in the telephone directory. Besides the background map, the map database also contains the digitally stored boundaries of valuation areas and further specific information about the real property stock of single or two-family dwellings.

GISTAX also has access to purchases of single or two-family dwellings, these purchases are among other things the basis for obtaining a clear idea of the value levels . The map database, which includes the background map, boundaries of the valuation area and information about the real property stock, is available for the assessment technician at the local office, while information about the purchases is available in a central database at the Central Board for Real Estate Data in Gävle.

Above all, GISTAX makes the following four procedures possible:

- analysis of the real property stock
- analysis of purchases
- changes of the boundaries of the valuation area
- digitally produced valuation maps

In GISTAX it is possible, by the key window or survey window, to mark and to choose the local authority that you, for the moment, would like to work with. Analysis of the real property stock is made possible by marking each of the single or two-family dwellings in the map, as well as by obtaining information that would otherwise be difficult to collect about real properties, but which is now available through GISTAX. Those real properties within a specific densely-populated area, which have access to local authority water and drainage, can, for example, be marked by a particular symbol on screen.

GISTAX provides additional options and thus access to more and more readily available analysis alternatives. Analysis of the purchases provide other options. The purchases can either be presented by their coordinates on the map or statistically.

The background map of which the stock and the purchases are digitally composed has different layers, each one consisting of separate units of the system. The assessment technician has the option of choosing which part of the background map that will be shown on screen or whether the analysis should refer to the stock or to the purchase. When the assessment technician has decided on the requirements of change (of the digitally stored boundaries of the valuation areas) according to value levels, the task of updating then remains to be done. GISTAX can therefore, with the help of tools, remove and add areas according to value and change existing boundaries. ArcView as well as Arc/Info are used when changing boundaries of the valuation area.

Digitally produced valuation map and tax return forms

Since the review of the standard value map has been completed, the new standard value map can simply be produced, i.e. plotted out using the National Land Survey's plotter. The maps can be produced in optional scales and in varying materials. The map scales of 1:50000 and 1:100000 are normally used, and 1:10000 or 1:20000 for the densely-populated areas. The stored information is used at a further stage.

In the multipurpose cadastre system (a register of attributes of parcels of land, for example the centre coordinates of each property unit), information about the whole stock of the Swedish real estate has been entered. Naturally the information is utilized and stored as a database. This database is linked together with the database of valuation area boundaries. Each real property unit is then given the specific identification of the valuation area to which it belongs. In the latter part of the entire working process, this is used to print the identification of valuation area and other information at each real property declaration. An assessment value is also estimated and reported to the property owner. These latter stages of the process are handled by the tax authorities, i.e. by the Swedish National Tax Board.

Future trends in real property assessment in Sweden

A gradual follow-up of the costs of real property assessment and a comparison with other countries with comparable systems have led to a gradual decline in costs. The guiding principles in the work have been simplification and the requisitioning of more rational working methods. The simplification has occurred in organization and administrative routines as well as in valuation methods. Assessment based on register records has already been mentioned as an attempt at rationalization. When it comes to rational working methods, it can be mentioned that at the beginning of the 1980s test valuation, including examination and sorting out of irrelevant market data, was all carried out manually. Mapping was also done using traditional methods, that is, information such as valuation areas was drawn by hand on paper maps or on film. During the latter part of the 1980s, extensive computer support has been taken into use for the test valuation procedure, that is, examination and sorting out of irrelevant purchases, calculation of price trends and calculation of valuations, analysis and evaluation of the test valuation results. In the mid-1990s, another step was taken towards a quicker and more rational assessment using the 'GIS technique' for mapping work and other map associated working procedures. During the next few years, development should be directed at improving GIS support for all types of real property assessment in Sweden.

8 Computer assisted mass appraisal: the Queensland experience

A. Kirby

Introduction

Australia is a Federation of States and Territories, with each being responsible for the Regulation of most Land Uses and Land Titles. The valuation of State lands for Statutory uses is carried out by each State. This article discusses a Computerized Mass Appraisal (CAMA) system used in the State of Queensland and illustrates its flexibility and performance by use of a case study.

Queensland

Queensland comprises highly developed Coastal centres with the bulk of the population located in the Capital of Brisbane and provincial cities principally in the South-east corner. The northern and western areas of the State are sparsely populated. The range of property (and valuation) types reflect the population distribution ranging from general City Development through Residential and Tourist properties, small rural properties, to grazing properties exceeding a million hectares in area.

The valuation of Queensland

In Queensland, the Department of Lands (DOL) is the responsible agency for the valuation of any lands for rating and taxing purposes and for this purpose operates through ten Regions and twenty six of it's thirty seven offices under the *Valuation of Land Act 1944* (Qld). Property rates are levied in 128 Local Government (Authority) areas. Note a number of Local Governments do not levy property rates, while others are in the process of amalgamation.

For valuation purposes the State is divided into parcels of land which are mainly based on surveyed allotments. A Parcel of land means every part of an area of land which is separately held by an owner, or any part of an area of land which is directed (by the Chief Executive Officer DOL) to be valued as a separate parcel.

Number of parcels to be valued

The DOL holds a number of types of records relating to parcels. These records are:-

Issuing - Parcel record will have a valuation issued (to an owner) covering all parts of the parcel

Allocated - A property which forms part of an amalgamated issuing property. This valuation is not issued.

Super - An amalgamation of parts of an issuing property

Lease - A issued valued used for the calculation of lease rental payments.

Therefore, a property can have more than one valuation.

For the 1995 Annual Revaluation (January/February 1995), the DOL had recorded the numbers of valuations as outlined in Tables 8.1 and 8.2.

Table 8.1
Regions covered by new CAMA system

Property Issuing Status	Numbers of Valuations
Issuing	836,916
Allocated	21,472
Super	507
Lease	3,789

Source: IVAS (Database), Queensland Department of Lands.

A further 4146 Lease Valuations in the areas covered by Table 8.2 have been performed manually to date. Source DOL Lease Rental System Database, Queensland Department of Lands.

Table 8.2
Regions covered by old CAMA system

Property Issuing Status	Number of Valuations
Issuing	432,004

Source: Valuer General Database, Queensland Department of Lands

What is to be valued?

The *Valuation of Land Act* requires that the DOL must decide the unimproved value of land for the Acts under which local authorities (now Local Governments) are established. This Act (VOL) also sets out that the DOL is to make an annual valuation of all land at a date set by the Chief Executive of the DOL subject to a number of requirements set out in the Act.

The *Valuation of Land Act* sets out what unimproved value is in the following terms-

Unimproved Value of land means-

(a)   in relation to improved land - the capital sum which the fee simple of the land might be expected to realize if offered for sale on such reasonable terms and conditions as a bona fide seller would require, assuming that, at the time as at which the value is required to be ascertained for the purpose of the Act, the improvements did not exist.

Unimproved Value is used for Rating (Local Government Rates); Taxing (State Land Tax); Rents (Rentals for Queensland Government Leaseholds), and calculating some Federal Government Grants to States.

Frequency of valuations

Annual Valuations have been performed for most of Queensland in almost all years since the mid-1980s. Property owners are advised of their Property Valuations by a combination of Mailed Notices and Public displays of Property Valuation Rolls. The annual valuation has a Date of Valuation of the 1 January of the year, with owners being advised during February and March, with this Valuation first being used for Rating purposes from the 1 July of the same year.

Historical development of the system

In 1981 work by Departmental staff of the then Department of Valuer General commenced with the design for a CAMA system to support the requirement to produce valuations annually to replace the then existing five (5) to eight (8) year valuation cycle for Local Government areas. By 1985, Computer Assisted Valuations (CAV) Version 1 was operating, that is, producing some annual revaluations. Development work then commenced on a new CAMA aimed at overcoming valuation problems which arose through the use of a system based on updating an existing valuation via a factor. The proposed system became Provide Unimproved Value Part 2 (PUV2), which is discussed later.

The focus of design then changed, to accommodate the requirement that the Valuation administration system, used by the Department of Valuer General, required redevelopment from a COBOL based batch system running on a mainframe computer, to a relational database management system, which was eventually to run on a minicomputer. This design work continued, with the assistance of some external consultants, through to 1989, when the Department of Valuer General was absorbed into the Department of Lands.

Although 'trickle' design work continued, much of the early design was reviewed, and what was eventually to become the Integrated Valuation and Sales System (IVAS) for DOL was designed from 1990 onwards. As this design work continued to evolve, it became apparent that the internal resources available to the DOL would not be adequate to build the new system. Therefore, a contracted Project Manager was employed in late 1992, and special recoverable funding secured from the State Treasury in early 1993 when the final design and construction of IVAS began with the employment of significant numbers of contract consultants to complement internal staff.

IVAS contains a CAMA in a subsystem called CAV (Computer Assisted Valuation), the design and development of which in the main mirrored the development of IVAS. The implementation of IVAS commenced in the first DOL Region in May 1994, with six other Regions following by October 1994. Two of the balance three Regions were implemented after the completion of the 1995 Annual Revaluation Program, in March and April 1995.

The 1995 Annual Revaluation Program has recently been completed using the IVAS CAV and CAV Version 1.

Philosophy of system

- The cornerstone of any valuation are the comparable sales upon which every valuation is based (Lockwood and Reynolds 1992).
- A CAMA is a tool used by valuers in producing a predicted property valuation, and then a valuation, for which the valuer is ultimately

responsible for its accuracy.

- A valuation prediction for a property can be reliably made by applying a factor to an existing valuation for that property.
- Properties can be aggregated into groupings known as Sub-Market Areas (SMA) which contain properties whose valuations will move similarly during a given period.
- Where parts of SMA groupings vary in value over a given time period, or numbers of SMA's increase or decrease during a time period, Categories defining parts of an SMA, or a number of SMA's can be varied as required.
- The system be kept relatively simple by performing any required regression modelling in a PC environment using commercially available packages.
- The basis of valuation not be directly linked to the CAMA, but be held externally in either a paper based or electronic format.

The evolution of sub market areas (SMA's)

The base unit of CAV is the Sub Market Area, being a grouping of properties, determined by geographical or physical features, which have been identified as having values that will move similarly over time. SMA's are defined by Valuation Number which is a unique number which identifies a property parcel which is to be valued by the CAMA. Both CAV Version 1 and IVAS CAV use SMA's, which in the case of IVAS CAV, have in the main been inherited from CAV Version 1. So how have SMA's been determined?

SMA's were originally based on Australian Census Collection Districts, which were analysed and aggregated using cluster analysis techniques based on socio-economic factors. These 'original' SMA's have in most cases been radically altered in the light of valuers knowledge and perception of what constitutes land markets for various types of land overtime. Therefore, SMA's as they are constituted today are a product of a number of years revaluation and continual refinement based on local experience.

Characteristics of the current system

The Queensland Department of Lands (DOL) operated two CAMA systems as outlined above until April 1995. A batch CAMA system comprising a suite of COBOL programs and dating from the early 1980s (CAV Version 1), operated in three of the DOL's ten Regions and produced predicted valuations for that part of the 1995 Annual Revaluation Program Assisted Valuation (CAV). Valuations for these three Regions will in future be produced using IVAS CAV.

IVAS is an Integrated Valuation Administration and Valuation system which provides support in the processes of valuation administration and valuation under the Valuation of Land Act. IVAS mirrors in its functionality these two areas with the following subsystems covering the Valuation Administration and valuation systems respectively

The Valuation Administration area covers the following subsystems:

- Property Update
- Objections
- Appeals
- Issues
- Provide Information
- Security
- Standard Information

The Valuing systems area covers the following:

- Prepare Unimproved Value (Part A)
- Computer Assisted Valuations

The following is a brief outline of the function of each of the IVAS Subsystems.

Property update

- Enquire on Property and sales information
- On-line and overnight maintenance/update and validation of property and sales information
- Production of on-line Reports
- Overnight update of property information.

Objections

- On-line recording and maintenance of objections lodged against revenue valuations and rating categories
- On-line recording of decisions on objection
- Setting down and notification of conferences
- Production of reports.

Appeals

- On-line recording and maintenance of appeals lodged against objections, appeal decisions, and against client valuations
- On-line recording of hearing information and decisions on appeals
- Production of reports.

Issues

- Produces and issues notices of valuations to landowners and councils on a regular basis (daily, weekly, fortnightly, monthly)
- Provides for the scheduling and associated issue of revaluations on a flexible basis
- Applies the proposed values to the property record
- Produces revaluation display reports; e.g. owner revaluation display list
- Produces statistical reports
- Provides bulk information from the issue process to other government departments and local authorities.

Provide information

- System reports for sale to external clients
- Produces property and sales reports and statistical reports
- Report production from any point on the network
- Printing of reports locally in some cases and centrally dependent on Report size.

Security

- User security by registration of users and password access.

Standard information

- System information kept updated by common tables
- Valuation.

Prepare unimproved value

- Access to records created in Property update for the addition/amendment of values
- Quality control Reports
- Ability to provide approval for various specified functions.

Computer assisted valuations

Values can be updated according to property location, land use, other specified category criterion, within nominated groupings.

This chapter will outline the CAMA CAV contained in IVAS (and associated Subsystems).

193

General overview of CAV

IVAS CAV allows Valuer's to perform bulk revaluations and provide new values for properties. The new values are based on a pre-specified percentage factor applied to the current value on the properties which have been selected using location and/or particular attributes as selection criteria. The percentage factor can result in either an increase or decrease to the value. Reporting on this process is also provided.

The Computer Assisted Valuation subsystem can be divided into four areas:-

* Set revaluation date
* Review SMA's, and categories
* Formulate CAV requests
* Reconcile and review predicted values for market conformity.

Figure 8.1 represents a schematic of the IVAS CAV Revaluation process. In the diagram various CAV Subsystem transactions are represented in the boxes, with mandatory activities being joined by firm lines, and optional activities joined by broken lines.

Set revaluation date

The date for the Local Government Area or Areas is set by the *Valuation of Land Act* and is the same statewide for those Local Government Areas to be revalued as part of the Annual Revaluation Program.

Review SMA's, and categories

Sub Market areas which continue in use from year to year are reviewed and updated in the light of recent sales evidence, market trends, as well as developing land uses. A number of Reports allow for quality control of this process. For example, Properties Missing SMA's.

Categories which identify either parts of an SMA, or numbers of SMA's, are recorded for later use in the production of bulk valuation predictions. These CAV Categories can be defined using combinations of a range of attributes including locality, land use, sub-market area, street, tenure, total area, valuation number, current value, and town plan zoning.

These categories are retained for ongoing use in subsequent revaluations.

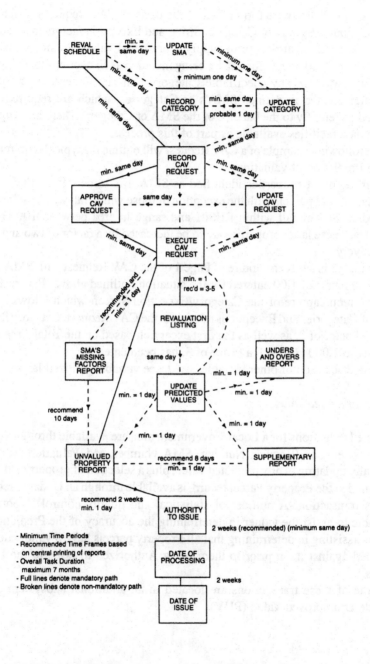

Figure 8.1 Functional diagram of IVAS CAV revaluation

195

Formulate CAV requests

Valuation predictions are formulated on the basis of CAV Requests which are a list of attributes by way of Category, SMA, and Exception factors to be applied to different sets of attributes to supply a predicted value. Predicted property values can be further categorized by being included as Exceptions to an SMA or Category based on any specifiable Category Criteria. Exception groups are properties located in defined SMA's or Categories, which are required to be adjusted differently to the balance of the SMA or Category. There are Approval and Update facilities available as part of this process.

The following example of a CAV Request will outline the typical requirements for the Prediction of valuations.

A grouping of properties identified as SMA 4 is to be left at it's Existing Valuation for all parcels with the exception of those which fall within a Category entitled RES01 or fall within RES01 and range in area between 100 Ha and 1,000 Ha. These latter properties are to be increased by a factor of two and three respectively.

Figure 8.2 is a screen capture of Page 1 of the CAV Request with SMA 4 and the Basic factor of 1.00 entered for the situation outlined above. Figure 8.3 is also a screen capture of the Category/Exception Screen which allows for the input of Categories and Exceptions relating to the CAV Request. Category RES01 and it's Factor of 2, as well as the first exception based on the Total Area range (100 Ha to 1,000 Ha) with a factor of 3, has been entered.

For a discussion of other variables used, see variables utilized later.

Review predicted values

Predicted valuations for a Local Government area are available through various Report selections (Request Number, SMA Number, and Valuation Number). Manually updating of any predicted value, plus a selection of property attributes contained in the Property Parcel record, is available through an Update Predicted Values transaction. A number of statistical and quality control Reports are available to assist the valuer in determining the accuracy of the Prediction, as well as assisting in determining that all Property parcels have a valid valuation recorded against them prior to them being Authorized to Issue to the DOL's clients.

Some of these transactions are located in an additional subsystem called Provide Unimproved Value (PUV).

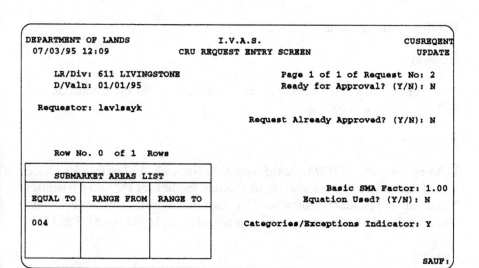

```
DEPARTMENT OF LANDS                  I.V.A.S.                      CUSREQENT
07/03/95 12:09              CRU REQUEST ENTRY SCREEN                 UPDATE

    LR/Div: 611 LIVINGSTONE              Page 1 of 1 of Request No: 2
    D/Valn: 01/01/95                     Ready for Approval? (Y/N): N

  Requestor: lavlsayk
                                         Request Already Approved? (Y/N): N


    Row No. 0  of 1  Rows

   ┌─────────────────────────────┐
   │    SUBMARKET AREAS LIST      │              Basic SMA Factor: 1.00
   ├──────────┬───────────┬──────┤          Equation Used? (Y/N): N
   │ EQUAL TO │RANGE FROM │RANGE TO│
   ├──────────┼───────────┼──────┤      Categories/Exceptions Indicator: Y
   │ 004      │           │       │
   │          │           │       │
   │          │           │       │
   └──────────┴───────────┴──────┘
                                                              SAUF:
```

Figure 8.2 CAV request page 1

```
DEPARTMENT OF LANDS                  I.V.A.S.                      CUSREQENT
07/03/95 12:09              CRU REQUEST ENTRY SCREEN                 UPDATE

Category Name:  ES01  Factor:  2.00  Equation: (Y/N) : N   No 1 of 1 of Page 1

                                          Row No. 0  of 1  Rows

┌──────┬────────┬──────┬─────────┬───────────────┬─────────────────────────┐
│ Excpt│ Factor │ Eqtn │ Criteria│ Except Criteria│ Exception Criteria Range│
│ No   │        │ Used │ Code    │ Equal To       │   From      │    To     │
├──────┼────────┼──────┼─────────┼───────────────┼────────────┼────────────┤
│ 1    │ 3.000  │ N    │ TOTA    │                │ 100HA      │ 1000HA    │
│      │        │      │         │                │            │           │
│      │        │      │         │                │            │           │
│      │        │      │         │                │            │           │
│      │        │      │         │                │            │           │
│      │        │      │         │                │            │    SAUF:  │
└──────┴────────┴──────┴─────────┴───────────────┴────────────┴────────────┘
```

Figure 8.3 CAV request category/exception screen

Database management

Hardware

IVAS runs on two Unisys Sequent minicomputers, a 790 for production and 490 for enquiry and backup.

Software

IVAS operates over a TCP/IP based Wide Area Network to 37 offices Statewide with the user interface being via either 'dumb' terminal or PC using Windows based terminal emulation software. The Operating System Software is Dynix, while Application software has been developed using Ingres 6.4 ABF and C.

Database

IVAS comprises 11 Databases (10 Regional, 1 Corporate) with Regional sizes from 750 Megabytes to 2.2 Gigabytes, and Corporate of 8 Gigabytes.

Variables utilized in mass appraisal process

A CAV Request to produce predicted values may include the variables set out below.

LA/Div -	Local Government Area or Division (Part) of a LGA
Page Number -	CAV Request Page Number
Request Number -	CAV Request Identifier
Date of Valuation -	Annual Revaluation Date
Requestor -	Person who prepared the CAV Request
Ready for Approval -	Indicator to show Request formulation completed
Request Already Approved -	Indicates whether an Approved Request has previously been Executed
SMA(s) -	SMA defined by Property Valuation Number
Basic SMA Factor -	Basic factor change to be applied to an SMA or SMA Range.
Equation -	Equation representing valuation model to be applied to SMA or SMA Range
Category -	Valuation Category as described above
Category Factor -	Factor change to be applied to the Category
Category Equation -	Equation representing valuation model to be applied to a CAV Category

Exception Number -	Exception Identifier
Exception Factor -	Factor change to be applied to the Exception
Exception Equation -	Equation representing valuation model to be applied to the Exception
Exception Criteria Code -	Code for Criteria upon which Exception is based
Exception Criteria -	Criteria upon which Exception is based (same Criteria as Category)

Clearly, not all of the above variables are mandatory for any Request - variables used will depend on Request complexity. However, variables such as LA/Div, SMA, and Date of Valuation would be required in all cases.

Locational identifiers including GIS

The following locational identifiers are held in IVAS. It can be seen by comparison with the above list that many of these are not directly referenced via IVAS CAV.

Region -	DOL Administrative Region
District -	A smaller area of a DOL Region
LA/Div -	As above
Real Property Description -	Title Description relating to predicted valuation, held as Lot Number, Plan Number, and Parish.
Property Address -	Street address of Property in the form Street Number, Street Name, and Town/Locality. Locality can be used to define CAV Category.
Zoning -	Town Planning Scheme Zoning

Additional Attribute information , such as Access Type and Frontage Type, is held in IVAS. This is not used by IVAS CAV, and is not comprehensively examined here.

Use of GIS

The use of GIS in conjunction with IVAS CAV has been limited to date with GIS technology on 'full' trial in one Region. The DOL has produced paper based valuers field maps comprising combinations of 'layers' including predicted valuation, SMA, Land Use and Property Valuation Number. Layer Information from cadastral , topographic , and colour orthophoto sources has also been used. Applications have included maps of Predicted Values (for manual review), Land

Uses, SMAs (for boundary review), and sales for an area of interest based on direct graphical selection from the Statewide Digital Cadastral Database. The location of property improvements for valuation purposes, has also been undertaken.

Algorithms/appraisal software

CAV allows property parcels included in a CAV Request to be altered by a simple factor i.e. the Predicted Value (NEWVALUE) equals the Existing Value (OLDVALUE) multiplied by a factor. For many market situations this has proved to be adequate. That is, where the particular market represented by an SMA, Category, or Exception, has moved uniformly over a given time period.

Where, on the basis of available sales information, it appears that a type of variable adjustment is required, four options are available to a valuer. These particular options were selected for inclusion in CAV, based on the operational experience by DOL valuers of the likely adjustment functionality required for mass appraisals.

The four 'variable' options available to the valuer are as follows:-

Option 1 - NEWVALUE Vs OLDVALUE

Predicted Value (NEWVALUE) is based on Existing Value (OLDVALUE) by entering the appropriate coefficient, or coefficients, into the following equation, as the result of a modelling process which is outlined later. The available equation format is:-

$$NEWVALUE = P_1 \times OLDVALUE + P_2 \times OLDVALUE^2 + P_3 \times OLDVALUE^3 + P_0$$

$P_0, P_1, P_2,$ and P_3 are coefficients in this, and each of the following three options.

Option 2 - NEWVALUE Vs OLDVALUE and AREA

Predicted Value (NEWVALUE) is based on Existing Value (OLDVALUE) and Area (area in square metres of the property). The available equation format is:

$$NEWVALUE = P_1 \times AREA + P_2 \times OLDVALUE + P_3 \times OLDVALUE \times AREA + P_0$$

Option 3 - NEWRATE Vs OLDRATE

OLDRATE is the Existing Value divided by the area of the property to which it relates. Predicted Value (NEWVALUE) is based on calculating an existing rate, updating it in accordance with the following formula, and then applying the result to the property area. The available equation format is:

200

$$NEWRATE = P_1 \times OLDRATE + P_2 \times OLDRATE^2 + P_3 \times OLDRATE^3 + P_0$$

Option 4 - FACTOR vs AREA

Factor is the increase (or decrease) to be applied to the Existing Value, while Area is the total area in square metres of the property. This enables the factor variation, to be applied to an Existing Value, to be varied in accordance with parcel area. The available equation format is:-

$$FACTOR = P_1 \times AREA + P_2 \times AREA^2 + P_3 \times AREA^3 + P_0$$

Modelling software

In accordance with the design philosophy, valuation modelling software is a commercially available shareware package called NONLIN. However, for numerous valuation models not requiring higher order equations, many calculators or common spreadsheets are suitable to the task. Similarly, for the production of tables of Predicted value estimates, a number of Spreadsheet macros have been written using Quattro Pro which is currently the DOL Standard. The following brief example shows the typical use of the modelling package.

Example

From market data it appears that a particular SMA has increased variously since it's last Revaluation. The lower and upper segments of the market have increased fairly steeply, whilst the mid market level has increased at a lesser rate. The situation can be represented by the following table in which a number of 'sale properties' are listed with their Existing Values, and their relevant Predicted Values based on the sale of the property.

Table 8.3
Sale properties with predicted values

Existing Value (OLDVALUE)	Predicted Value (NEWVALUE)
$1,000	$1,500
$14,000	$23,000
$26,000	$34,000
$36,000	$42,000
$50,000	$70,000

NONLIN produces the following analysis using the model

$$NEWVALUE = P_0 + P_1 \times OLDVALUE + P_2 \times OLDVALUE^2 + P_3 \times OLDVALUE.$$

SMA analysis

Proportion of variance explained (R^2)   = 0.9997
Adjusted coefficient of multiple determination (Ra^2) = 0.9987
Durbin-Watson   = 3.531

Table 8.4
Calculated parameter values

Par't'r	Estimate	Standard Error	t	Prob(t)
P_0	-1,164.92	1,046.55	-1.11	0.46596
P_1	2.65529	0.21452	12.38	0.05132
P_2	-7.9768 E-005	1.05577 E-005	-7.56	0.08377
P_3	1.1019 E-009	1.35653 E-010	8.12	0.07798

Table 8.5
ANOVA for SMA analysis

Source	DF	SS	Mean Sq	F Value	Prob (F)
Reg'n	3	2.536351 E+009	8.454504 E+008	996.01	0.02329
Error	1	848,837.1	848,837.1		
Total	4	2.5372 E+009			

202

The following output matrix is a subset of output generated by a simple macro which uses Oldvalue, the relevant 'P' Coefficients, and the interval of value (Step Value) for the Oldvalues to produce a range of proposed values for a nominated Oldvalue range.

Table 8.6
Output data from SMA analysis

OLDVALUE	NEWVALUE	Predicted Newvalue	Residual
1,000	1,500	1,411.712	88.2883
14,000	23,000	23,398.292	-398.2915
26,000	34,000	33,316.532	683.4683
36,000	42,000	42,456.491	-456.4909
50,000	70,000	69,916.974	83.0258

Table 8.7
Predicted values and factor increases from 'Macro' based on analysis

OLDVALUE	NEWVALUE	Factor
1,000	1,400	1.4
14,000	23,400	1.671
26,000	33,300	1.281
36,000	42,500	1.181
50,000	69,900	1.398

Predicted values based on the output from the macro are compared with all available sales evidence to determine whether or not the predicted values will 'fit' the valuation situation. This is principally in situations where other than a uniform increase is indicated. In all cases, the percentage of available sales versus their predicted values, for various time periods leading up to the date of valuation, are calculated to ensure a consistent level of valuation.

Statistics versus sales

On occasions statistical prediction will conflict with what the market evidence will indicate as being a property's value. Hence, in the above example it is probably more statistically accurate to remove PO. However, this would result in poor predictions for many low valued properties. A further factor to account for is that all predictions are subject to a rounding factor e.g. the range $1,001 to $10,000, round to $100.

Appraisal/administrative linkup

The Property Update Subsystem is the hub of the IVAS system as it is responsible for on-line and batch update of property and sales information. The IVAS database is maintained through the creation of property change schedules which may either be sent directly to the Issues Subsystem for dispatch (of valuation change) to clients, or to the Prepare Unimproved values Subsystem for the manual input of valuation or other changes. CAV uses the information held in the IVAS database (see foregoing) to produce predicted values which are also held in the IVAS database. These mass appraised values are also issued to clients through the Issues Subsystem.

Operational performance

The 1995 Revaluation program was the first using IVAS CAV. Due to nature of the DOL's business, IVAS CAV is only used during the period October to January for the annual Revaluation Program. Predicted values may be produced either on-line for a maximum of 1,500 properties per CAV Request, or overnight for larger numbers of predicted valuations.

The performance output of CAV is dependent on many factors such as system load (in current and other databases) and request complexity. However, an order of magnitude is that by running a single CAV Request, consisting of 806 valuations, comprising two SMAs with one Category based on one category criteria, predicted values were produced in 4 minutes and forty-five seconds, while a further four minutes were required to produce a revaluation listing of these values and associated comprehensive property data such as rate calculations, land use, zoning, owner, and legal description. Each database is capable of running four jobs (e.g. CAV Predictions or Reports) concurrently with unlimited numbers able to be queued for on-line or overnight execution.

Total Local Government predicted valuations were produced using as few as one CAV request for small Local Governments, and up to 120 Requests for the largest Local Government Areas. Some of the CAV requests would have been discarded due to application errors, while an unspecified number of Requests would have been produced multiple times as well as being modified and produced again.

Case study

Overview

The purpose of the following case study is to assess the results of a revaluation using the IVAS CAV system. To achieve this, the revaluation of the residential component of the then Gold Coast City was selected for study.

Study area and data

Gold Coast City has had over the last twenty years one of the highest growth rates for any local government area in Australia. It has as one boundary the southern Queensland border, and is generally regarded as Australia's premier beachside tourist destination. The City incorporates one of the most diverse ranges of urban land types in the state, from detached residential properties (canal and dry), commercial and industrial activities, highrise and resort style condominiums and golf courses.

The growth rate of an area effects the valuation of the area in the creation of new properties (by resurvey) and changing land use patterns (green field development and urban redevelopment).

The revaluation program commenced in early August 1994 and was completed on the 27 January 1995. Essentially, the revaluation period is set by the availability of sales evidence on which to base a Valuation at a particular time, and after its' issue to clients, the necessity to finalize objections to Valuations prior to their use from 1 July.

The residential revaluation program was completed by four Gold Coast based valuers who are responsible for all DOL Valuation business areas which include the annual Revaluation. Valuations in Gold Coast were allocated (to valuers) on the basis of market type (rather than by geographical area). This case study will examine the Residential valuations within the Gold Coast City which include detached properties on canal and dry land, rural homesites, duplex properties, three storey walkup, as well as single (attached units) and multiple strata (highrise) properties.

Method

The Gold Coast is divided into 61 SMA's of which 55 comprise a Residential component which is any land used for single unit residential purposes within any Zone or land located within any of the seven Residential zones and used for a purpose commensurate with that zone.

Nineteen CAV Categories based on combinations of Primary Land Use, Secondary Land Use, Zone, and Total Area criteria were used to identify Residential land. A total of 59 Approved CAV Requests were used to produce the valuations. However, some of these Requests may have been executed more than once as a result of 'Updating' or being Executed in an Unapproved form or may replace 'original' Requests. At least one Revaluation listing was produced for each CAV Request.

Results

Analysis of CAV request types

Base factor (F) or equation (E) only	21
Base F or E with exceptions (E)	9
Base F or E with category F or E with or without E	29
Total number of CAV requests	59

Valuations

Analysis of predicted valuations

Estimated altered predicted valuations	861
Estimated unaltered predicted values	41,309
Total number of valuations	42,170

Human resources

Maximum Staff involvement	4
Maximum work days	122
Estimated total staff hours	1,778
Average valuations per staff member per day (7.25 Hours)	Abt 43

Grievances

Grievances lodged by clients	267
Grievance numbers as a percentage of total predicted valuations	0.63%

206

Evaluation of performance

A simple measure of the effectiveness of a revaluation of an area could be the amount of grievance it generates. It is however difficult to draw any reliable conclusions from the amount of grievance activity as a result of a new valuation of an area. For example, the previous revaluation of Gold Coast resulted in 2,131 grievances for all land uses versus 375 on this occasion. The author's personal experience with the Gold Coast over a ten year period is that grievance levels seem to be related to numerous factors including the stage of the real estate market cycle, often localized issues, and the incidence of, and increases in, Land Taxes which are directly linked to value levels (and hence affected by steep market movements).

The most that therefore can be concluded, is that the grievance result for the 1995 revaluation is at least in keeping with other years produced with CAV Version 1.

Conclusion from study

IVAS CAV provides a relatively cheap cost effective way (in comparison to manual systems), for producing bulk numbers of valuations for use for revenue purposes in a relatively short inflexible timeframe. Judged by the number of predicted values which require manual change, and the number of grievance actions by clients, the system appears to successfully meet the requirements for a mass appraisal valuation system.

Operational problems of CAV IVAS

Human resources

Many of the people that used IVAS CAV were relatively new to the DOL. Consequently a significant number of valuers had no experience in carrying out mass appraisals. This factor was also complicated by the revaluation being carried out for the first time using the IVAS CAMA.

Some grievance matters can be attributed to non-familiarity with the IVAS CAMA resulting in proposed changes to predicted values not being made. This was evident in the areas of value exceptions not being made, and entered manual valuation changes not being saved to the database.

Initially the functionality of some key transactions did not support business. For example, it is not uncommon to have more than one valuer 'working' in an SMA, hence parts of the SMA need to be able to be predicted separately. This requirement was not available until the Revaluation had commenced.

Some IVAS transactions did not perform to specification in the production environment. This was principally a result of transactions not being specifically designed for a Very Large database (VLDB) and testing being performed using limited datasets in a non-production environment. The outcome of this was a combination of further development work being required, especially in performance enhancement, and predicted valuations being initially produced without some quality control reports. Additionally, due to problems with a number of IVAS transactions, a number of valuations which normally would have been produced using CAV had to be carried out manually.

Under operational conditions it became apparent that there were limitations on the complexity of CAV Requests. For example, Exceptions to CAV Categories were limited to five valuation ranges per Exception, with a maximum of about 30 combined Category and Exception Criteria per Request Page. The practical effect on the production of predicted values was minimal.

The bottom line in all this is that the DOL has many core business areas and hence competing demands for resources. The annual revaluation is one of these business tasks which simply must be completed within a relatively fixed time, and resource envelope, with any attendant quality constraints.

Developmental/future trends

Refinement of CAV

Predicted valuations are based on existing valuations, however, to improve valuation level with respect to valuation date, 'Final' predicted values may in future be based on an 'Initial' prediction plus any manual adjustments.

Private sector contracting of the Annual Revaluation program has been trialled by the DOL, and is under active consideration for widespread adoption.

Provide unimproved value part 2 (PUV2)

An alternate way to produce any valuation is by using a unit by a rate methodology. That is, a valuation is most simply 'X' Units (square metres, hectares etc.) multiplied by 'Y' Rate (dollars per square metre, per hectare etc.) to give an end figure. Any valuation can be 'built up' by aggregating any number of Unit by

Rate calculations. Each rate is directly referenced to a line in a valuation basis, called a Basis Line Entry (BLE).

A BLE comprises a BLE No (an identifier); a Regional Land Category (an RLC is a description of the physical nature of land); a Regional Land Category Break up (a subdivision of RLC based upon additional features); a Market (an economic grouping of properties determined by geographical or physical features); a Unit (of Value, say square metres); and a Rate (in the form of a Dollar Range).

Some 150,000 Properties have had information collected to be used in the PUV2 system, and a PC based prototype system is currently being coded.

Some advantages

Consistent valuation terminology; direct linkage between valuation and valuation basis: ability to maintain relativity between valuations over time; and ability to predict unimproved and improved valuations.

GIS

GIS technology in conjunction with IVAS CAV will be used in all Regions of the DOL as soon as funding allows. Contingent on a drop in GIS Software prices, it is anticipated that GIS will move off the desktop, and be commonly used in lap top computers by field valuers. The integration of IVAS CAV and GIS will be pursued in the future, however the exact direction of this development is as yet unclear.

References

Lockwood, A. and Reynolds, W. (1992), 'Computer Assisted Valuations : The South Australian Experience', *The Valuer*, pp. 109-111.
NONLIN Nonlinear Regression Analysis Program (computer program) (1994), Nashville, Author Phillip H. Sherrod.
Valuation of Land Act of 1944 (Qld).

9 The New Zealand experience with computer assisted valuation

A. Pegler

Background to the New Zealand experience

Valuation New Zealand

Valuation New Zealand has existed as a department of state for almost 100 years. It has responsibility for the cyclical revaluation of all properties within New Zealand. Some 420 people are employed at 28 different locations. The valuations assessed by Valuation New Zealand are used as a rating base by 74 separate local authorities as well as 8 regional authorities. The most recent information available indicates that the valuation roll is used as base for raising some $1.5 billion of revenue for local government. The task of assessing a capital value (improved value), land value and value of improvements for each of the 1.5 million properties that comprise New Zealand over a three year time frame requires the application of significant human resources. While most of the resources of Valuation New Zealand are focused on preparing and maintaining valuation rolls a range of commercial valuation services are also provided to local and central government agencies. The sale of property related information has become important in the last few years.

Valuation New Zealand has a computerized record system with a network linking to an IBM AS/400. Currently the network comprises approximately 130 devices and this number is likely to grow over the next few years.

Methodology up to 1979

For the first 70 years of Valuation New Zealand's existence valuations were carried out in a traditional manner by manually compiling values using either one or more combinations of the three accepted approaches. This generally resulted in individual valuers making 8-10 valuations per day.

In the 1970s there was significant pressure on government departments to reduce expenditure. For an organization such as Valuation New Zealand where approximately 65% of expenditure relates to personnel it became critical that productivity be improved. Figure 9.1 charts the change in the ratio of Valuation Records per Employee since 1960.

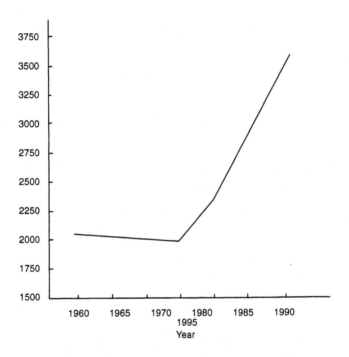

Figure 9.1 Valuation records per employee

Research

Significant research into the predictability of values using multiple regression analysis (MRA) in the valuation of single residential properties was commenced a little over twenty years ago. At that time it was recognized that with the increasing sophistication of computers that there was a potential for this technology to be harnessed for the benefit of valuers involved in mass appraisal type applications.

212

Research and a number of pilot studies were undertaken at a variety of sites around New Zealand for a period of 8 years. This testing was necessary as we sought to refine the nature of the descriptive data that was to be collected to enable accurate estimates of value to be generated. In the initial pilot studies up to 50 separate data elements were captured. Many of these variables reflected the interior amenities of houses such as the number of bedrooms and bathrooms. In those times a significant issue was the cost of data in a computer system. The research sought to reduce the number of variables so that those storage costs would be reduced. While the cost of storage is today of less concern, the number of variables is still critical in that there is a real cost in collecting the data as well as a cost in maintaining it in a correct state.

In 1978 the Government approved the implementation of computer assisted valuation techniques. This approval was necessary only insofar as it required the commitment of government financial resources to proceed with the necessary data capture.

Implementation

Since 1979 computer assisted valuation methods using MRA techniques have been an integral part of Valuation New Zealand's processes. The use that has been made of the techniques has not however been all embracing. Due to the characteristics of settlement within New Zealand with comparatively small population centres and yet quite diverse real estate developments, the application of computer assistance has been limited to the estimation of Capital Values/ Improved Values of single residential properties. Land values are estimated using traditional processes. There is a further limitation in that for communities with fewer than 800 houses we believe there is inadequate evidence of property sales to develop equations which are sufficiently robust to produce acceptable estimates. For all commercial, industrial, other non single residential properties and single residential properties in smaller communities, we are reliant upon the application of traditional manual methods of valuation.

The New Zealand MRA approach - an overview

Data collection

In most parts of New Zealand the data to be used in the computer assistance programme has been captured for at least 15 years. The initial data capture exercise was the most time consuming. Typically the additional time associated with the collection of the data used, colloquially known as 'mass appraisal data', would have amounted to between five and ten minutes per residential property.

With one exception all the data is related to external characteristics of the property and these can be determined without the need for an interior inspection of the house. The mass appraisal data is largely objective. Subjective data has been kept to an absolute minimum. It is always difficult to ensure reasonable consistency of subjective data, and the overall quality of the data will be enhanced if the number of opinion based variables on which a valuer has to make a judgement are reduced to the minimum. Appendix 9.1 contains a list of the current mass appraisal and other data which is used in the computer assistance process.

Valuation New Zealand is advised by the local council of any building work that requires council approval. This advice means that the property records are continually being maintained including the various data fields. With the exception of new construction there is usually very little change to the property characteristics over time. The changes that do occur usually only require the alteration of individual data fields which can be completed very quickly.

Sales system

An integral part of the computer assisted valuation regime is the establishment of a comprehensive sales database. Since 1981 Valuation New Zealand has had in place such a system. By law vendors are required to advise of the transfer of all real estate. This means that the details of every property that is sold within New Zealand are entered onto our database. The information that must be conveyed to us is the sale price, the name of the parties to the transfer, the date of agreement to sell and the date on which transfer was effected. Usually advice of sales is received within a month of settlement occurring, and we therefore have a very comprehensive source of information on which to base any valuations.

The process of sales analysis to predictions

Understanding the available data The condescriptive analysis is a prerequisite to the multiple regression analysis. This analysis seeks to identify the particular property characteristics present within the sales samples. From this preliminary analysis the valuer/analyst selects the various property characteristics that are considered likely to be of relevance in explaining the variation in sale prices and which will likely have relevance to the wider property population.

Depending on the number of properties to be valued, sales that occurred within the preceding eighteen months are subject to analysis. If the area is large with a number of distinct communities, they may be analysed separately. The input of the valuer in these decisions is considered important as they bring 'on the ground' knowledge of the locality. At this stage decisions are likely to be made about the sale date. In most cases each separate month or quarter is treated as a distinct and separate variable which will be simply analysed along with all other variables.

Regression analysis The analysis is undertaken on a stepwise regression basis. The analyst studies the results of the initial run. In particular they will be wishing to maximize the R^2 which is a measure of the equation's ability to explain the variation in sales price. More importantly however, the analyst will be wishing to minimize the standard error of the estimate. This statistic indicates the general level of accuracy of the estimate. At the point in the regression analysis where an equation produces an acceptable balance between the R^2 and the Standard Error of Estimate the analyst will be expecting the variables which have been entered to be stable and explicable. It is desirable that variables have an impact which a valuer would expect, i.e. garages add value rather than deduct value which could imply that there is an unacceptable degree of multicollinearity between property characteristics.

In complex areas it would be usual for the analyst to run many regressions. The initial run will be based on the analysts intuitive assessment of how the market is likely to treat particular property characteristics. In situations where the regression does not produce acceptable statistical results it will be necessary to respecify the variables so that the prices are able to be better explained through the analysis process.

During the course of the regression analysis it is probable that some of the sales evidence is suspect. It is suspect in that the computed value shows significant variation from the actual price. The most common reason for a property being an 'outlier' is that the data does not correspond with the actual situation at the date of sale. While data is maintained between valuations there can be important characteristics which change over time, e.g. an expansive water view that was previously available may have been built out, or extra floor space may have been added and no advice was received. In some instances the analyst will identify these outlier sales to the local valuer and request that they be further investigated to ascertain why they are not conforming to the expected pattern. Three separate regression analyses are completed.

The Predict

This analysis seeks to explain the variation in price by analysing the observed property characteristics only. The results of this analysis will be most accurate where there is a high level of homogeneity in the housing stock being analysed. In areas where a valuer will normally have little difficulty in establishing values for the range of property types, the regression analysis results will also be accurate. Basically this means where there is a comparatively narrow range of values, where the age, style and attributes of the houses are quite similar the results will be very good. In more diverse areas the analyst is presented with a greater challenge to produce an equation which is reasonable in a high proportion of cases and of assistance to the valuers in most cases.

The Index

This analysis seeks to explain the variation in the ratio of sale Price/Existing Capital Value for each property. The variables that are analysed are locality, level of existing capital value and age of property.

The same sales that were used in the Predict analysis are used in the Index analysis. Generally the answers that are generated through this analysis will be more consistent than those produced by the Predict. This is because the existing Capital Value captures all of the existing market related considerations in the one figure and with fine tuning can be updated to produce a close estimate of current value. Also in the New Zealand context the existing capital value is frequently referenced as a basis for determining current market value when properties are bought and sold. This estimate will not be accurate when the current property characteristics have not been captured within the existing capital value, e.g. new rooms may have been added to the dwelling but the existing capital value reflects the situation prior to the addition.

The Modindex (Modified Index)

This analysis is an amalgam of the variables used in both the Predict and Index estimates. It incorporates many of the descriptive property characteristics as well as including the existing capital value and in some cases the existing land value.

Once again the sales that are used in the analysis are the same as for the other two. The accuracy produced in the Predict equation is generally enhanced at this stage by the inclusion of the old values. It does however suffer if the market has moved randomly away from the existing values and in cases where the existing values do not incorporate current property characteristics.

Production of estimates of values

At the conclusion of the analysis the three equations selected from each of the separate analysis are firstly re-applied to the last six months sales evidence and secondly to the population of houses generally. This output which will show three capital value estimates for each property is advised to the valuer who indicates whether they are acceptable for use. If the estimates are acceptable they may be printed onto a field record sheet which will be used by valuers as a worksheet in the field to establish final valuations. Alternatively they will be left on lineflow.

There will be instances where the valuer is dissatisfied with the results and may suggest alternative ways of analysing the data. This analysis can go on in an iterative manner until the valuer is satisfied with the results.

Concerns about MRA predictions

One of the major concerns for valuers of the MRA based predictions is that there is no certainty in result from revaluation to revaluation. This uncertainty is particularly apparent when relativities between properties can be upset as a consequence of the analysis. This reversal is simply a consequence of a different group of sale properties with different characteristics being analysed each period. The variables (and weightings) that are identified as explaining the difference in price at the time of analysis will invariably be different from former periods. The net affect of these results is that valuers are suspect of the results and property owners will be unaccepting of what they consider to be inexplicable changes.

To some degree the inclusion of the existing capital value within the regression analysis will minimize the extent of inexplicable reversal of relativities. The problem however, does remain real and one which requires careful management.

Valuers responsibility

Determining land values Prior to the analysis commencing, the valuer will advise what process is to be used for the assessment of land values. Frequently the changes in land values will be constant, certainly within small localities and often over much larger areas. In most cases there will be a low level of sales evidence available on which to establish the current market value and the sales that have occurred will be insufficient to determine that changes to existing relativities are justified. The most common situation therefore will be that the existing land values of large groups of properties will be increased/decreased by a common factor. This index will then bring them to an assessment of current market value with the valuer making a final determination of the reasonableness of the change when viewing the property.

Establishing bench marks Once the valuer has received the MRA generated estimates of capital value he/she will proceed to establish a selection of 'bench mark' properties. These bench mark properties will be used as the basis of the final valuations. This means that all valuations made will relate to the value that has been ascribed to the benchmark properties. The valuer is now ready to commence the task of valuing all the properties. The normal process is for the valuer to first compare the subject property with the most appropriate benchmark and arrive at a preliminary value. The valuer will then look to the computer estimates for support. Hopefully one or other of the computer estimates will be within close proximity to his/her preliminary assessment. If this is the case the valuation will be completed without the necessity to justify it further by proceeding through a summation approach.

Level of property inspection Depending on the completeness of the field records the valuation process may involve an on site and interior inspection of the house (not always possible when many houses are unoccupied during the day). Alternatively if the field record is complete and there have been no changes to the property since last inspection the valuation may be made from the roadway. In some instances where there is a high level of similarity among the houses, coupled with no physical changes to the properties, the valuations may be completed without viewing of the property. (In these cases the acceptability of the resultant valuation will be directly related to the accuracy of the base data).

Conclusion of the valuation task Having determined both a capital value and land value the valuer enters the figures onto the field record sheet or notates the lineflow appropriately and upgrades any data which is deemed to be inaccurate. At this point the valuer has finished his or her task. The field record card or lineflow is then passed to support staff who will then enter the new data into the computer. At some date in the future all owners of property within the area will receive a notice advising them of their property's new valuation and importantly, informing them of their opportunity to object if they disagree with the value.

Importantly the valuer takes responsibility for the accuracy of the valuations issued to property owners. While the valuer does rely on the computer analysis, the correctness or otherwise of the valuations issued is solely the responsibility of the valuer.

Case study

Locality

This case study relates to the revaluation of part of Kapiti District. This community comprises approximately 12,000 properties and is located on the west coast some 40 kilometres to the north of Wellington. It is primarily a dormitory suburb of Wellington with an electric train system linking the centres. It is also one of the areas in New Zealand which is showing high population growth. Additionally it is sought after as a retirement area, and also has a reasonable size commercial centre.

The residential development that makes up this community covers the full spectrum of New Zealand house development ranging from minimum standard weekend cottages, through low income group housing schemes to high class residential accommodation. Diverse property characteristics such as the contour of the lot, the availability of good sea views and the wide range in house types make this area quite a difficult candidate for computer assistance. House values lie within the general range $60,000 NZD to in excess of $600,000 NZD.

Kapiti has been broken into some 5 district locality groups. Analysis and valuation is undertaken within each separate group. The reason for the establishment of these subsets is that the results of analysis are best confined within localities that broadly separate market entities. It also means that the number of variables that are needed to explain the various market differences can be reduced with the results generally being more robust.

This example focuses on the application of computer assistance within one such subset - Raumati Beach of 1,900 single residential properties. While the sales analysed in this case study are based in 1988-89 the process is illustrative of the approach used since then through 1995.

Condescriptive analysis

Some 213 sales that occurred between July 1988 and October 1989 were subject to extensive condescriptive analysis. This particular group of sales produced a range of prices from $30,000 through $325,000 with a mean price of $113,974. Further analysis provided at this point indicated that the market had generally been quite stable throughout this period with little movement in prices.

Regression analysis

The Predict The initial analysis produced very disappointing results with an R^2 of 0.662 and a SE of 0.2085. This analysis was based on a multiplicative model having Ln(Price) as the dependent variable. This model identified a large number of sales as 'outliers'. Further transformations of variables were used as well as considering a straight additive model. Results did not vary significantly from the initial analysis.

At this stage it became evident that there was a group of 35 properties that consistently fell outside of acceptable parameters irrespective of how the data might be analysed or the variables transformed.

An informal inspection of these 'outlier' properties was carried out. From this inspection it was evident that our data was incorrect in 10 cases. In the balance of these outlier sales it was clear that while the property characteristics were correct as recorded the prices did not conform to the pattern that had been set by the other 178 sales.

After the data that had to be corrected was complete some 25 sales were detected from further analysis. The mean price of this reduced group of 188 sales was $115,174 which indicates a general spread of the 'outlier' properties across the full price range.

Further analysis was then carried out with the results being significantly improved. Appendix 9.2 reproduces the substance of the final regression run.

219

As is clearly evident the R^2 has increased to 0.857 while the SE now stands at 0.124.

The Index Following the problems in establishing good Predict estimates there was no surprise that the regression runs to produce a good Index equation were similarly difficult. In the initial analysis the results were not spectacular but following some further transformations of variables and the deletion of the obvious outlier sales from the sample the equation shown at Appendix 9.3 was settled on as producing an acceptable level of accuracy.

The Modindex As this was the last equation to be determined the analyst started with the clear indication that the results would likely follow the accuracy attained in the Predict and Index. The equation shown at Appendix 9.4 was selected as generating the best possible accuracy from the diverse sales sample.

Results of analysis

The results of the analysis are not at the level that would generally be desirable. They do however fall within the range that is typically generated by the regression analysis process. In very homogeneous areas R^2 as high as 0.98 and a SE of 0.05 could be expected. In areas such as Raumati Beach where the property types, contours of site and availability of views are very diverse an R^2 of 0.85 and SE of 0.12 are more usual.

Sales versus estimates

The results of the Predict, Index and Modindex equations were then applied back against all the sales that had taken place during the month of October 1989 which is the market level of the estimates. This process compares the computer produced estimates with all the observed prices, some of which have previously been identified as falling outside of the market pattern. In the Raumati Beach area the Predict equation produced estimates that were within +10% of the price in 65% of the sales sample. For the Indexes and Modindex the results were 60% and 65% respectively. Clearly in this area the most consistent answers were produced by the Modindex and Predict which even so were unable to generate a satisfactory estimate on 35% of observed sales. Of greater relevance however was the fact that for 85% of the sales at least one of the estimates was within +10% of the actual price. This meant that valuers in the field would need to be particularly diligent in completing all valuations if the results were to be acceptable to the property owners.

This particular analysis does produce a biased answer in that the same sales that were the basis of the estimates are used to measure the accuracy of the estimates. A more meaningful analysis is to produce the estimates from only a sample of the available sales. The results of the analysis can then be applied to the control group which were not analysed. In Raumati Beach there were insufficient sales to use this approach, however see the later discussion on the analysis of subsequent sales.

Estimates on all house properties

Concurrently with the above process the analyst also applied the equations to all the house properties. In the Raumati Beach area estimates were provided for 1,900 houses. Table 9.1 shows the mean and range of the predict, Index and Modindex estimates along with the existing capital value.

Table 9.1
Summary of estimates

	Mean Estimate	Minimum Estimate	Maximum Estimate
Predict	127,570	9,000	504,500
Index	126,821	13,500	652,000
Modindex	125,128	11,000	510,500
Existing Capital Value	91,890	9,000	541,000

Valuers reaction

On receipt of the Sales versus Estimates listing and the listing showing the estimates for all the houses the valuer saw that there was a reasonable degree of variability between the three estimates. He recognized however that Raumati Beach is a diverse area and considered that without the guidance provided by the estimates maintaining uniformity among the valuers would be difficult.

Field work

Three valuers were assigned to the revision of values in Raumati Beach. Their objective was to conclude the task with a production rate of 40.0 properties per valuer day. This figure included all 2,603 properties that comprise Raumati Beach and not just the single residential house component. The small team

221

surpassed their productivity goal by valuing at an average rate of approximately 45.0 properties per valuer day.

The valuers viewed every property from the street, went on site when verification of property attributes was necessary and inspected the interior of houses whenever possible if the property had significantly changed since the last full inspection. Significant reliance is placed on the completeness of our computer record as well as the manual permanent data record which is held on each property.

Prior to computer estimates being part of the valuation process the revision of this area was typically completed at a rate of 12.5 properties per valuer day. This production was generally achieved in an environment where the valuer went onto every property and whenever possible made an inspection of the interior of each house or building.

Support staff

When the valuers have finished their work they pass the completed field record sheet to the support staff. These people have the task of inputting the new revision values as well as all the data which has changed into the computer. Depending on the degree of change associated with each property this task would typically take 15-20 seconds per property.

Use of the estimates

The only way to make some assessment of how much use was made of the estimates by the valuers was by comparing the estimates with the value actually fixed. A 5% random sample was analysed with the results being listed in Table 9.2.

Table 9.2
Use of computer estimates by valuers

	Mean	Within + 10% of assessed value
Predict	124,095	48.6%
Index	123,566	75.2%
Modindex	121,709	58.0%
Assessed Value	129,657	

The statistics produced are a very harsh measure of usage. In fact for 88% of the sample at least one of the estimates was within + 10% of the assessed value. This means that in only 1 case in 9 was the valuer not necessarily assisted by the provision of the estimates. Important to remember is that the valuer will have included in his or her valuation the property attributes as they existed at the date the property was viewed. By comparison the estimates are based on data which was recorded at least 3 years ago. From the analysis however it would appear that the estimates were of significant assistance and the feed back from the valuers would support that conclusion.

Analysis of subsequent sales

As a further test of the accuracy of the revised values, sales which were received after the original analysis had been concluded have been compared with the assessed values. The results of this analysis involving the 34 sales which had occurred between November 1989 and January 1990, is shown at Table 9.3.

Table 9.3
Analysis of subsequent sales

	Mean	% within + 10% of Price
Valuation	108,294	82.3%
Price	107,411	

Computer assisted applications other than MRA

Indexation

Given the operational limitations that have been placed on MRA, clearly there are many hundreds of thousands properties that fall outside the catchment area. As discussed previously Index methods can be applied using MRA processes. VNZ has developed this method to have a broader application than those limited by MRA. It is used in two ways, firstly as an alternative approach to using MRA. The second usage is to apply indexation to MRA generated values as a final adjustment prior to the valuations being issued. This final adjustment will reflect any market movements that have taken place since the MRA generated values were originally derived.

223

The actual process involves the valuer determining a series of indices which when applied to 'existing' Capital and Land Values, results in a proxy for current values. The indexes developed by the local valuers do not usually result from the same level of statistical sophistication that is integral with MRA. At its most simple the index is simply the division of sale price by the previously assessed capital value. The derived index can then be applied to existing capital value of comparable properties to produce a proxy for sale price. They are however, developed from the valuers in-depth knowledge of locality and in many instances will capture the essence of unofficial market transactions.

Indexes have been developed in this way for many years and have been applied across all property types. These indexes are deemed successful in precisely the same situations that were identified with the MRA index. This process certainly enables a preliminary estimate of value to be made with final determination of value remaining with the valuer. The application of these indexes is currently centralized but is shortly to be distributed to districts using some customized PC-SAS software. In this way districts will be able to take responsibility for the whole process.

Income and summation approaches

A number of VNZ offices have established PC based systems to generate computer estimates of values on the income and summation approach. These applications are generally limited to specialized properties in the case of the summation approach, and commercial and industrial properties for the income approach.

The detail of application will be dependent upon the number of properties in any particular area and the valuer's assessment of the realizable benefits of data input and maintenance versus the costs of manually completing the valuation task.

The future

Portable computers

Hand-held computing devices were successfully used in a 'one-off' large scale valuation exercise in 1993. The units used, Hewlett Packard LX95 Palmtop, were the best of a very inadequate range of portable computing products available on the New Zealand market at that time.

The Palmtops were used as both a data collection device and a basic processor. Their use was successful and the contract was completed within expectations. Since 1993 we have sought to identify a suitable hand-held product which can be used. Very real benefits have been identified in having valuers take their work into the field in electronic form, update it and pass it back to the main database without further input operator intervention. In 1995/96 a 'limited pilot' application will be undertaken which should result in a computer based substitution for line flow and other paper records. The ability to 'build in' robust controls will mean that valuation quality will be enhanced, data quality will improve and the opportunity for processing error on input will be eliminated.

Conclusion

Valuation New Zealand's experience with computer assisted valuations have been successful. They have enabled significant improvements in productivity to be realized, while at the same time ensuring that the valuer is dominant in the process and not subservient to it. The nature of New Zealand's property development does however mean that there are some very real limitations in using the statistically robust process available for large residential housing areas in all areas of valuation. Valuation New Zealand continues to seek solutions to that particular problem while also looking at other areas of computer technology to further improve the quality and productivity of the whole valuation process.

Appendix 9.1

Property characteristics currently used in computer assisted valuations

Roll number- reflection of locality
Date of sale
Sale price
Property Category - for residential defines year built or quality of dwelling
Existing roll capital value
Existing roll land value
Section size
Zoning
Condition of walls and roof
Construction of walls and roof
Class of surrounding improvements
Position of site
Contour of site
Nature of landscaping
View
Scope
House type
Modernization
Effective year built
Area of main living level
Total area of house
Poor foundations
Deck
Laundry/workshop area
Large other improvements on site
Car access to site
Formed driveway
Number of garages being integral part of dwelling
Number of garages being free standing from dwelling
Is property a typical

Appendix 9.2

Predict equation for Raumati Beach

		DF	Sum of Squares	Mean Square
R Square	0.85721	Regression	13	16.11674	1.23975
Standard Error	0.12422	Residual	174	2.68473	0.01543
		F = 80.34944	Signif F = 0.00000		

Variables in the Equation

Variable	B	SE B	Beta	T	Sig T
Ln Total Floor	0.44774	0.03344	0.51533	13.389	0.0000
LN House Age	-0.09999	0.02084	-0.16519	-4.798	0.0000
Other Views	0.11385	0.02634	0.13857	4.323	0.0000
Water Front	0.23584	0.04972	0.14119	4.743	0.0000
Location 1 & 2	-0.13585	0.02797	-0.14830	-4.857	0.0000
Regular Lot	-0.12643	0.02878	-0.13342	-4.393	0.0000
Garage OIS	0.16619	0.04178	0.11794	3.978	0.0001
LN UMR Garages	0.11949	0.03265	0.15857	3.660	0.0003
Steep Contours	-0.05452	0.02178	-0.07801	-2.504	0.0132
Poor/Fair Cond.	-0.10802	0.03932	-0.08349	-2.747	0.0066
Tile Roof	0.10167	0.04014	0.07546	2.533	0.0122
LN FS Garage	0.07026	0.02839	0.09412	2.475	0.0143
Quality Modern	0.10217	0.04637	0.07250	2.203	0.0289
Constant	3.01010	0.17671		17.034	0.0000

Variables not in the Equation

Variable	Beta In	T
Easy Contour	-0.02234	-0.527
Ave/Good Lands	-0.00573	-0.175
Water Views	-0.02391	-0.748
Old House	0.00204	-0.058
Early Bungalow	0.01887	0.604
Two Storey	-0.03266	-0.964
Car access	-0.00691	-0.218
Formal Drive	-0.01615	-0.452
Good Wall/Roof	0.03369	0.923
Wood Walls	0.04251	1.393
Solid Walls	0.03133	1.046
Iron Roof	-0.02680	-0.720
Jul 1988	-0.01916	-0.613
Aug 1988	-0.03189	-1.067
Sept 1988	-0.01351	-0.466
Oct 1988	0.00303	0.102

227

Appendix 9.2 (contd)

Predict equation for Raumati Beach

Variables in the Equation					Variables not in the Equation		
Variable	B	SE B	Beta	T	Sig T		
					Variable	Beta In	T
					Nov 1988	0.00478	0.162
					Dec 1988	-0.04505	-1.531
					Jan 1989	0.02339	0.802
					Feb 1989	-0.00220	-0.075
					Mar 1989	0.03655	1.243
					Apr 1989	-0.04973	-1.663
					May 1989	-0.00249	-0.085
					Jun 1989	0.03997	1.360
					Jul 1989	-0.02194	-0.735
					Aug 1989	-0.01648	-0.548
					Sep 1989	0.05111	1.745
					Area 15081	-0.01378	-0.451
					Area 15082	-0.00285	0.092
					Area 15092	0.03078	0.952

Appendix 9.3

Index equation for Raumati Beach

		DF	Sum of Squares	Mean Square
R Square	0.26666	Regression	6	2.28796	0.38133
Standard Error	0.18645	Residual	181	6.29214	0.03476
		F = 10.96924	Signif F = 0.00000		

Variables in the Equation

Variable	B	SE B	Beta	T	Sig T
CV125PLS	-0.20250	0.04785	-0.27890	-4.232	0.0000
CV650-65	0.10804	0.03134	0.23871	3.447	0.0007
Dec 1988	-0.13726	0.05964	-0.15080	-2.302	0.0225
Mar 1989	0.12563	0.05834	0.13803	2.153	0.0326
Area 15092	0.09466	0.04085	0.15296	2.317	0.0216
Jul 1989	-0.20851	0.09538	-0.14085	-2.186	0.0301
Constant	1.41205	0.01917		73.649	0.0000

Variables not in the Equation

Variable	Beta In	T
CV65-75	0.02408	0.349
CV75-90	0.07805	1.073
CV90-125	-0.10458	-1.462
Old House	-0.10835	1.498
House 1940-49	0.06899	1.064
R9 1950-59	0.00705	0.105
R6 60-69	0.03763	0.550
R7 70-90	-0.02829	-0.393
Aug 1988	-0.07639	-1.193
Sept 1988	-0.10693	-1.677
Oct 1988	0.07837	1.220
Nov 1988	0.02801	0.428
Jan 1989	-0.00255	-0.040
Feb 1989	-0.00374	-0.058
Apr 1989	-0.08005	-1.247
May 1989	-0.53703	-0.008

Appendix 9.3 (contd)

Index equation for Raumati Beach

Variables in the Equation					Variables not in the Equation		
Variable	B	SE B	Beta	T	Sig T	Variable	Beta In	T
						Jun 1989	0.10873	1.703
						Jul 1989	-0.08908	-1.391
						Aug 1989	-0.04886	-0.762
						Sep 1989	0.11821	1.814
						Area 15081	0.01630	0.241
						Water Front	0.02498	0.363
						Area 15082	0.03713	0.565

Appendix 9.4

Modindex equation for Raumati Beach

		DF	Sum of Squares	Mean Square
R Square	0.86838			
Standard Error	0.11863	Regression	8	16.61898	2.07737
		Residual	179	2.51898	0.01407
	F = 147.61938		Signif F = 0.00000	

Variables in the Equation							Variables not in the Equation		
Variable	B	SE B	Beta	T	Sig T		Variable	Beta In	T
LN Old VI	0.26011	0.04368	0.38868	5.955	0.0000		Steep Contour	-0.04316	-1.503
LN Old LV	0.24877	0.03369	0.24823	7.681	0.0000		Easy Contour	0.02906	1.049
LN Total Floor	0.26525	0.04928	0.30260	5.383	0.0000		Ave/Good Lands	0.02505	0.810
LN House Age	-0.07703	0.02160	-0.12614	-3.567	0.0005		Water Views	-0.03743	-1.345
Large OIS	0.12592	0.03999	0.08857	3.149	0.0019		Other Views	0.03131	0.946
Dec 1988	-0.09659	0.03740	-0.07105	-2.583	0.0106		Old House	-0.00151	-0.045
Location 1 & 2	-0.07624	0.02772	-0.08249	-2.750	0.0066		Early Bungalow	0.03083	1.040
Regular Lot	-0.06594	0.02884	-0.06897	-2.286	0.0234		Quality Modern	0.03442	1.107
Constant	5.27804	0.46244		11.413	0.0000		LN Lot Size	0.43203	0.014
							Two Storey	-0.00968	-0.306
							Car access	-0.03262	-1.100
							Formed Drive	-0.01297	-0.382
							LN UMR Garage	0.05120	1.576
							LN FS Garage	-0.00948	-0.339
							Good Walls	0.03116	0.926
							Poor/Fair Cond.	-0.04745	-1.654
							Wood Walls	0.01744	0.605

Appendix 9.4 (contd)

Modindex equation for Raumati Beach

Variables in the Equation						Variables not in the Equation		
Variable	B	SE B	Beta	T	Sig T	Variable	Beta In	T
						Solid Walls	0.02820	1.020
						Iron Roof	-0.02610	-0.956
						Tile Roof	0.02280	0.803
						Jul 1988	-0.05255	-1.883
						Aug 1988	-0.02514	-0.906
						Sept 1988	-0.03145	-1.148
						Oct 1988	0.01938	0.706
						Nov 1988	0.00773	0.277
						Jan 1989	-0.00467	-0.169
						Feb 1989	0.00319	0.116
						Mar 1989	0.05193	1.882
						Apr 1989	-0.04285	-1.568
						May 1989	-0.00327	-0.119
						Jun 1989	0.03060	1.104
						Jul 1989	-0.03479	-1.259
						Aug 1989	-0.02396	-0.863
						Sep 1989	0.04801	1.739
						Area 15081	-0.01403	-0.504
						Water Front	0.03388	1.092
						Area 15082	0.00253	0.092
						Area 15092	0.03794	1.323

10 Computer assisted valuation in Tasmania

D. Thomas

Introduction

Tasmania is an Australian State lying south of the main island. The population is distributed in four major centres (Hobart, Launceston, Devonport and Burnie), compact country towns and rural communities. Decentralization of population makes statistical mass appraisal difficult as sales volumes are low, sub-markets are small and property varied. This chapter will study the history and evolution of Computer Assisted Valuation (CAV) techniques in Tasmania including the development of a hybrid regression model to accommodate heterogeneous market groups. It will also provide a Case Study showing the application of the Proportionality Model.

Historical development

Office of the Valuer General (OVG)

The Office of the Valuer-General exists under provisions of the Land Valuation Act 1971 to provide Tasmania with a centralized rating and taxing valuation service for State and Local Government. Since its inception the Division's activities have expanded to include responsibility for maintenance of a comprehensive property database as one of the core modules in a statewide land information system.

The organization currently employs a mixture of professional valuers, field assistants and clerical support located at three sites around the State. During high volume periods work is outsourced to private valuation firms who operate under the supervision of internal managers.

The Valuer-General is currently responsible for the maintenance of over 225,000 valuations situated in 29 municipalities and is required under legislation to value each property individually at least every ten years. The present cycle is five years for urban municipalities and seven years for outlying rural jurisdictions.

Tasmanian rating system

The Act requires the Valuer-General to return three valuations:

Land Value:	The value of the land only,
Capital Value:	The value of the property including land,
Assessed Annual Value:	The annual gross rental of the property,

which are used in various ways for rating and taxing purposes. The Commissioner of Taxes uses Land Value to apply Land Tax to holdings based on the following classifications:

- Principle residence,
- Rural, or
- General

Following recent amendments to the Land Tax legislation , Principle Residences will be exempt from Land Tax from the 1996-97 financial year.

Local municipalities have the right to impose rates using the three values above individually or in any combination. Presently Councils prefer to use Assessed Annual Value only.

Computerization

Traditionally, the OVG and Commissioner of Taxes have had a close relationship in respect to property taxation which led to the joint development of a computer system in the early 1980s. This database, called Valtax, aimed to computerize and streamline manual records, providing on line property information. The Commissioner of Taxes was responsible for ownership details, while the OVG maintained the valuation roll.

Following the creation of the Department of Environment and Land Management and development of an integrated Land Information System, Valtax became obsolete and was replaced by a comprehensive valuation database, separate from the Commissioner of Taxes. This system, known as Vistas, retained the original Valtax database, but allowed flexibility in developing multiple CAV techniques, management statistics and automating valuation processes.

Introduction of CAV processes

Government downsizing in the 1980s led to the Valuer-General developing a CAV programme in 1986, with the intention of using advanced technology to aid the revaluation of properties. Consultants from South Australia had successfully developed a Simple Regression Model which regressed current sale price on previous statutory value. The South Australian Model was preferred as it required minimal data capture, was easy to understand, simple to apply and required only a basic knowledge of statistics. Initial runs produced satisfactory results when applied to the original manual valuation base, however, as the model matured, certain weaknesses became evident. These problems included:

- Model disintegration through inconsistent valuation approaches;

- Model variances exponentially expanded over multiple CAV revaluations compounding inaccuracies;

- Non-linearity in the regression equation which becomes apparent at fringe price levels;

- Inconsistent market variations;

- Suitability to homogeneous market groups only; and

- Low sale volumes in every neighbourhood group.

By the end of 1990 it was clear that the complexity of property types within heterogeneous city markets made Simple Linear Regression an unreliable model, necessitating a review of CAV techniques and development of more sophisticated models. Austerity measures by the State Government meant that specialist systems were impractical, necessitating development of CAV models suitable for personal computers using commercially available software.

Models

The Office of the Valuer General currently uses the following models for CAV programmes:

- Simple Linear Regression;
- Multiple Linear Regression;
- Base Home;
- Matrices; and
- Proportionality Model.

Simple linear regression

As mentioned above, this model was developed in South Australia and regresses Sale Price on the previous statutory Capital Value. It is effectively used in homogeneous neighbourhoods where housing is of a consistent price range, type and quality. Accuracy is reliant upon consistency of the valuations originally produced and property dynamics over the revaluation cycle. Good documentation is required for supplementary valuations under taken over the cycle so that value creep may be contained. Maintenance of the model requires regular monitoring runs to assess market performance, outliers identification and valuation consistency.

Traditional multiple linear regression

This model has been effective in homogeneous areas where prices are contained within a small spread. With the option of using Simple Linear Regression or the Proportionality Model (a hybrid multiple regression method), this technique is rarely used.

Base home

The government Housing Commission developed large acreage housing estates between 1945 and 1980. These houses are similar in design, size, quality and outlook enabling the use of Base Home matrices. A standard house value matrix is developed for an area based on a house, land and general improvements (fencing and paving) package. Adjustments for outbuildings and extensions are made from look-up tables and added to the base value. The system is simplistic, easy to apply, though tends to be inaccurate where Commission tenants have undertaken extensive internal modifications. Such properties are manually adjusted.

Matrices

The OVG has adopted South Australia's matrices/look-up table format for rural CAV projects. Property components are classified by a column/row code number which relates to specific look-up tables. These matrices cover house values, farm buildings, land improvements, land rates (i.e. $/ha) and rural residential block prices. Once coded, revaluations are undertaken by analysing sales and upgrading the various matrices. Property values are automatically updated.

Currently, data is being captured as part of the initial valuation programme. The first rural revaluations using this model have commenced. Its effectiveness will be monitored during the 1995/96 financial year.

Proportionality model

The Proportionality Model is a hybrid multiple linear regression model, developed during research in 1992 to over come existing Simple Linear Regression CAV problems. Development of this Model is explained below.

Model development

The aim of the research programme was to establish comprehensive CAV methods that adequately sustained predicted values over diverse property groups, locations and time frames, producing a more efficient and effective property tax base. The project investigated the following areas:

- Sales volume;
- Variable selection;
- Model performance;
- Sub-market identification;
- PC based software; and
- Methodologies and processes.

Sales volume

Annual sales volume equates to about 10% of the State's property portfolio, providing inadequate data to sustain reliable models for CAV's relying on neighbourhood-based sub-markets. For statistical methods to be effective either time adjusted historical sales data must be used or bench mark valuations created. Both methods were found to be inadequate and inconsistent with the principles of the research programme. The first usually failed to recognise market fluctuations and the latter relied heavily on subjective valuer opinion. Any model developed had to be sustainable using existing sales volumes. To achieve this, it was necessary to create a large volume of sales by either sub-market cross pollination or using sales of a diverse range of properties within the same Model. This was done through the development of the Proportionality Model.

Variable selection

After completing a strategic analysis of the existing system and identifying weaknesses in methodologies, research concentrated on global literature covering a wide spectrum of CAV issues. It was considered that variable identification and selection were the most important issues in developing a robust model. The six categories of explanatory variables identified by the Resivalu Model (De Rosiers, 1991) were supported in the Tasmanian research. They were:

- Building characteristics
- Land characteristics
- Fiscal variables
- Location and neighbourhood characteristics
- Access variables; and
- Time and cyclical factors.

Tasmanian research approached variable selection by examining the various components that make up a property's constituted value. Carbone and Longini (1977) expressed property in terms of quantitative and qualitative variables affecting real estate both individually and collectively. To avoid extensive (and expensive) data capture, the influence of variables on sale price or a property's value was flow charted (Figure 10.1). This approach considered the impact each individual variable had on sale price through categorizing its relationship to the Generic Model.

It was found that the majority of CAV studies used numerous variables in the regression equation. Studies relied heavily on dichotomous variables to segment property characteristics as model developers tried to replicate actual real estate attributes. Lockwood (1984) found that an initial attempt to adopt all variables was impossible, because many were not represented in the sample, or occurred rarely to be statistically reliable for estimating property values. To over come this problem, a review into how property values were constituted, particularly the treatment of time, building area, other improvements, age and location, was undertaken.

The treatment of time in regression analysis has been well documented using percentage adjustments (qualitative), monthly ranking (quantitative), paired sales and transgeneration into a trigonometric form (Cosine Curve) (Jensen, 1991; Gloudemans, 1990; and Matthews and Wichern, 1978). While under taking analysis of property value trends it was discovered that the market fluctuated, rather than steadily increasing or decreasing. With such variance, use of the above methods to adjust sales could result in the assessed value being in error. To improve accuracy, sales were adjusted by a fixed value increase or percentage as reflected by a monthly running median price. It is recognised that this method is convoluted compared to other forms of time adjustment, but it gives the valuer more control over the dependent variable. Physical adjustment to sale price was applied while sales data under went cleansing in a spreadsheet format. Recent projects within the OVG have experimented in treating time as a quantitative variable to speed up the process.

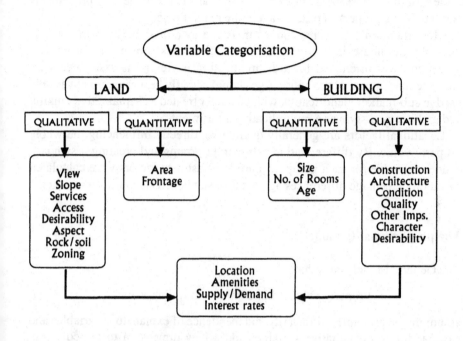

Figure 10.1 Variable categorization

In all studies, building area was the most significant variable in the regression analysis. Secondary space created major problems because it included attics, rumpus rooms and other living space that added value to the property. It was debated whether such space should be considered as a dummy variable with the risk that it may not be included in the analysis once stepwise regression techniques were applied. By transforming the building size to an Effective Area, calculated by converting all accommodation into square metre equivalents based on the full value rate of the main building area, all secondary accommodation was represented in the regression equation.

Similarly, other improvements, such as fencing, paving, garages, tennis courts and swimming pools, were treated as having a collective added value to the overall property and not individual components of value (unlike American studies). This enabled the Model to eliminate many dummy variables by converting other improvements into a percentage of the property's total value.

For instance a tennis court may add $10,000 to a $100,000 property, but the same court may add $30,000 to a $400,000 residence. The value of improvements is relative to a property's price strata in the market place.

Most traditional CAV techniques treat age as a quantitative variable, for example, the house is twenty-five years old. Studies showed that a buyer's perception was orientated towards architectural style and is associated with character and appeal of the house. Age should actually be a categorical variable used in sub-market identification with character treated as a qualitative ranking and architectural style as a multiplicative adjustment.

Locational factors are generally qualitative, directly influencing the whole property value. By differentiating sub-market groups and creating a standard residential value for each group, locational adjustment factors were calculated based on percentage differences against the established standard sub-market.

The proportionality model

The Generic Model states that:

$$\text{Property value} = \text{Land value} + \text{Building value} \tag{1}$$

assuming the principles of linearity, independence of explanatory variables and strict additivity. Qualitative variables add a new dimension to the equation, adjusting the quantitative variables individually or collectively into an additive/ multiplicative model expressed in the formula:

$$\text{Property value} = QG\,[(QB \times BV) + (QL \times LV)] \tag{2}$$

where:
QG is the general or collective percentage adjustment;
QB and QL are building and land qualitative variable adjustments,
BV and LV are building and land quantitative variables.

Most research has centred on developing Models that represent valuation principles through independent variables. To provide satisfactory results, data were linearized and added to the equation. The Proportionality Model assumes that variability in price, as measured by the standard deviation, is proportional to expected price. Logarithmic transformation of sale price enables extreme values at both ends of the regression line, which are susceptible to bias predictions, to have variances that are proportional to their values. Transformation into a logarithmic base allows an error of $10,000 in $100,000 to be proportional to $50,000 in a $500,000 residence. This model is represented by the equation:

$$\text{Log } Y = a + b_1 X_1 + b_2 X_2 + \ldots + b_k X_k \tag{3}$$

which is equivalent to a model representing a compounding percentage adjustment:

$$Y = C^a \times C^{b1X1} \times C^{b2X2} \times \ldots \times C^{bkXk} \qquad (4)$$

Significant variables that affect property were categorized as Quantitative (Land size, effective building area, percentage of other improvements), Qualitative (ranking) (Slope, View, Access, Condition, Quality, Character and Style), or Adjustment (weighting) (Location, wall type and style). Style was identified by ranking, then entered into the equation as an adjustment variable.

Adjustments for wall type and style were formulated from sales analysis, with location being calculated using a base home and comparing the variance in price between similar properties in each sub-market group. The Proportionality Model is represented by:

$$\text{Log (Price)} = (\text{Constant}) + b_1X_1 + b_2X_2 + \ldots + b_iX_i \qquad (5)$$
$$+ \text{adjwall} + \text{adjsty} + \text{adjloc} + \varepsilon$$

Where bX are coefficients (i.e. effective area, slope, character etc.),
Adjwall is the wall type adjustment,
Adjsty is the architectural style adjustment,
Ajdloc is the location adjustment, and
ε is the error component.

Model performance

Table 10.1 shows the reliability/accuracy of the Proportionality Model in homogeneous and heterogeneous sub-markets. The model has been tested in complex neighbourhoods where properties are diverse and cover the whole price spectrum. Its accuracy in all cases was superior to the South Australian Model and traditional Multiple Linear Regression techniques.

Operational problems

Field testing of the Model was carried out during the 1994/95 financial year as part of an urban revaluation. Accuracy between predicted value and subsequent actual sale prices was mediocre, with large discrepancies in some valuations. This was caused by the following factors.

Price sensitivity The research cell was made-up of a wide selection of property in the $75,000 to $250,000 price spectrum. The property market in the area generally supported properties up to $150,000 before substitution influenced buyer perceptions. Houses over this value tended to become over capitalized.

241

Table 10.1
Model reliability in research suburbs

Suburb	Market	Mode	R	Reliability		
				5%	10%	15%
Lenah Valley	Homogeneous	PM	0.913	63.5%	92.5%	100%
New Town	Heterogeneous	PM	0.902	52%	86%	97%
Prospect	Homogeneous	PM	0.910	52%	92%	100%
Lindisfarne	Homogeneous	PM	0.954	76%	96%	100%
Howrah	Homogeneous	PM	0.979	90%	100%	

To over come the problem, effective area:

- Either had to be weighted to compensate for its abnormal size;
- Transformed to a power base (i.e. square root); or
- Readjusted according to standard house rates.

Abnormal size In addition to the problems outlined above, extreme land and building sizes created inconsistencies. Where small/large houses on small/large blocks of land existed, over/under valuing occurred. It is important that land attributes be forced into the equation, though compensation for over or under size is needed. One method being trialed is substituting a manually assessed land value for all land characteristics. This is seen as a short term solution as:

- At every revaluation land value must be assessed and added to the data manually;

- Values are susceptible to valuer bias;

- Land value as a substitute for locational adjustments fails to consider location as a general qualitative variable affecting both land and building values; and

- Use of land value restricts cross-pollination of sales data and transportability of the model.

No final conclusion has been made in regard to this matter until extensive field testing has been completed.

Data capture While checking outlying sales it was found that the quality of data capture showed inconsistencies, particularly in codings for condition and quality. Data capture was outsourced without instigating a quality control program. Inaccuracies in significant variables compromised the model. Future programs will employ staff internally to avoid any recurrence as corrupt data corrupts the total CAV process.

Sub-market identification

Development and analysis of sub-markets is essential for CAV techniques to work. Sub-markets may be based on:

- Style of houses
- Socioeconomic group
- Type of development
- Locational aspects.

Understanding sub-market dynamics will allow the valuer to develop reliable adjustment factors. Originally, sub-markets developed by the OVG were simplistic using either architectural style or location as a basis. Research found that subtle variances within these large groups which, once weighted, provided more reliable results. It is important that these weightings are correctly calculated, as they can adversely affect the final output.

One important issue is added value of land. It was discovered during the sales analysis stage that the full value of land may not be totally reflected in the property's complete value. This was true for new houses in older areas, where such homes commanded higher land values than the established properties. Sub-market identification became a mixture of logic and experimentation.

CAV methodologies and processes

Every mass appraisal operation has its own methodologies and processes. The OVG in Tasmania is no different. The following steps outline the CAV process adopted for revaluations in an urban area:

Step 1:   Sales with property attributes and weighting adjustments are down loaded into MS Excel for cleansing. Non-market transactions and data errors are removed. Market value trends are assessed, with time adjustments to sales being applied during this stage of the process.

Step 2:   Field sales analysis is undertaken with data being corrected where necessary.

Step 3: Spreadsheet information corrected and adjustment weightings added. Data then loaded into a Windows based statistical program, currently Systat for Windows, for manipulation.

Step 4: A raw data run is undertaken including the following:

- Sale histogram, scatter plot of sale verses previous statutory value and sales ratio plot

- Correlation analysis, sub-market box plot and descriptive statistics

- Simple linear regression analysis and diagnostic output analysed

- Proportionality Model run with diagnostic output analysed

- Both models compared for accuracy, with outliers flagged and checked against sales analysis.

Step 5: Weightings adjusted, spreadsheet data corrected.

Step 6: Both models are rerun with diagnostics and reliability testing. If results acceptable coefficients are applied to the property portfolio. Adjustment factors are placed in a look-up table which is activated when properties down loaded into spreadsheet.

Step 7: All properties with adjustment factors and attributes are down loaded from the main database into spreadsheet. The regression equation is applied. The predicted value is compared against the last sale price which is included in the down loading process. Large discrepancies are flagged for field inspection.

Step 8: A random sample is manually valued and compared to the predicted value. If results are good, all estimated values are up-loaded from the spreadsheet into the main database, being held for monitoring. Poor or inconsistent values may be kerbside adjusted, or the model re-calibrated, or properties flagged for manual valuation.

Step 9: Sales subsequent to the valuation process date are compared to the property's predicted value. If market trends are changing, predicted values, as a whole, can be adjusted before release.

A number of the above steps will be automated as model development matures.

Future application

Future research will concentrate on improving the Proportionality Model and experimenting with variations in the use of variables, particularly land attributes. Simple Linear Regression will continue to be applied in homogeneous housing groups where reliability is satisfactory. The long term application of the Proportionality Model is depended upon:

- Continued existence of the OVG. Under new State/Commonwealth agreements open competition is encouraged. Councils have indicated a strong wish to manage their own valuation affairs which appears to be supported by recent changes within the Tasmanian Government. If devolution occurs to the 29 municipalities, research and development would virtually cease through lack of resources and technical skills.

- Continued commitment to model research. Most studies have been undertaken on an *ad hoc* basis by staff committed to improving valuation processes with limited input from statistical consultants.

- Limited resources are presently being invested in the development of CAV statistical applications. Adequate resources are required to capture necessary data and provide ongoing comprehensive sales analyses, or model development will be curtailed.

These problems are not unique to Tasmania. Property taxation is a major revenue source for governments globally and with a small investment in human and technological resources, the return could be immense.

Summary

The Proportionality Model is suitable for both small and large heterogeneous jurisdictions with low sale volumes. The model provides long term robustness and the ability to be transported across sub-markets and municipalities without the constraints experienced by other traditional regression techniques.

Case study

New Town is located north of the city centre, just outside the inner residential area. Bounded by New Town Creek to the north and Elphinstone Road to the south, the area consists of heterogeneous properties ranging from Georgian

245

architecture to Contemporary styles. The majority of the houses were constructed during the late Federation to 1940s and demographically cover a mixed socioeconomic population. Providing a good mix of land and building sizes, styles and character, property values range from $80,000 to $300,000. Demand for properties in the area is strong which resulted in consistent appreciation even during the recession years. (See Figure 10.2).

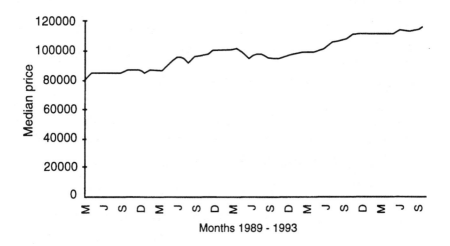

Figure 10.2 Market trend New Town 1989 - 1993

This case study concentrates on research under taken during January/March 1994. The data is real and has not been modified for this chapter.

Sub-market segregation

New Town was divided into five defined main sectors, then into sub-markets within these sectors based on period of development and socioeconomic demographics. Exclusive neighbourhoods were removed as these represented large land holdings and mansions which were out of keeping with the general housing within the research area.

A sales analysis was completed which included data not previously captured. Considering the span of model development, this case study will illustrate only the 1850-1930 period homes. Table 10.2 shows the sales adopted and variables included in the analysis.

Table 10.2
Descriptive statistics

	Price
Number of cases:	41
Minimum:	70,000
Maximum:	201,000
Mean:	117,279
Median:	110,000

Sale price spread

Figure 10.3 shows the sales distribution skewed to the left with a high concentration of prices between $80,000 and $140,000. Predicted values in the higher price bracket will need to be checked for over assessment. Research shows that the valuation of these properties can be influenced by the large proportion of general housing included in the equation. This also occurs where one group (either style or sub-market) dominates the cases included in the statistical analysis.

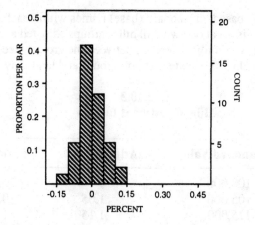

Figure 10.3 Sale price spread

Box plot of sub-market price distribution

A box plot of sales grouped into sub-markets allows a valuer to compare sale spread, median prices and extreme values. This is helpful in studying locational analysis when developing a locality weighting adjustment factor. In Figure 10.4, groups 21 and 24 have similar dynamics, while sales in 25 are skewed to the lower end of the price scale and have a broader range. Group 23 comprises more 'up-market' houses.

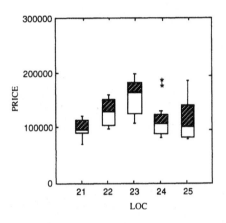

Figure 10.4 Box plot of price distribution

Adjustment factors

Location weighting is based on standard (base) homes within each sub-market. The principle locality is set at one with all other groups adjusted accordingly. In this study, land value is the only difference between the groups (see Table 10.3). Research in other localities indicate that both house and land may vary.

Table 10.3
Value adjustment factors

SM	Standard Value	Adjustment	Main Rd
21	100,000	1	0.9
22	105,000	1.05	0.945
23	115,000	1.15	1.035
24	100,000	1	0.9
25	90,000	0.9	0.81

Wall weightings are calculated by comparing values of different wall types in various style categories (see Table 10.4). For New Town the following was adopted. Similarly, standard homes within style categories were compared and weighted, with Modern/Austerity period (1940-1965) being set at one.

248

Table 10.4
Wall weighting adjustments

Wall Type		Architectural Style	
Weatherboard	0.9	Victorian	1.25
Brick	1	Federation	1.25
Concrete	0.85	Bungalow	1.24
Vertical Board/Stucco	0.9	ArtDeco/1930s	1.06
		Modern/Austerity	1.00

Regression output

Below is the stepwise regression output for the Proportionality Model from data contained in Table 10.5.

Table 10.5
Regression statistics

DEP VAR: LPRICE   N:41   MULTIPLE R: 0.981   SQUARED MULTIPLE R: 0.962

ADJUSTED SQUARED MULTIPLE R:0.950   STANDARD ERROR OF ESTIMATE:0.060

VARIABLE	COEFFICIENT	STD ERROR	STD COEF	TOLERANCE	T	P(2TAIL)
CONSTAN	9.191	0.287	0.000	-	32.047	0.000
EFFAREA	0.004	0.000	0.495	0.370	8.549	0.000
LOCADJ	0.518	0.163	0.127	0.773	3.170	0.003
WALLADJ	0.412	0.214	0.080	0.723	1.926	0.063
STADJ	0.274	0.118	0.093	0.777	2.332	0.026
PEROI	0.618	0.415	0.058	0.812	1.487	0.147
C	0.061	0.014	0.189	0.645	4.301	0.000
Q	0.172	0.030	0.283	0.519	5.793	0.000
S	-0.048	0.014	-0.152	0.668	-3.518	0.001
SIZE	2.692	0.581	0.263	0.384	4.632	0.000

ANALYSIS OF VARIANCE

SOURCE	SUM-OF-SQUARES	DF	MEAN-SQUARE	F-RATIO	P
REGRESSION	2.796	9	0.311	86.089	0.000
RESIDUAL	0.112	31	0.004		

WARNING: CASE 15 HAS LARGE LEVERAGE (LEVERAGE = .489)

DURBIN-WATSON D STATISTIC   1.974

FIRST ORDER AUTOCORRELATION -0.026

Diagnostics

The Probability plot for the regression output shows a linearized line becoming slightly unstable at the higher end. Considering the heterogeneity of property types, this result is acceptable (see Figure 10.5).

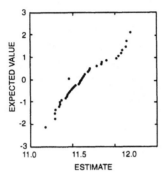

Figure 10.5 Probability plot

Residual plot for the regression output shows no model deficiencies but identifies three properties that require further investigation (see Figure 10.6).

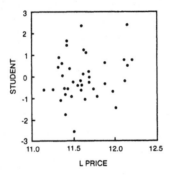

Figure 10.6 Residual plot

Reliability testing

Table 10.6 shows the Proportionality Model's regression output and reliability results. Reliability testing is the residual divided by price represented as a percentage. Accuracy standards satisfactory for CAV purposes are given in Table 10.7.

Table 10.6
Proportionality model output with reliability percentages

CASE	STUDENT	PREDICT	PRICE	RESIDUAL	PERCENT
10	-2.5317	114,100	100,000	-14,100	-14.1%
1	-1.7447	98,493	90,000	-8,493	-9.4%
31	-1.4339	176,768	165,000	-11,768	-7.1%
21	-1.0771	90,950	86,000	-4,950	-5.8%
11	-1.0399	120,207	114,000	-6,207	-5.4%
8	-0.9265	101,960	97,000	-4,960	-5.1%
24	-0.8002	94,025	90,000	-4,025	-4.5%
36	-0.9128	138,375	132,500	-5,875	-4.4%
28	-0.6652	165,873	160,000	-5,873	-3.7%
22	-0.6121	112,661	109,000	-3,661	-3.4%
30	-0.5670	131,083	127,000	-4,083	-3.2%
23	-0.6026	80,502	78,000	-2,502	-3.2%
14	-0.6014	72,210	70,000	-2,210	-3.2%
38	-0.5289	92,650	89,950	-2,700	-3.0%
27	-0.5596	95,757	93,000	-2,757	-3.0%
39	-0.4116	107,345	105,000	-2,345	-2.2%
4	-0.3989	112,329	110,000	-2,329	-2.1%
40	-0.3284	147,034	144,500	-2,534	-1.8%
35	-0.2687	121,729	120,000	-1,729	-1.4%
3	-0.2411	100,158	99,000	-1,158	-1.2%
17	-0.1837	109,044	108,000	-1,044	-1.0%
16	-0.1848	185,762	184,000	-1,762	-1.0%
26	-0.0126	121,084	121,000	-84	-0.1%
5	0.0626	87,199	87,500	301	0.3%
33	0.1416	111,116	112,000	884	0.8%
9	0.2548	118,383	120,000	1,617	1.3%
13	0.4059	92,860	95,000	2,140	2.3%
41	0.4599	80,931	83,000	2,069	2.5%
20	0.5433	184,990	190,000	5,010	2.6%
37	0.6109	84,377	87,000	2,623	3.0%
15	0.7918	194,243	201,000	6,757	3.4%
12	0.6687	139,762	145,000	5,238	3.6%
18	0.8046	175,150	182,500	7,350	4.0%
2	0.9012	80,266	84,000	3,734	4.4%
7	1.1194	109,347	116,000	6,653	5.7%
6	1.1578	107,397	114,500	7,103	6.2%
29	1.2496	106,172	113,500	7,328	6.5%
25	1.4549	85,365	92,000	6,635	7.2%
32	1.6738	85,461	92,500	7,039	7.6%
19	2.4340	169,232	190,000	20,768	10.9%
34	2.3796	97,772	110,000	12,228	11.1%

Table 10.7
Accuracy standards

	5%	10%	15%
Homogeneous	70%	95%	100%
Heterogeneous	65%	95%	98%

In a heterogeneous area, if 95% of the predicted values are within 10% of the sale price, the model is accepted.

In the case of New Town Table 10.8 shows the results achieved using the Proportionality Model.

Table 10.8
New Town results

Range	5%	10%	15%
Reliability	68%	92.5%	100%

Figure 10.7 shows a histogram of the distribution of frequencies allows the valuer to determine if the model tended to over or under value properties.

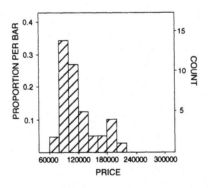

Figure 10.7 Frequency distribution

In Figure 10.7 the accuracy of the predicted values is normally distributed with a slight tendency to over value. The distribution is acceptable and falls within the required standards.

Conclusion

Based on the above statistical analysis, the coefficients expressed in the regression output would return a reliable CAV revaluation in New Town for properties within the prescribed architectural styles. This model could be expanded to include all property groups if required.

References

Carbone, R. and Longini, R.L. (1977), 'A Feedback Model for Automated Real estate Assessment', *Management Science*, Institute of Management Sciences, USA.

Des Rosiers, F. (1991), 'RESIVALU: An Hedonic Residential Price Model for the Quebec Region, 1986-87', *Property Tax Journal*, vol. 10 no. 2, June.

Gloudemans, R. J. (1990), 'Adjusting for Time in Computer Assisted Mass Appraisal', *Property Tax Journal*, vol. 9 no. 1, March.

Information and data, Office of the Valuer General, Dept Environment and Land Management, Tasmania

Jensen, D. (1991), 'Modelling Time Effects in Computer Assisted Mass Appraisal', *Property Tax Journal*, vol. 10 no. 1, March.

Lockwood, A.J.M. (1984) 'Computer Assisted Valuations - A Comparison of Options', *The Valuer*, AIVLE, January.

Matthews, J.P. and Wichern, D.W. (1978), 'A Time Adjusted Model for Sales of Real Property', *CAAS News*, IAAO.

Thomas, D.St.A.C. (1995), 'Proportionality Model - The Tasmanian Experience', *Appraisal Journal*, vol. 2 no. 3, May/June.

Powers, S.C. (1992), 'Comparing Model Structures', *Property Tax Journal*, vol. 11 no. 1, March.

Appendix 10.1
Sale schedule for 1850-1930 houses - New Town

CASE	LOC	DATE	PRICE	CV	SIZE	NOR	WALL	R	B AREA	S	V	A	C	Q	C	ST	EFF OA	PERO A	PERO I	A RATIO	LPRICE	EFF AREA	LOC ADJ	WALL ADJ	ST ADJ
1	21	8	90,000	53,000	0.0300	3	STON	GI	125	5	1	3	4	3	5	1	0	0.00	0.047	0.59	11.40756	125	0.90	1.00	1.24
2	24	2	84,000	62,500	0.0192	3	STUC	GI	65	4	1	3	3	3	4	2	0	0.00	0.056	0.74	11.33857	65	1.00	1.00	1.24
3	22	5	99,000	53,000	0.0873	5	WB	GI	114	3	1	3	3	2	6	3	8	0.04	0.047	0.54	11.50288	122	1.00	0.90	1.24
4	23	4	110,000	72,500	0.0622	5	WB	GI	126	5	1	3	3	3	7	3	0	0.00	0.069	0.66	11.60824	126	1.15	0.90	1.24
5	21	4	87,500	65,000	0.0400	4	BK	GI	82	5	1	2	3	3	7	4	0	0.00	0.076	0.74	11.37939	82	1.00	1.00	1.24
6	21	6	114,500	69,000	0.0450	5	BK	GI	119	5	1	3	4	3	6	4	0	0.00	0.069	0.60	11.64833	119	1.00	1.00	1.25
7	21	7	116,000	62,000	0.0465	6	WB	IT	138	5	1	2	4	3	5	4	0	0.00	0.050	0.53	11.66135	138	1.00	0.90	1.24
8	21	6	97,000	56,000	0.0390	4	WB	GI	114	4	1	3	4	3	6	4	0	0.00	0.030	0.58	11.48247	114	1.00	0.90	1.25
9	21	9	120,000	77,500	0.0950	5	WB	GI	121	5	1	3	4	3	7	4	0	0.00	0.068	0.65	11.69525	121	1.00	0.90	1.24
10	21	8	100,000	61,000	0.0814	5	WB	GI	125	4	2	3	3	3	4	4	0	0.00	0.065	0.61	11.51293	125	1.00	0.90	1.24
11	22	8	114,000	55,000	0.0665	4	WB	GI	96	5	1	1	4	4	7	4	0	0.00	0.087	0.48	11.64395	96	1.00	0.90	1.24
12	21	10	145,000	77,500	0.0898	5	BKR	TI	175	4	3	3	2	3	7	4	0	0.00	0.050	0.53	11.88449	175	1.05	1.00	1.24
13	21	8	95,000	48,000	0.0352	4	WB	GI	89	4	1	3	4	3	6	4	0	0.00	0.048	0.51	11.46163	89	1.00	0.90	1.24
14	23	7	70,000	51,000	0.0450	4	WB	GI	106	5	1	3	2	2	6	4	0	0.00	0.050	0.73	11.15625	106	1.00	0.90	1.24
15	23	3	201,000	170,000	0.0892	7	BK	GI	210	3	3	3	3	3	7	4	0	0.00	0.118	0.85	12.21106	210	1.15	1.00	1.24
16	24	6	184,000	130,000	0.0903	5	BK	TI	166	5	1	3	4	4	7	4	0	0.00	0.080	0.71	12.12269	166	1.15	1.00	1.24

Appendix 10.1(contd)
Sale schedule for 1850-1930 houses - New Town

CASE	LOC	DATE	PRICE	CV	SIZE	NOR	WALL	R	B AREA	S	V	A	C	Q	C	ST	EFF OA	PERO A	PERO I	A RATIO	LPRICE	EFF AREA	LOC ADJ	WALL ADJ	ST ADJ
17	24	6	108,000	70,000	0.0697	4	WB	GI	120	3	1	3	2	3	6	4	9	0.04	0.040	0.65	11.58989	129	1.00	0.90	1.24
18	24	4	182,500	105,000	0.1173	5	BK	GI	152	5	1	3	4	4	5	4	0	0.00	0.076	0.58	12.11451	152	1.00	1.00	1.24
19	24	8	190,000	150,000	0.0080	7	BK	GI	186	5	1	3	3	3	7	4	24	0.07	0.050	0.79	12.15478	210	1.00	1.00	1.24
20	25	3	190,000	145,000	0.0829	6	BK	GI	185	5	1	3	5	4	8	4	0	0.00	0.104	0.76	12.15478	185	0.90	1.00	1.24
21	25	6	86,000	72,500	0.0465	4	BK	GI	123	5	1	3	2	3	5	4	0	0.00	0.055	0.84	11.36210	123	0.90	1.00	1.24
22	21	10	109,000	68,000	0.0400	4	BK	GI	122	3	1	3	4	3	6	5	0	0.00	0.080	0.62	11.59910	122	1.00	1.00	1.06
23	21	9	78,000	56,000	0.0300	3	WB	GI	84	5	1	2	3	3	4	5	0	0.00	0.125	0.72	11.26446	84	1.00	0.90	1.06
24	21	7	90,000	55,000	0.0372	5	WB	GI	107	5	1	3	4	3	5	5	0	0.00	0.110	0.61	11.40756	107	1.00	0.90	1.06
25	21	7	92,000	58,000	0.0250	4	BK	GI	81	5	1	2	4	3	7	5	10	0.03	0.035	0.63	11.42954	91	1.00	1.00	1.06
26	21	6	121,000	80,000	0.0750	5	BK	GI	137	5	1	2	4	3	4	5	0	0.00	0.110	0.66	11.70355	137	1.00	1.00	1.06
27	21	2	93,000	66,000	0.0500	4	BK	GI	106	5	1	3	4	3	6	5	0	0.00	0.023	0.71	11.44035	106	1.00	1.00	1.06
28	22	10	160,000	88,000	0.0957	5	BK	GI	190	3	3	2	4	3	7	5	0	0.00	0.060	0.55	11.98293	190	1.00	1.00	1.06
29	22	2	113,500	65,000	0.0613	4	STUC	GI	116	3	2	3	3	3	5	5	0	0.00	0.050	0.57	11.63956	116	1.05	1.00	1.06
30	23	9	127,000	65,000	0.0800	5	WB	GI	152	4	3	3	4	3	6	5	0	0.00	0.075	0.51	11.75194	152	1.05	0.90	1.06
31	23	5	165,000	102,500	0.1219	5	BK	TI	183	3	4	3	3	3	6	5	0	0.00	0.063	0.62	12.01370	183	1.15	1.00	1.06
32	24	6	92,500	56,000	0.0526	4	C	GI	112	5	1	3	2	3	4	5	0	0.00	0.089	0.61	11.43496	112	1.00	0.85	1.06

Appendix 10.1(contd)
Sale schedule for 1850-1930 houses - New Town

CASE	LOC	DATE	PRICE	CV	SIZE	NOR	WALL	R	B AREA	S	V	A	C	Q	C	ST	EFF OA	PERO A	PERO I	A RATIO	LPRICE	EFF AREA	LOC ADJ	WALL ADJ	ST ADJ
33	24	6	112,000	82,500	0.0750	5	BK	GI	124	5	1	3	4	3	6	5	0	0.00	0.090	0.74	11.62625	124	0.95	1.00	1.06
34	24	9	110,000	85,000	0.0472	4	STUC	GI	95	3	1	2	4	3	6	5	0	0.00	0.088	0.77	11.60824	95	0.95	0.90	1.06
35	24	10	120,000	77,500	0.0423	6	WB	IT	152	3	1	1	4	3	6	5	0	0.00	0.084	0.65	11.69525	152	1.00	0.90	1.06
36	24	8	132,500	115,000	0.0733	7	BK	GI	211	4	1	3	2	3	5	5	0	0.00	0.056	0.87	11.79434	211	0.95	1.00	1.06
37	24	6	87,000	65,000	0.0508	4	WB	GI	139	3	1	2	2	2	5	5	0	0.00	0.090	0.75	11.37366	139	0.90	0.90	1.06
38	24	9	89,950	70,000	0.0559	4	BK	GI	100	5	1	3	3	3	5	5	0	0.00	0.078	0.78	11.40701	100	1.00	1.00	1.06
39	25	3	105,000	85,000	0.0547	4	BKV	IT	131	5	1	3	4	3	6	5	0	0.00	0.123	0.81	11.56172	131	0.90	1.00	1.06
40	25	7	144,500	90,000	0.0691	5	BK	GI	150	5	1	3	5	4	7	5	0	0.00	0.080	0.62	11.88103	150	0.90	1.00	1.06
41	25	6	83,000	65,000	0.0309	4	BK	GI	101	5	1	2	3	3	5	5	0	0.00	0.046	0.78	11.32660	101	0.90	1.00	1.06

11 The valuation of residential property using regression analysis

R. Almy, J. Horbas, M. Cusack and R. Gloudemans

Introduction

In 1991, property taxes provided U.S. state and local governments with $168 billion in revenue. Most ($162 billion) goes to local governments, and property taxes constitute 75% of local governments' total tax revenue and 30% of their total general revenue. Comparable statistics for Arizona are 79 and 28% and for Illinois, 78 and 38%. (It might be noted that some Illinois school districts receive more than 90% of their revenue from local property taxes.)

The national government plays a negligible role in property tax administration, allowing each state government to design its own property tax system. Most states delegate primary responsibility for property tax administration to local governments. There are about 13,500 local assessment jurisdictions responsible for compiling property registers and for valuing taxable properties. There are more than 100 million parcels of real property in the U.S. Some assessment jurisdictions have fewer than 100 parcels. The largest, Los Angeles County, California, has more than two million. Cook County, Illinois, has more than 1.5 million parcels of real property (more than one million are residential) and is considered the second largest assessment jurisdiction in the U.S. There are 2.1 million parcels of real property in Arizona, of which 1.2 million are residential.

The California State Board of Equalization first used multiple regression analysis (MRA) operationally in property tax administration to value single-family houses in about 1968, although its usefulness in property valuation was recognized in 1919. The State of Arizona and Cook County, Illinois, were among the earliest jurisdictions outside California to use the technique.

In Arizona, county governments are primarily responsible for property assessment. They are supervised and assisted by a state government agency, the

Arizona Department of Revenue. As part of its assistance role, the Department began in the early 1970s to develop regression models for residential property for Arizona's fifteen county assessors.

Cook County, Illinois began to use regression analysis in 1976 as part of a program to reform assessment practices.

State of the art in residential CAMA systems

Overview

Of the two broad orientations to valuation, single-property valuation and mass valuation, mass valuation has perhaps made the greatest advancements toward a true science in the last two decades. For the first five decades of the twentieth century, the state of the art in mass valuation was a manual application of the cost approach using a cost manual. Two connected developments in the 1960s made the development of mass valuation science possible: computers became accessible to academics and governments and statistical packages containing multiple regression analysis became available. Beginning in the 1970s, the International Association of Assessing Officers (IAAO) set out to consolidate the body of knowledge contained in dozens of journal articles and conference papers, first in Improving Real Property Assessment: A Reference Manual in 1978, and second in 1990 with the publication of Property Appraisal and Assessment Administration. These works articulated a formal statement of the mass valuation process and the steps in developing mass valuation models.

Today's CAMA system includes a flexible database management system, a market model module (usually using MRA), a comparable sales selection module, an income capitalization module, a cost module, and a sales ratio analysis module. The system may be an integrated package or a collection of individual program modules, possibly including generic database, spreadsheet, and statistics packages. By developing market, income, and cost models, an assessor's office can generate multiple estimates of a property's value, test them, and evaluate overall valuation performance, in conformity with contemporary professional standards.

Contemporary mass valuation emphasizes cost-effectiveness and quality assurance. Valuation quality assurance measures include ratio studies before and after the revaluation exercise, tests of valuation models, and extensive reviews of individual value estimates. Modern CAMA systems help these processes.

CAMA systems nowadays can provide crisp graphic images of perimeter sketches. They may be linked to a geographic information system (GIS), which helps spatial analyses important in market area identification, land valuation, and in estimating building obsolescence. They may incorporate an imaging system containing digital pictures of properties, which eliminates the need for some field inspections. Some assessors use hand-held computers in the field in data collection to eliminate the need to fill out a paper data collection form and to permit on-the-spot data edits, thereby eliminating the need for follow-up field inspections.

Accurate property data are valuable to more than assessors. They provide incentives for local government agencies to develop integrated computer systems and to share the costs of implementing new technology for data maintenance and analysis, such as computerized mapping and GIS systems. If data access laws allow it, governments can recover part of these investments by selling data products to the private sector.

As CAMA systems evolve with developments in information technology, certain environmental conditions seem constant: changing property values, changing legislation, and fiscal constraints. Meanwhile, performance expectations continue to rise.

Market analysis and stratification

Preliminary steps in mass valuation involve stratification (classifying properties according to characteristics that identify a submarket) and analysis. Model builders evaluate the completeness and accuracy of the data on the properties that will be used in model calibration. It is also helpful to profile the properties that will be valued, discover market relationships, and identify the types of properties for which the model will be valid. CAMA systems should provide these analytical capabilities.

Time trends should be analysed. When price levels change significantly, the effects of those changes on sales prices must be analysed, and sales should be adjusted to the price level on the valuation date to avoid imparting a bias in the models. There are four accepted methods for analysing the effects of time: paired sales analysis, resales analysis, sales ratio trend analysis, and multiple regression analysis. Of these, sales ratio trend analysis and regression analysis are most amenable to automation, and the CAMA system should help these analyses. Separate analyses by property type and area should be made, because market trends can vary substantially.

Similarly, the CAMA system should help analysis of location attributes at the levels of market areas, neighbourhoods, and sites. The traditional approach to location in CAMA modelling, which is used in both Arizona and Cook County, is to have valuers delineate discrete geographic areas (market areas and neighbourhoods). A separate model is developed for each area. Subareas (such as neighbourhoods or small pockets of properties) are treated as separate variables in the model. Such variables can be binary in form, or they can be linearized to form a location desirability index.

The fixed neighbourhood approach has substantial advantages. Separate models capture differences in market forces among areas, which are often substantial. Further, because they are more geographically specific, models can be simpler. When Arizona began market area models in the early 1980s, performance immediately improved even though the models were greatly simplified (Gloudemans, 1981). Each area can be reviewed through ratio studies and other quality control methods and needed refinements readily identified.

The fixed neighbourhood approach also carries disadvantages. More models may have to be developed. Neighbourhood boundaries must be maintained. Neighbourhood codes must be created and updated as new areas are developed and boundaries shift. Multiple models also reduce sample sizes, which makes model calibration more difficult. Finally, there is the possibility of inconsistency in values among areas, which is most noticeable along the borders. The latter problem can be reduced by choosing boundaries that correspond to natural or manmade barriers such as rivers, railroad tracks, and major streets.

A more recent strategy for making location analyses is 'global response surface analysis' (GRSA). It involves the development of a single model for an entire jurisdiction with adjustments made for distance from various 'value influence centres' or VICs (German, 1982; O'Connor and Eichenbaum, 1988). The method begins with a single model without location variables. Sales ratios comparing predicted values with sales prices are computed and displayed as a contour map of the model area. Areas that are under-appraised will have low ratios and areas that are over-appraised will have high ratios. Next, VICs are located on the map at points near pockets of low and high ratios. VICs can be either points or lines associated with premiums or decrements for location, such as the city centre, premium residential areas, shopping centres, or slums. For each parcel, distances from each VIC must be computed. These distances (or some mathematical transformation of them) are then used as variables in a second regression model. Sales ratios are again computed, additional VICs identified, new distance variables computed, and the model rerun. The process continues until all significant location influences have been accounted for, as indicated by an absence of pockets of low or high sales ratios.

GRSA requires that parcels be geographically referenced, which can be an expensive and time-consuming front-end project. Preferably the geographic coordinates of at least one point in the parcel would be known, although GRSA has been successfully used with resolutions no finer than the block level. This is necessary to automate the calculation of distance variables. The global model must be capable of incorporating all major value influences in the jurisdiction and, thus, may be complex. Explaining the model may also be difficult, as property owners may more readily identify with neighbourhoods. Lucas County (Toledo), Ohio, and New York City currently use the technique.

Cluster analysis has been advocated as a technique for grouping properties based on data similarities, including location attributes and socioeconomic data. The objective is to minimize differences within strata and maximize differences among strata. The method received much attention in the early days of CAMA (Stenehjem, 1974) but has grown out of favour. A purported advantage was that it did not rely on the subjective judgments of valuers to define area boundaries. It ensures consistency in the valuation of properties having the same identified features. The method has substantial deficiencies. First, values can be inconsistent for adjacent parcels. At the extreme, two adjacent parcels can be appraised with different models because one building is bigger or otherwise different from the other, causing them to be assigned to different clusters. Second, the approach poses administrative difficulties, as the models should be updated simultaneously to help ensure consistency. Quality control is difficult, particularly between areas. The method works best when the market responds more to physical than to location differences.

Cluster analysis can also be used to combine previously defined areas that are too small for modelling purposes. For example, in Jefferson County, Colorado (suburban Denver), the method was used to combine adjacent sections into market areas for modelling purposes. Variables included average sale price, average size, average age, and the number of miles east/west and north/south of a common reference point. A similar approach has been used to combine smaller counties in Colorado for commercial modelling (Gloudemans, 1991).

CAMA systems also should help ratio studies, which compare valuations (either existing valuations or proposed valuations) with independent indicators of market value, usually sales prices. They are the primary tools by which assessors can evaluate where assessment performance is good and where it can be improved. Although ratio studies must be customized, there is general professional agreement on how the data used in ratio studies should be processed, what statistics should be computed, and what are appropriate performance goals (IAAO, 1990).

Valuation

Objectives of CAMA models include predictability, explainability, and stability. Predictability refers to the accuracy of the model in predicting values. In MRA, it is measured by such goodness-of-fit statistics as R^2 and the standard error of estimate. Explainability refers to the ease of explaining and defending the model. Simple models that conform to appraisal theory are easier to explain. Models that have many variables, complex statistical transformations, or unintuitive coefficients are difficult to explain, both to appraisers and to the public. *Stability* refers to the consistency of models and resulting values over time. Although models must reflect changes in price levels, the form of the models should be similar and coefficients should not fluctuate widely. Again, simple models are likely to give more stability than complex ones.

Mass appraisal models can take one of three fundamental forms: additive, multiplicative, and hybrid. In an 'additive' model, the effects of each variable are assumed to be independent and therefore can be added. The variables, however, can be nonlinear or interactive, for example, the square root of land area, or quality rating multiplied by square feet of living area. Additive models can be readily calibrated using multiple regression analysis and, if the variables do not involve complex transformations, can be easy to explain. On the other hand, additive models fail to recognize interactive relationships between variables and can be inadequate in complex markets. Also, additive models cannot be readily decomposed into land and building values, largely because of problems in apportioning the constant. Most jurisdictions currently use additive models, particularly for residential properties, due to the ease of explaining them to taxpayers.

In a multiplicative model, variables are either raised to powers or, in the case of binary variables, they serve as powers. The results are multiplied together rather than added. Multiplicative models are calibrated by regressing the logarithm of the dependent variable (sale price) on the logarithm of the specified model. Except for binary variables, the independent variables become logarithms. Binary variables remain as such and serve as exponents in the model. Technically, calibration is simple, since ordinary least square MRA is used. Estimated property values are found by simply taking antilogarithms of the regression estimates. To be evaluated properly, however, the resulting model coefficients must be converted from their logarithmic format, which requires some mathematics. Multiplicative models are well suited to commercial and other properties where sales prices exhibit wide variation. In such cases, percentage adjustments work better than dollar adjustments. They also work well in large residential areas and eliminate the collinearity problems of simpler models.

Hybrid models, also known as 'generic' models, combine both additive and multiplicative features. The basic hybrid or generic model takes the format:

$$SP = \Pi GQ \times (\Pi LQ \times \Sigma LA + \Pi BQ \times \Sigma BA)$$

where ΠGQ = product of general qualitative features such as neighbourhood and time of sale adjustments, ΠLQ = product of land qualitative features such as street type and view, ΣLA = sum of land quantitative features such as lot size, ΠBQ = product of building qualitative features such as grade and percent good, and ΣBA = sum of building quantitative features such as main living area and basement area. The basic hybrid model can be readily decomposed into land and building values.

The basic hybrid model cannot be calibrated by least squares MRA because it is neither totally linear nor multiplicative in format. It can be calibrated by either adaptive estimation procedure or nonlinear MRA.

Finally, the most flexible model structure is a general hybrid model, which can take any format. This permits one to use additional additive terms, such as garages, swimming pools, and outbuildings. A simple example is:

$$SP = B_1{}^{NBHD1} \times B_2{}^{NBHD3} \times B_3{}^{NBHD4} \times [B_4 \times LOTSIZE + QUAL^{B5} \times COND^{B6}$$

$$\times (B_7 \times TLA + B_8 \times FINBSMT + B_9 \times UNFBSMT) + B_{10} \times$$

$$GARAGE + OBY]$$

where LOTSIZE = lot size (square feet), TLA = total living area, FINBSMT = finished basement area, UNFBSMT = unfinished basement area, GARAGE = garage stalls, OBY = cost value of outbuildings and yard improvements, and the other terms are as defined above. This model has land, building, garage, and outbuilding components, each of which is affected by neighbourhood. Given present technology, such a model can only be calibrated by nonlinear MRA or artificial intelligence.

As a general matter, there are currently three calibration tools available in mass appraisal: regression analysis, adaptive estimation procedure, and artificial intelligence. In addition, automated comparable sales provides a method of estimating values using comparable sales and coefficients derived from one of the above three methods.

Multiple regression analysis (MRA) has been the traditional market calibration workhorse. Ordinary least square regression will directly calibrate additive models, which are often used for residential property. This approach has the advantage of being widely understood and accepted. By definition, the technique finds that model that minimizes the sum of the squared errors and for which the average predicted value equals the average sale price. These are powerful features. The technique is also accompanied by powerful diagnostics, which permit one to evaluate 'goodness of fit' and the importance of individual candidate variables. Variables that fail to make a significant contribution to the explanation of sale price can be automatically excluded.

On the negative side, multiple regression requires that the model be additive in form. This can be a serious limitation when dealing with complex markets, particularly if there is wide variation in sales prices. As mentioned above, *loglinear MRA* can be used to calibrate completely multiplicative models, although goodness-of-fit statistics (such as R-square and the standard error of estimate) become difficult to interpret and additional mathematics are required.

All in all, loglinear regression is a good alternative when the market is multiplicative in nature and the modeller possesses the necessary mathematical expertise.

Nonlinear MRA presents a method for calibrating the generalized hybrid model. This is done through a trial-and-error process designed to minimize the sum of squared errors. Only some CAMA packages and general statistical packages (including SPSS and NCSS) include nonlinear MRA. Although it may appear a panacea, nonlinear MRA has serious limitations. First, because of its iterative nature, run times are much longer. Second, the diagnostics are not as complete or reliable as in linear MRA. Third and most important, the coefficients can be highly unstable (as indicated by their standard errors). In particular, the user cannot place minimum significance levels on the candidate variables, but rather must completely specify the desired variables beforehand. Also, the model is likely to give an unsatisfactory solution if terms in the model are highly collinear or if one attempts to 'over-calibrate the model'. For example, incorporating a component such as

$$B_1 \times SQFT^{B2}$$

is likely to produce unstable results. This suggests that nonlinear MRA should not serve as one's primary calibration technique. The method can, however, be used to find the solution to hybrid models after ordinary MRA has been used to research the appropriate variables.

Adaptive estimation procedure (AEP) or 'feedback' is a technique for calibrating the basic hybrid model:

$$SP = \Pi GQ \times (\Pi LQ \times \Sigma LA + \Pi BQ \times \Sigma BA).$$

Like nonlinear MRA, feedback operates on a trial-and-error basis, although it seeks to minimize the absolute rather than squared errors. Feedback, which incorporates technology used in missile guidance and engineering, was originally developed and marketed by professors Robert Carbone and Richard Longini and presented to the assessment community in the late 1970s (Carbone and Longini, 1976). There are at least two commercial providers of feedback modules (AEP, Inc., and Microsolve, Inc.).

All feedback programs operate on a trial-and-error basis (see Schreiber, 1985). Sales are sorted from least to most recent and read one at a time. Variables are categorized as general qualitative (GQ), land qualitative (LQ), land quantitative (LQ), building qualitative (BQ), and building additive (BA). An additional distinction is made between qualitative binary and linearized variables. As in nonlinear MRA, coefficients for qualitative variables are exponents of multipliers, while coefficients for additive variables are dollar amounts. As each sale is read, the software adjusts the coefficients so as to reduce the sum of absolute errors.

However, 'dampening' and 'smoothing' factors are employed to prevent the algorithm from 'unlearning' knowledge accumulated from previous sales. The sales file is read forward and backward successively until no further improvements can be made or until a specified number of passes is reached. The procedure stops with a forward pass through the file, so that the most current sales are processed last.

Feedback has obvious advantages. Most important, it provides a way of calibrating the basic hybrid model and yields separate land and building values. Also, by working to reduce the sum of absolute rather than squared errors, it is less influenced by outliers than MRA. On the negative side, feedback does not employ a standard algorithm and will not find 'the optimum' solution. The final model depends on the algorithm itself, which is proprietary and typically only partially documented, on the chosen dampening and smoothing factors, and on other parameter settings. Hence, if pressed, one may find it difficult to explain or defend the process. Like nonlinear MRA, feedback does not have variable screening capabilities, so that the final variables must be determined beforehand. Feedback also lacks the repertoire of diagnostics available with MRA. In particular, there are no statistics related to variable significance (partial t- or F-values). Users should also be aware that feedback per se is a standalone technique. The CAMA system must have other modules to edit the data, perform transformations, and port a file to feedback for analysis. The user may not be able to modify the input file in feedback and, in order to test a new model structure, would thus have to exit feedback to create a new input file (see Ward and Steiner (1988) for an empirical comparison of MRA and feedback.)

Artificial intelligence (AI) can also be used in mass appraisal model calibration. One existing system is REX (Regression EXpert), which features an interactive graphical statistical package that provides statistics, graphics, and recommendations to help guide the user to a final model (Gale, 1986). In addition, exploratory work has been done on AI-based CAMA systems requiring no or little user intervention.

Borst presented one approach, termed artificial neural networks, at the 1991 annual IAAO Technical Seminar in Montreal (Borst, 1991). Basically, the modeller defines the input neurons (predictor variables), output neuron (sale price), hidden neurons (passes through the sales file), and training tolerance (acceptable percent error). The software (Borst used Brainmaker) develops coefficients that maximize the number of facts (sales) that meet the required training tolerance. After each pass through the file, the results are 'back propagated' and the coefficients refined so as to increase the success rate. The iterative nature of the technique and necessity of prespecifying the predictors is reminiscent of feedback. The technique can capture nonlinear relations and fit various model structures, including the generic structure. Borst reports that in tests the technique produced results superior to MRA or feedback.

The methods described above can help calibrate all three approaches to value. In mass appraisal, the sales comparison approach generally takes the form,

$$ESP = f(X_1, X_2, ..., X_n)$$

where ESP = estimated sale price and $(X_1 ... X_n)$ are property characteristics. Depending on the form of the model, one or more of the methods described above can be used to calibrate the model. Success will depend, of course, on the adequacy of sales, data reliability, and ability of the model to capture market interactions. To achieve adequate sales and help ensure stability, several years of sales can be used. Sales ratio statistics should be computed to test the consistency of the models and values should be field reviewed, with emphasis placed on management by exception.

In addition, the traditional sales comparison can be automated and market calibrated. The approach takes the form:

$$ESP = SP_c + \Sigma (ADJ_1 ... ADJ_n)$$

where SP_c = sale price of comparable property and $\Sigma(ADJ_1 ... ADJ_n)$ = sum of adjustments made for the various property characteristics postulated to affect value. The adjustments can be based on the coefficients calibrated by MRA or an alternative technique. Hence, using a distance metric the system can be programmed to select, say, the five most comparable sales for each subject property and apply appropriate adjustments for differences in physical features. One can then compute ESP as, say, the median or mean of the adjusted comparables. The CLT and Sigma systems employ versions of this approach. Of course, such systems can also be programmed in-house or with generic software.

This approach, known as automated comparable sales analysis, has the advantage that the estimate of value is rooted in actual comparables, as in the traditional sales comparison approach. The approach also tends to negate any price-related biases that may be inherent in the underlying model, since ESP is computed primarily by reference to parcels in the same price range. On the negative side, because ESPs begin with different comparables, values will be less consistent from parcel to parcel. Such systems also involve comparatively long processing times, since the sales file must be successively searched for each subject parcel.

The income approach involves the estimating of market rents, vacancy and expense ratios, income multipliers (which can be also viewed as a market approach application), and overall rates. Mass appraisal model can be used to help calibrate each.

Market rents can be estimated as a function of property characteristics:

$$\text{Market Rent} = f(X_1, X_2, ..., X_n)$$

where $X_1 ... X_n$ are variables relating to property characteristics. Market rents should be expressed on a per-unit basis, for example, rent per apartment unit or rent per square foot of gross leasable area. Important independent variables include size, effective age or condition, and economic area or neighbourhood. Market rents used in the analysis can be gathered by questionnaire, through field interviews, or during the appeals process. The models can be effectively calculated by additive regression. Expense ratios can be calculated similarly:

$$\text{Expense Ratio} = f(X_1, X_2, ..., X_n)$$

Again, important independent variables include size, condition, and location, as well as property type. If the model is formulated so that the variables are calculated with respect to standard or typical features, the constant in the model can be interpreted as the typical expense ratio. Of course, development of expense ratios in this manner assumes adequate expense data, which are more difficult to collect and analyse than gross income data. Where adequate data are not available, industry norms can sometimes be used.

Once expense ratios have been estimated and used to compute net operating income (NOI), overall rate (OAR) models can be developed:

$$\text{OAR} = \text{NOI/SP} = f(X_1, X_2, ..., X_n)$$

The independent variables should include factors that help explain variations in overall rates, such as location, building condition, and (sometimes) land/building ratios. Again, if these variables are expressed about the average, the constant from the model will reflect the typical OAR.

Gross income multipliers (GIMs) often provide a practical and effective alternative to net income capitalization:

$$\text{GIM} = \text{SP/GI} = f(X_1, X_2, ..., X_n)$$

Theoretically, the model should include those variables important in estimating OARs, as well as those that relate to expense ratios, since GIM includes no expense allowance. From a practical viewpoint, however, the same variables, particularly location and condition, tend to be important on both counts, so that a GIM model may be no more complex than an OAR model. Gross income models, of course, do not require the collection and analysis of expense data. On the other hand, appeal boards may prefer net income capitalization, at least for some property types.

The cost approach involves three essential steps: land valuation, estimation of replacement cost new (RCN), and estimation of depreciation. Cost tables are used to estimate RCN, although the tables can be converted to equation form for quicker processing and updating (Ireland and Adams, 1991). Market calibration of depreciation schedules is essential to success of the cost approach.

Derivation of market-based depreciation schedules begins with the calculation of improvement residuals (sale price less land value), which are divided by RCN to yield percent good. Percent good is then plotted against age or effective age:

$$\% \text{ Good} = (SP - LV)/RCN = f\,(age)$$

From the plot, one can visually construct a smoothed percent good table. Or, if one prefers, depreciation tables can be derived in a similar manner by plotting the complement of percent good against age or effective age:

$$\% \text{ Depreciation} = 1 - (SP - LV)/RCN = f\,(age)$$

Loglinear MRA can also be used to calibrate the relationship:

$$\% \text{ Depreciation} = B_0 \times AGE^{B1}$$

$$\log\,(\% \text{ Depreciation}) = \log\,(B_0 \times AGE^{B1})$$

The formula captures nonlinear relationships between depreciation and age (the farther the exponent is from 1.00, the more nonlinear the relationship).

Values generated by the cost approach should be market calibrated before finalization. The simplest method is simply to compute sales ratios and divide the target appraisal level by the actual level to obtain trend factors:

$$\text{target ratio/actual ratio} = \text{trend factor.}$$

This can be improved by calibrating the following model to get separate land and building trend factors:

$$SP = B_1 \times LV + B_2 \times RCNLD$$

where RCNLD = RCN less depreciation (the constant is constrained to zero). For example, coefficients for B_1 and B_2 of 1.23 and 0.95, respectively, would suggest that land values should be increased by 23 % and building values decreased by 5 % to achieve full market value. Further refinements on this basic model also are possible.

Considerations by property type

The following discusses specific modelling considerations that apply to various types of residential property.

Single family residences Because of the availability of sales and relative homogeneity, single family residences generally lend themselves well to modelling, particularly in larger jurisdictions. Some analysts prefer a global approach, although models based on geographic area stratification are most common. Usually, simple additive MRA (or feedback) will suffice. If prices vary widely, however, multiplicative MRA may improve results.

Experience has shown that 80 to 85 % of explainable variation in sales prices is usually accounted for by four characteristics: living area, construction grade, effective age, and neighbourhood. Items of secondary importance include garages, basements, swimming pools (depending on the climate), fireplaces, heating/cooling, lot size, and situs (view, street type, etc.). Items of marginal importance, which may provide some additional improvement, are baths, porches, building style, exterior wall type, roof type, topography, and utilities. In addition, several other items may be important is specific areas, such as golf course frontage, ocean view, or renovation.

Single family residential models can be kept simple and explainable with little if any loss in predictive accuracy.

Condominiums and cooperatives Condominium and cooperative units are generally best appraised by the sales comparison approach because of their relative homogeneity and the difficulty in determining land and common area values in the cost approach. Condominiums and cooperatives also lend themselves well to modelling. If modelled on a global basis or by market area, binary variables should be included for each complex or group of similar complexes (except, of course, for the reference complex). Such variables will capture the 'essence' of each complex, including location, common area facilities, construction grade, and condition. In fact, few additional variables are needed, the most obvious being unit size and golf or water frontage.

An alternative approach is to develop a 'mini model' for each large complex or group of similar, smaller complexes (Gloudemans, 1983). Very few variables will be required in each model. Sometimes, unit size may be all that is needed:

$$SP = B_0 + B_1 \times SQFT \text{ or } SP = B_0 \times SQFT^{B1}$$

Few if any other variables are required because they would not vary among units in the complex. Accordingly, few sales are required (in some cases as few as ten sales over a two- to three-year period may suffice). Moreover, where sales are lacking, appraisers can 'smooth out' models by reference to nearby or comparable complexes.

Besides unit size and golf/water frontage, other variables that can be important in condominium models are story, end unit (binary variable), condition, garages and patios, and interior amenities. During sales analysis, care should be taken to subtract any significant personal property value from the sale price of furnished units.

Multi-family residential Models for multi-family residential properties can take several forms (Fruitman and Gloudemans, 1989; and Shenkel, 1974). First, market values can be estimated directly, as for single family residences, although the dependent variable should usually be expressed on a per-unit basis:

$$SP/UNIT = f \text{ (property characteristics)}.$$

Property characteristics often important in such models include location, average unit size, average baths per unit, construction grade, age and condition, parking, common area facilities, and land size or land/building ratio. If adequate sales are available, the modeller can stratify by number of units and/or geographic area. Alternatively, variables relating to the number of units can be included. Subsidized properties should be excluded, modelled separately, or characterized through a binary variable. Usually a simple additive model will suffice.

Second, a gross income approach can be used. Such a model will have two parts: one to estimate market rents and one to estimate GIMs. Once developed, GIMs can be applied against either estimated rents or actual rents, if the latter are available and appear reasonable. In any case, one must be careful to use consistently either potential gross rents (100% occupancy) or effective gross incomes (after vacancy and collection loss allowances) throughout the analysis. Gross rent multipliers for multi-family residences are well accepted by most appraisers and are used by many large jurisdictions.

Finally, models can be constructed to estimate and capitalize net income. Of course, this requires the collection and analyses of expense data, which can be difficult. Fortunately, multi-family properties can usually be adequately modelled through one of the two approaches above, thus avoiding the need to collect and model expense information.

Communicating the results

The values produced by a valuation model and desirably the model itself must be presented to the public. The manner in which this is done affects the acceptance and supportability of a revaluation, as well as overall perceptions of the assessor's office. The ability to show clearly how values were calculated will help resolve complaints and lend credibility to a reappraisal. Taxpayers are entitled to know, at least in a general sense, how their values are calculated. Clear explanations are one measure of good public service.

Ease of explaining a mass appraisal model begins with the structure of the model itself. Sales-based models with many variables and exotic transformation are difficult or impossible to communicate and, for technical reasons (i.e., multicollinearity), may have seemingly irrational coefficients. By contrast, simple models are easier to explain and more likely to have stable, reasonable coefficients.

Similar considerations apply to cost and income models. Sound model structures will be more readily understood and accepted by professional appraisers and taxpayer representatives, and more easily defended before appeal boards.

Despite simplification, most taxpayers find multiple regression and other mass appraisal equations inherently difficult to understand. The base home approach which is more fully described in the section on the Arizonza system, converts valuation models into a table format that can be used to show specific properties were valued in an easy-to-understand manner.

Update strategies

As mentioned, besides accuracy and explainability, an objective of CAMA modelling is stability. In jurisdictions where reappraisals are infrequent, stability is of minimal concern. However, if revaluations are frequent, taxpayers question large value changes that cannot be explained by market conditions. Several techniques to help ensure stability are available.

First, model specification should be the same or similar over time. This is particularly important if properties are reappraised annually or biennially since changes in model structures can cause unnecessary value shifts. Of course, sometimes models must be changed of necessity. Previous models may have been poorly specified or overly complex. The market itself may have changed, so that new variables are required. Or better information, for example, geographic coordinates or improved neighbourhood boundaries, may have become available. In such cases, models should be respecified and improved. However, barring such circumstances, modellers should strive to keep model specifications similar.

Second, if properties are appraised annually or biennially, use of three or more years of sales can lend stability. In this way, some of the sales used to calibrate the previous model will be used in the new model. Of course, time adjustments should be applied as required.

Third, constrained regression (Thompson and Gordon, 1987) can be used to minimize coefficient changes. In particular, coefficients for variables of marginal importance, such as patios and detached structures, may differ widely. Constraining these variables to reasonable ranges can improve model stability with minimal loss in model accuracy. The CLT and Sigma mass appraisal systems both feature constrained regression. Feedback and nonlinear MRA also permit such constraints. (The same effect can be achieved in statistical packages by adjusting the dependent variable and rerunning the model.) Stability in feedback and nonlinear MRA may also be enhanced by beginning the starting coefficients with their ending values from the previous revaluation.

Fourth, linearized values can be obtained from global or regional models. The preferred method of deriving values or weights for linearized variables is through binary variables. However, this approach may produce inconsistencies and instability, particularly where few observations are available, say for a given roof type. Stability can be improved by combining modelling areas for purposes of deriving such weights before beginning work on individual models. Although requiring added front-end work, this will be more than offset by reduced time in the development of individual models. Further, once these weights are determined, they can be expected to remain relatively stable over time, so that small changes every, say, five or six years, may be sufficient.

Fifth, specific modelling techniques can be used to incorporate previous model results. The most prominent technique of this type is Bayesian regression (Jensen, 1987). Bayesian regression is a way of giving partial weight to a previous and new correlation matrix, so that the resulting model will reflect both the old and new data without incorporating the old sales. Proper use of the technique requires advanced mathematics and statistical software.

The system in Arizona

Background

Arizona was one of the first sites to implement an MRA-based appraisal system. In the early 1970s the Arizona Department of Revenue contracted with a CAMA vendor to develop a statewide CAMA system using MRA. At the time, there were fourteen counties in Arizona (now fifteen). The two major counties, Maricopa (Phoenix) and Pima (Tucson) had computer centres servicing the assessor's office. The rest were connected by terminal to the Department of Revenue's system. Thus, the CAMA system was implemented at three sites: Maricopa, Pima, and the Department of Revenue.

The regression system was implemented in 1973 for all fourteen counties in essentially the same format. There were twenty-five hard-coded regression variables based on fourteen property characteristics. Many of the variables were complex interactive terms. There was one model per county. Location adjustments were based on 'neighbourhoods' which the software constructed by combining contiguous assessor's map numbers similar in terms of predefined property characteristics until at least 30 sales were obtained. Appraisers completed data entry forms which told the software which maps were contiguous. The neighbourhood adjustment process was only fully implemented in Maricopa County.

The system succeeded in improving assessment ratio statistics. Appraisal levels were consistent between counties and CODs improved. However, the system was complex and unexplainable. Users could not fine-tune or modify it. This, along with the resulting increased values, made it unpopular. Seven of the fourteen counties abandoned the system and returned to the cost approach; the other counties valued atypical or problem properties on the cost system.

Problems came to a head when the Sedona Taxpayers Association protested the system to the state legislature. Sedona is a wealthy retirement community lying partly in Coconino County and partly in Yavapai County about 100 miles north of Phoenix. Thus, one model was used on one side of the county line and another on the other side. The Sedona Taxpayers Association pointed to nonsensical terms and results in both models and inconsistencies between the models. They and others succeed in convincing the legislature that the system was not fair or understandable.

In 1977, the Arizona legislature responded by hiring the IAAO Research and Technical Services Department to review the system, along with the organization and procedures of the Property Tax Division, and make recommendations for improvement. The IAAO recommended major changes, including redesign of the CAMA system and establishment of an assessment standards section in the Property Tax Division in charge of appraisal procedures and modelling. The legislature welcomed the recommendations and appropriated the required funding. The Department of Revenue created and filled the new positions and developed a detailed plan for implementation of the IAAO recommendations.

Base home concept

An early task of the implementation plan called for replacement of the MRA system with a simpler system. This system, initially implemented in 1980, came to be known as the 'base home approach' (BHA). Except in Maricopa County (which continued the previous system in modified form), the previous MRA system was replaced with a simpler system with fewer variables and less complex terms developed using the Statistical Package for the Social Sciences (SPSS). Once developed, the models were converted to the base home format. This was accomplished as follows:

1   Identify the typical or base home in each county by construction class. Since there are seven classes (LM through R6), this implied seven base homes for each county. The base home for each quality class was based on the typical square footage, year-built, heating and cooling, garage stalls, and so forth for homes of that class. Appendix 11.1 shows the original base homes in Coconino County (Flagstaff) for the 1980 tax year.

273

2   Determine the base home value. This was done by simply applying the MRA models to each of the seven base homes in the county (second line from bottom in Appendix 11.1).

3   Determine adjustments for variations from the base home. This involved analysing the model and determining how much to add or subtract for differences from the base home. As a simple example, if the model showed a coefficient of $3,250 per garage stall, and the base home had a two-car garage, then $3,250 would be subtracted for homes with a one-car garage. These adjustments were expressed in an adjustment table and entered into computer screens. Appendix 11.2 shows the computer-generated report of the base home adjustment table corresponding to the base homes in Appendix 11.1. The value for a subject property was computed by selecting the appropriate base home value and applying the required adjustments.

Although the simplified system had little impact upon assessment ratio statistics, its understandability was immediately popular among assessors, appraisers, and taxpayers alike (most notably the Sedona Taxpayers Association). Users could examine the base home tables for reasonableness and consistency, and make needed modifications. Taxpayers could replicate the calculations and satisfy themselves that values were fair and consistent.

Technically, the BHA approach represents no more than a repackaging of the regression model. However, the approach appears to have significant advantages. For one, the regression constant is 'folded' into the base home value and need not be separately explained. The base home value, representing the typical value, provides a more stable and intuitive starting or reference point than the regression constant. Second, the repackaging permits users and taxpayers to visualize how each characteristic used in modelling impacts value. Where property characteristics are used more that once or as part of interactive terms, the repackaging shows the net impact of the characteristic upon value. This permits appraisers to catch and correct questionable results before valuation. Also, interested taxpayers can step through the calculations and satisfy themselves of their reasonability without having to wade through the regression equation itself.

Evolution of system

As mentioned, a major deficiency of the Arizona system was the lack of predefined market areas and neighbourhoods. The use of only one model per county tended to overvalue less desirable areas and undervalue more desirable areas. While implementing the initial base home system in 1980, the Department of Revenue and counties embarked on an ambitious program of defining market areas and subareas throughout the state (except Maricopa County which continued to use the neighbourhood formation process described above). 'Market areas' consisted of large geographic areas similar in terms of major location factors and value trends. The number of such areas ranges from two in several smaller counties to sixteen in Pima County (Tucson). Subareas are groups of similar, usually contiguous subdivisions or small towns. There are typically four to eight subareas per market area.

By 1981 market areas had been defined and separate regression models were developed for each. Accordingly, the BHA was modified to define one base home per market area rather than per construction grade.

In 1982, subareas were completed and used in regression modelling. In each market area, one subarea was identified as most typical (the base sub-area), so that base home tables showed upward adjustments for premium areas and negative adjustments for less desirable areas.

The introduction of market and subareas led to substantial improvements in uniformity measures such as the coefficient of dispersion (COD). It also gave the BHA a geographic orientation, further increasing its effectiveness and appeal.

At the same time, the technique was extended to condominiums and town homes with excellent results (CODs averaged less than 10.0). In this case, one base home was defined for each subarea (complex or group of similar complexes). The base home value expressed the typical value for the subarea and the adjustments table showed adjustments for relevant characteristics used in modelling, mostly size, land values (used to reflect golf course frontage and the like), and 'add items' value (balconies, etc.).

Current system

The MRA and base home systems in Arizona today are much as they were in 1982. Models continue to be updated annually and follow a simple, consistent format. Approximately three years of time-adjusted sales are used in modelling. This and consistency in model specification tends to produce highly stable models that change only with value trends. In fact, changes in base home value from year to year provide a good gauge of price trends. Sometimes, when the market has been highly stable in an area, the base home value in adjusted as necessary instead of remodelling. Both mainframe and PC versions of SPSS are now used in modelling. Of course, market and subareas are continually being refined to account for growth and market shifts.

A continuing problem has been a dearth of location or site-related data. Before the development of market areas and subareas, models included only improvement characteristics. This was because the data base essentially had no land data (lot size was provided for but usually not captured). Shortly after completion of market and subareas, the system was modified to include 'situs adjustments'. These adjustments are computed as the difference between the land value of a subject parcel and the average land value of the subarea. For example, if the average land value of a subarea is $16,000 and an individual parcel has a land value of $25,000 (perhaps because it is larger or has a premium view), the situs adjustment for the parcel is $9,000. The situs adjustment is applied as the final step in the BHA. In effect, it provides a way of capturing location adjustments within subareas. Appendix 11.3 shows a contemporary market model value calculation sheet (note the situs adjustment in section VII).

Aside from the introduction of situs adjustments, primary changes in the system have related to the automation of the process for converting regression equations to the base home format. This is accomplished by a spreadsheet program. The modeller enters the base home characteristics (these normally do not change from year to year) and the regression coefficients. The program then computes the base home value and adjustment table, which are used to update the mainframe tables (this too could be potentially automated). Since model specifications are consistent, changes to the conversion program are rare.

Simplified MRA models and the BHA approach have served Arizona well. The residential mass appraisal system, once the centre of controversy, now performs quietly and effectively year after year, receiving little attention and requiring relatively few resources. CODs are generally excellent (average of about 10.0) and values are stable and explainable. Although no comparative statistics are available, the system undoubtedly is highly cost-effective. Since the reforms of the early 1980s, several counties have returned to the MRA-based system and others have extended it to more areas and a wider range of properties (about 95 % of all single-family residential and condominium parcels in the state are currently valued with MRA).

Of course, additional improvements are easily envisioned. From a modelling viewpoint, additional land variables could improve predictability (potentially replacing situs adjustments). In this regard, the Department has recently introduced a PC land valuation program that stands to enhance the capture and evaluation of land data. Valuation reports showing value calculations for a subject parcel, which now must be manually completed (Appendix 11.3), could be automated.

The system in Cook County, Illinois

Background

The Cook County Assessor's Office (CCAO) decided to computerize the valuation of residential properties in 1970 as part of a concerted effort to update its assessment practices. The office's goals were to produce more accurate valuations, provide greater taxpayer assistance, make better use of automation, and increase professionalism. In 1972, a decision was made to change the system used in the valuation of residential properties with six or fewer dwelling units from one based on construction cost data to one based on actual sales data. Based on its successful use in California, MRA was selected as the calibration method used to develop residential valuation models. The current assessor, Thomas C. Hynes, who was elected in 1978, has remained dedicated to the goal of making continuous improvements in assessment practices, and he has successfully introduced both legislative and procedural improvements.

The legislative framework for property tax administration in Cook County differs from the rest of the state. Outside Cook County, properties are to be revalued *en masse* at four-year intervals. However, Cook County has had authority since 1959 to revalue a portion of its properties every year. This allows the assessor's office to use its staff more efficiently. Initially, the county was divided into four reassessment districts known as 'quadrants', one of which was revalued each year on a cyclical basis so that all property was reassessed once every four years.

In 1992, the assessor sought legal authority to reduce the number of reassessment districts from four to three. The objectives were to make the overall level of valuation in the county more uniform and improve tax equalization. This was accomplished in two stages. First the reassessment districts were realigned to minimize the number of instances in which a taxing district straddled the boundaries of reassessment districts. Under the original quadrennial reassessment district scheme, parts of forty-one taxing districts in Cook County were in two or more reassessment districts. The City of Chicago, a city of three million situated on the western shore of Lake Michigan, was in all four. The second realignment put the City of Chicago in one district. There are now two suburban districts. The office's ultimate goal is to reduce the number of districts to two, but current fiscal constraints preclude the hiring of sufficient staff to meet this goal.

Reducing the number of reassessment districts from four to three implied a 33 % increase in the annual appraisal work load from 375,000 parcels to 500,000. Fiscal constraints prevented a commensurate increase in funding additional staff. Staff and budget constraints necessitated an increased use of automation and a change in modelling strategy.

Evolution of the system

The 1972 decision to use MRA entailed developments in several areas. Software had to be acquired and installed. Staff had to be trained in new procedures. There was a need to upgrade the property characteristics data base.

Initially, regression software developed by the California State Board of Equalization was used. In addition to its regression capabilities, it had a database module and the capability to produce scatter plots, a useful diagnostic tool. It was a mainframe, batch, and keypunch card oriented system. As was typical of assessment systems in that era, the Cook County Management Information Systems Department provided computing support (programming, data entry, and job control). In 1979, an enhanced version of the California software was installed. Two members of the staff were trained in using the software.

In 1972, the residential property characteristics data base was suitable only for the existing cost approach, which was developed in the 1940s and refined in the 1950s. It contained little about what makes properties desirable or undesirable in the marketplace. Only key characteristics were computerized. (Old characteristics retained in the new regression system included a classification code, land area, building area, and building age.) In addition to individual property characteristics, it was necessary for the office to delineate residential neighbourhoods, a task that initially was performed by consultants. More than 400 neighbourhoods were identified. Initially a model was developed for each neighbourhood. With the realignment of reassessment districts in the 1980s, the office abandoned the practice of modelling each neighbourhood and began to develop township-wide models, reducing the total number of models to thirty-eight. (Essentially for traditional legal and administrative reasons, townships constitute separate revaluation projects.) Sometimes the office identifies sub-neighbourhood areas.

Typically, neighbourhood effects are captured by creating a linear desirability index based on average sales prices. Although they can be criticized on theoretical grounds, the neighbourhood linearized variables have proven to be statistically powerful, and they sometimes are used in transformations with other variables, for example, square feet of living area or building class. Neighbourhood variables also are important to taxpayers in Cook County. 'Neighbourhood' is an important social concept. The City of Chicago has been described as a 'city of neighbourhoods', and this neighbourhood identification has been carried throughout Cook County as the children of city dwellers have spread to suburban areas. Other techniques of location identification, such as value influence centres (VICs), would not be appealing to homeowners, who strongly identify with neighbourhood delineations.

Only two site variables currently are available: lot size and site desirability (coded as 'above average', 'average,' or 'below average'). Additional site variables have been successfully tested for future use.

A county wide field canvass to collect the needed data on more than 800,000 residential properties was ruled out in 1972 because of funding and staff constraints. The office decided to use a taxpayer questionnaire to acquire the necessary data. This strategy would allow the office to collect information on numbers of rooms and other interior features quickly and inexpensively. (To this day, the office refers to its residential property descriptor form as 'the Q.') The questionnaires were mailed to all residential property owners in 1973. A follow-up questionnaire was mailed to 400,000 non-respondents in 1975. Although the eventual response was satisfactory, some data problems emerged. The number of non-responses and questionable responses was greater than the office could check in the field. A stopgap solution was a 'default' program which filled missing data fields with values typical for the specific building type in each neighbourhood. Predictably, this cost-effective solution had the disadvantage of creating some data errors which confounded regression analysis and contributed to assessment regressivity. Of course, some keypunch errors went undetected and uncorrected as a result of inadequate computerized edit routines.

The first revaluation in Cook County using MRA took place in 1976. By 1979, all small residential properties had been revalued using regression analysis. Despite the data problems, the accuracy of valuations was much improved. Some of the improvements were not popular. Neighbourhood influences were better reflected in the new values. The old cost system undervalued older properties, a problem which the use of regression corrected. Consequently, owners of older properties in good neighbourhoods received dramatically higher assessments.

For one four-year reassessment cycle, assessment notices contained a list of salient property characteristics and an invitation to inform the assessor's office if any were in error. Unfortunately, the volume of changes swamped the data entry division of the county MIS department, and some corrections were never made. In order to improve service and accountability, the assessor's office sought permission to acquire its own computers, develop some of its systems, and assume responsibility for data entry. Steady progress has been made in these areas. Since 1989, the assessor's office has done all of its data entry and substantially improved the accuracy of property record updates.

The assessor's office has employed other cost-effective strategies to deal with the historical problem of data accuracy. CCAO model builders have worked for ten to fifteen years with the database and can recognize data inaccuracies in each of the thirty-eight townships. They create variables to overcome the inaccuracies and do not use unreliable characteristics in model specification. The office makes more than 100,000 field inspections each year. Consequently, the database has been incrementally improved since 1978.

The refinement of the database and strong historically rooted township regression models have stabilized Cook County's mass appraisal process. In the last ten years, Cook County has achieved industry-accepted measures of valuation uniformity (coefficients of dispersion) in a highly diversified market.

Modellers now can develop MRA models on PCS using SPSS for Windows. The office has an ongoing research program to test new computer technology and modelling techniques, such as improvements in cluster analysis and other diagnostic tools. In 1996, the office plans expand the 'global' model concept from township models to multi-township models.

Other CAMA advancements are prevalent throughout the CCAO. The residential appeals department uses an automated sales comparison approach in analysing appeals. Condominium and cooperative valuation now is performed on PCS. These systems are refined versions of applications originally on the minicomputer.

Although the desirability of a county-wide field survey to ensure that every property is described completely and accurately is recognized, the county has never been able to justify the expenditure of approximately $30 million to make the survey. However, building perimeter sketches are not computerized in the current system, necessitating the maintenance of paper property records. Given the number of parcels involved and the number of people (including taxpayers) who might want to see a record, property record storage and retrieval are an ongoing source of frustration.

Goals

The current computer systems largely have been developed in-house by the County's Management Information Systems Department and by the Office's systems department. Program maintenance and system integration are difficult. In recognition of the limitations of patchwork systems, the CCAO has undertaken several initiatives to increase its use of modern technology. The first was to commission a paper entitled 'The State of the Art in Computer Systems for Large Urban Assessment Jurisdictions' by Almy, Gloudemans & Jacobs. In 1993 the office commissioned an automation feasibility study by Cole-Layer-Trumble Company (CLT), a large mass valuation and CAMA system contractor. The study was to outline strategies for updating the property inventory update, further automating the office including systems to value commercial and industrial properties and incorporating geographic information systems, and identifying ways to generate revenues to help pay for some of the investments in data collection and technology.

In conjunction with the CLT study, the CCAO has conducted a pilot study of the use of pen-based computers and digital cameras in data collection. As part of this study, new property characteristics were collected and tested. Included in the test were a simplified set of residential property type codes, simplified building descriptive variables, and additional site variables, such as street type and street desirability. Pen-based computers have been improved significantly since the pilot project began, and the CCAO would like to make a transition to electronic data collection in the next six years.

Another problem has been explanation of MRA-based values to taxpayers. Because of the limited data and an emphasis on predictive accuracy, models usually contain many transformations and can appear complex. Some variable coefficients may appear unreasonable. The County has experimented with the Base Home Approach as an explanatory tool. A prototype 'generic' base home approach has been developed using the spreadsheet program, Quattro Pro for Windows. The program prompts the modeller to enter the regression equation and base home for each model area (township). This would be done after the model is completed. To generate a value by the base home approach, a clerk or appraiser enters the characteristics of the subject property and hits a function key. The program then generates a valuation report in the base home format.

The program is 'generic' in that regression models need not be in a standard format as in Arizona. Instead, any model can be entered regardless of the number and form of data transformations and interactive terms. The program determines the contribution of each characteristic on value by initializing all characteristics to the base home and then incrementally changing them to match those of the subject property. As each characteristic is changed, the estimated value is recomputed and stored. The difference in values at each step represents the contribution of that characteristic to the total property value. Currently, the County is in the process of converting the spreadsheet program to a program that will run on its minicomputer so that base home reports can be generated by entering only the property's identification number.

Use of the base home approach does not solve a problem that occurs when taxpayers appeal their assessments on the basis of an error in a minor characteristic, such as a garage type. Taxpayers feel they are automatically entitled to an assessment decrease. A decrease may not be warranted, particularly when the coefficient assigned to the variable during the modelling process does not truly reflect the contribution of the characteristic to property value. A policy of automatically making such adjustments may damage the overall uniformity of value estimates. Although use of the base home approach will make it possible to explain the calculation of value estimates, it may lead to problems in explaining the contribution of individual characteristics to a property's value.

A new system is being developed to value new buildings and alterations to existing dwellings. The CCAO will experiment with artificial intelligence (AI) systems in coming years. Since CCAO's current model builders have many years of modelling experience, the initial intuitive step of choosing the correct variables in the AI software may not be that helpful. Because AI systems replicate the intuitive processes of experienced modellers, future less experienced modellers may find AI easier than MRA, but may not acquire a thorough understanding of how CAMA valuation modelling.

The CCAO has just completed a seven-year automation plan. It is a cost-effective response to the CLT study. The backbone of the automation plan is a county-wide geographic information system (GIS) and an integrated database. Under the plan, not only would data be captured electronically in the field but also all paper-driven office procedures would be automated.

References

Almy, R. R., Gloudemans, R. J., Denne, R. C. and Miller, S. W. (1978), *Real Property Assessment: A Reference Manual*, Chicago, International Association of Assessing Officers.

Bernard, J. C. and Jensen, D. L. (1992), '*Automatic Cost Calibration: Case Studies*,' paper Presented at the 58th Annual IAAO Conference, St. Louis, Missouri.

Borst, R. A. (1991), 'Artificial Neural Networks: The Next Modeling/ Calibration Technology for the Assessment Community,' *Property Tax Journal*, March.

Carbone, R. and Longini, R. (1976), 'Reform of Property Tax Administration for Achieving Intrajurisdictional Equity,' *Assessor's Journal*, vol. 11.

Chizewsky, A. F. (1988), '*Simplifying the Base Home Approach*,' paper presented at the Third World Congress on Computer Assisted Valuation sponsored by the Lincoln Institute of Land Policy, Cambridge, Massachusetts.

Eckert, J. K., Gloudemans, R. J. and Almy, R. R. (eds), (1990), *Property Appraisal and Assessment Administration*, Chicago, International Association of Assessing Officers.

Fruitman, C. M. and Gloudemans, R. J. (1989), 'A Feasibility Study of CAMA for Apartment and Commercial Property,' *Property Tax Journal*, March.

Gale, W. A. (1986), 'REX Review,' *Artificial Intelligence and Statistics*, New York, Addison Wesley.

German, J. C. (1982), '*How a MRA Model Can Contain More Than Fifty Terms Successfully and Provide Consistent Decomposition of Value*,' paper presented at the First World Congress on Computer Assisted Appraisal sponsored by the Lincoln Institute of Land Policy, Cambridge, Massachusetts.

Gloudemans, R. J. (1981), 'Simplifying MRA-Based Appraisal Models: The Base Home Approach.' *Assessor's Journal*, December.

Gloudemans, R. J. (1982), '*Simplified Sales-Based Models for Condominium/ Townhouse Valuation*,' paper presented at the First World Congress on Computer Assisted Valuation sponsored by the Lincoln Institute of Land Policy, Cambridge, Massachusetts.

Gloudemans, R. J. (1985), 'Base Home Methodology,' in Woolery, A. and Shea, S. (eds), *Introduction to Computer Assisted Valuation*, Lincoln Institute of Land Policy.

Gloudemans, R. J. (1991), 'Modeling Commercial Properties Under Various Economic Conditions,' *Property Tax Journal*, March.

International Association of Assessing Officers, Assessment Standards Committee, (1990), *Standard on Ratio Studies*, Chicago, International Association of Assessing Officers.

Ireland, M. W. and Adams, L. (1991), 'Transportability of a General-Purpose Residential Market-Calibrated Cost Model,' *Property Tax Journal*, June.

Jensen, D. L. (1987), 'The application of Bayesian Regression for a Valuation Model Update in Computer Assisted Mass Appraisal,' *Property Tax Journal*, December.

Jensen, D. L., (1990), 'Artificial Intelligence in Computer Assisted Mass Appraisal,' *Property Tax Journal*, March.

O'Conner, P. M. and Eichenbaum, J. (1988), 'Location Value Response Surfaces: The Geometry of Advanced Mass Appraisal,' *Property Tax Journal*, September.

Schreiber, J. (1985), 'A Feedback Primer,' *Introduction to Computer Assisted Valuation*, Cambridge, Massachusetts, Lincoln Institute of Land Policy.

Shenkel, W. M. (1974), 'The Valuation of Income property by Multiple Regression Techniques,' *The Application of Multiple Regression Analysis in Assessment Administration*, Chicago, International Association of Assessing Officers.

Stenehjem, E. J. (1974), 'Statistical Stratification of Residential Properties: Theory and Methodology,' *The Application of Multiple Regression Analysis in Assessment Administration*, Chicago, International Association of Assessing Officers.

Thompson, J. F. and Gordon, J. F. (1987), 'Constrained Regression Modeling and the Multiple Regression Analysis-Comparable Sales Approach,' *Property Tax Journal*, December.

Ward, R. D. and Steiner, L. C. (1988), 'A Comparison of Feedback and Multiple Linear Regression Analysis in Computer-Assisted Mass Appraisal,' *Property Tax Journal*. March.

Appendix 11.1
Base Homes: Coconino County (1980)

	Construction Grade						
	Lm	R1	R2	R3	R4	R5	R6
SQFT	800	800	900	1,300	1,600	1,900	3,100
GRADE	Poor	Poor	Poor	Ave	Good	Good	Good
HEATING	None	None	Grav	FA	FA	FA	FA
COOLING	None	None	None	None	None	None	Refrig
CONDITION	Poor	Poor	Ave	Ave	Good	Good	Good
PATIO	None	None	Slab-1	Cov-1	Cov-1	Both-2	Cov-2
GARAGE	None	None	None	Gar-1	Gar-2	Gar-2	Gar-2
AGE	44	32	30	16	12	10	10
BHV	13,585	16,140	20,340	34,465	50,590	65,330	120,945
BHV/SQFT	16.98	20.18	22.60	26.51	31.62	34.38	39.01

Appendix 11.2
Base Home Adjustment Tables: Coconino County (1980)

QUAL	LM	R1	R2	R3	R4	R5	R6
BHV	13,585	16,140	20,340	34,465	50,590	65,33	

Size Adjustments (Per Square Foot)

BASE	800	800	900	1,300	1,600	1,900	3,100
ADJ.	3.58	5.05	7.72	12.42	18.25	22.68	31.64

Quality Adjustment (per Square Foot)

GRADE							
POOR	Base	Base	Base	-0.96	-2.50	-3.22	-4.54
AVE	0.36	0.50	0.67	Base	-1.25	-1.61	-2.27
GOOD	0.72	1.00	1.34	0.96	Base	Base	Base
HEATING							
FA	1.45	1.45	0.58	Base	Base	Base	Base
GRAV	0.87	0.87	Base	-0.58	-0.58	-0.58	-0.58
NONE	Base	Base	-0.87	-1.45	-1.45	-1.45	-1.45
COOLING							
REFRIG	1.45	1.45	1.45	1.45	1.45	1.45	Base
EVAP	1.45	1.45	1.45	1.45	1.45	1.45	0
WALL	0.36	0.36	0.36	0.36	0.36	0.36	-1.09
NONE	Base	Base	Base	Base	Base	Base	-1.45
CONDITION							
POOR	Base	Base	-1.10	-1.10	-2.20	-2.20	-2.20
AVE	1.10	1.10	Base	Base	-1.10	-1.10	-1.10
GOOD	2.20	2.20	1.10	1.10	Base	Base	Base

QUAL	LM	R1	R2	R3	R4	R5	R6

Lump Sum Adjustments

PATIO

NONE	Base	Base	-1060	-1770	-1770	-2390	-3010
SLAB-1	1060	1060	Base	- 710	- 710	-1330	-1950
SLAB-2	1770	1770	710	0	0	- 620	-1240
COV-1	1770	1770	710	Base	Base	- 620	-1240
COV-2	3010	3010	1950	1240	1240	620	Base
BOTH-2	2390	2390	1330	620	620	Base	- 620
BOTH-3	3365	3365	2305	1595	1595	975	335

GARAGE

NONE	Base	Base	Base	-2610	-5220	-5220	-5220
CPT-1	1305	1305	1305	-1305	-3915	-3915	-3915
CPT-2	2610	2610	2610	0	-2610	-2610	-2610
CPT-3	3915	3915	3915	1305	-1305	-1305	-1305
GAR-1	2610	2610	2610	Base	-2610	-2610	-2610
GAR-2	5220	5220	5220	2610	Base	Base	Base
GAR-3	7830	7830	7830	5220	2610	2610	2610

AGE: ± 115 per year. Base ages are:

44	32	30	16	12	10	10

Appendix 11.3
Market Model Value Calculation Sheet

I. MARKET AREA: _____ SUBAREA: _____ BASE HOME VALUE: _____

II. <u>SIZE ADJ</u>:   <u>Subject</u> <u>Base</u> <u>Difference</u> <u>Adj Factor</u>

           _____ - _____ = _____ x _____ = _____

III. <u>QUALITY (PER SQUARE FOOT) ADJUSTMENTS</u>:

<u>Component</u>	<u>Subject</u>	<u>Base</u>	<u>Adj. Factor</u>	<u>SQFT</u>
1. Class/Grade	_____	_____	_____	
2. Heating	_____	_____	_____	
3. Cooling	_____	_____	_____	

                        = _____ x _____ = _____

IV. <u>LUMP SUM ADJUSTMENTS</u>:

<u>Component</u>	<u>Subject</u>	<u>Base</u>	<u>Adj. Amount</u>
1. Patios	_____	_____	_____
2. Gar/Cpt.	_____	_____	_____
3. Pool	_____	_____	_____
Total Adj.			= _____

V. <u>PHYSICAL DEPRECIATION ADJUSTMENT</u>:

<u>Actual Age</u>		<u>Phy. Cond. Factor</u> *		<u>Effective Age</u>
_____	x	_____	=	_____

<u>Eff. Age</u>	Depr. Adj. <u>(per SQFT)</u>	<u>SQFT</u>	Accrued <u>Phy. Depr.</u>	Base Phy. <u>Deprec.</u>
_____ x	_____ x	_____ =	_____ +	_____ =
_____				

* GOOD = .70, AVERAGE = 1.00, POOR = 1.30

VI.   <u>SUBAREA (NEIGHBOURHOOD) ADJUSTMENT</u>:   = _____

VII. <u>SITUS ADJUSTMENT</u>:   Ave. Subarea
                         <u>Land Value</u>   <u>Land Value</u>

                        _____   - _____   =_____

VIII. <u>OTHER ADJUSTMENTS</u> _____   =_____

IX.   <u>TOTAL VALUE</u> :   =_____

                                               _____

12 Mass appraisal of condominiums

W. Riley

Introduction

One of the most widely used taxes in the United States is the property tax. It is the backbone of the local government revenue system and in only three instances has it been used by the national government. In most other counties, the property tax is also a small percentage of national revenue and a large percentage of local government revenue. In the broadest sense the general property tax is a tax based on wealth that possesses exchange value. Therefore, the tax is levied on the value of property (ad valorem) at a common rate in the same jurisdiction. The assessor or person in charge of ad valorem property appraisal is responsible for the appraisal of property at current value. This assures that the property tax burden is distributed uniformly by all property owners.

This chapter deals with the valuation of residential condominium properties and the development and application of computer assisted mass appraisal (CAMA) systems which will speed and enhance the assessors job in of achieving uniform current value estimates. For detailed discussions of mass appraisal and CAMA fundamentals other sections of this book can be reviewed or one can consult *Property Appraisal and Assessment Administration* published by the International Association of Assessing Officers, Chicago, Illinois.

This chapter will address mass appraisal v. single property appraisal issues as they relate to condominium properties, discuss the history and concept of condominium ownership, laws governing development, the advantages and disadvantages of condominium ownership, and valuation considerations. It will orient one to unique issues specific to condominium mass appraisal. A brief look at the steps of mass appraisal will identify major functions; however, we will address key system components and development matters as they relate to condominium valuation. Database development and model specifications will be considered and comparable sales reports and listings will be addressed. Finally, system archival will be considered in regard to current computer technology. System development and implementation in Worcester County, Maryland as part of a statewide CAMA implementation will be used to demonstrate condominium valuation in a mass appraisal system.

Mass appraisal v. single property appraisal

Mass appraisal is used for developing ad valorem appraisals. Mass appraisal is the process of valuing a group of properties as of a given date, using standard methods, and allowing for statistical testing.[1] This is different from single property appraisal which is the valuation of one particular property as of a given date. Assessors need skills in both single property appraisal and mass appraisal. Both require extensive market research, but the principle differences are in the scale of work and quality control methods in mass appraisal. The scale of mass appraisal requires many people working on the project and requires synchronization of both tasks and appraisal judgments.[2] Mass appraisals are based upon valuation models and can be prepared with or without computer assistance. Often mass appraisals are developed by teams of people and can be thought of as a production line. Mass appraisal models emphasize the use of formulas, tables, and schedules in order to value all property uniformly.

Computer assisted mass appraisal (CAMA) is a technique used to conduct mass appraisal. The International Association of Assessing Officers defines CAMA as a system of appraising certain types of property that incorporates statistical analysis such as multiple regression analysis (MRA) and adaptive estimation procedures (AEP) to assist the appraiser in estimating value. In the United States, standard six of the Uniform Standards of Professional Appraisal Practice (USPAP) outlines accepted methods and techniques needed to produce a creditable mass appraisal. The standard identifies the use of MRA and AEP as accepted techniques. While it is desirable to have CAMA systems that incorporates MRA and AEP analysis, acceptable and easily explainable systems can be implemented that do not rely on MRA or AEP.

In computer assisted mass appraisal, a database is assembled that includes data for each real property parcel. CAMA allows improved statistical analysis and speeded mass appraisal modelling. In the 1960s, CAMA systems were implemented on mainframe computers and were not wide spread. With the advent of enhanced microcomputer hardware and disk storage capacity, CAMA systems became readily available for most local governments in the late 1980s.

Automated appraisal applications, proven in mass appraisal, are spreading to the single property appraisal field for the speed of data analysis or appraisal report generation. Nunnink (1994) in describing RealWorks Appraisal Software for single property appraisal indicates savings of 6-8 and 8-10 hours, respectively in professional and clerical staff time per appraisal.[3] Although, mass appraisal and single property appraisal are different in some methods and techniques, time savings can be accrued through automation in both single property appraisal and mass appraisal.

To many, computer assisted mass appraisal connotes only the use of multiple regression analysis and adaptive estimation procedures. CAMA systems are much more than the application of these two valuation methods. The production of a creditable market value appraisal that is easily supported and explained to property owners is the goal of the assessor. To this end, mass appraisal systems must use methods from both single property and mass appraisal. This requires that the computer assisted mass appraisal models apply the same principles as a single property appraisal. CAMA appraisal models should allow for a cost, sales comparison, and income approach to value.

CAMA models can be developed for various types of real property such as single family residential, condominium, apartment, office, retail, and commercial and industrial properties. This chapter deals with the valuation of condominium real estate through mass appraisal CAMA. Therefore, it is important to understand what a condominium is, its legal underpinnings, how they are established and managed, the history of this ownership concept, and the advantages and disadvantages of condominium ownership. This background is useful so that one might understand unique issues in condominium valuation.

Concept of condominium ownership

A type of real property ownership is the condominium. It is a fee ownership of whole units or separate portions of whole buildings.[4] The procedure for defining the ownership interest is established by law. The statute embodies the mechanics and procedures for filing the record of an undivided interest in real property where their is fee ownership of the unit in a multi-unit property and joint ownership of common areas.

It is preferable not to call this real estate entity 'a property' or 'the entire property' because their is no one unity of ownership but an aggregate of combined sole ownerships and co-ownerships. The aggregate of individual property interest values is typically different from the value the real estate would have if it were a whole or entire property.[5]

Condominium has become a frequently used term but is often misunderstood. The concept is a creation of law which divides the property horizontally, as well as, vertically.[6] This means each unit is separately defined as to the exact horizontal square footage it occupies from the floor to ceiling and from wall to wall. This area is privately owned by the owner who has independent and exclusive use of the area.

The second portion of the owner's interest is the common area. Common areas include land, walks, driveways, elevator corridors, open space, and recreational amenities. Recreational amenities may include swimming pools, tennis courts, and golf courses. This second ownership interest is a share or individual interest of the common area.[7] It is usually a percentage interest of the common area of the development. The owner, however, cannot lay claim to a specific portion of the common area but only the right to use the entire common area.

Condominium statues

Condominium properties or sections of condominium projects are referred to as 'regimes' or 'condominium regimes'. The enabling statues for the establishment of condominiums are generally called Horizontal Property Acts and set the procedures for the organization and management of the condominium.[8] These statues provide that each apartment or unit together with an undivided interest in common areas will constitute real property.

The declaration establishing and describing the condominium is filed in the land records where title to real estate is recorded. The condominium declaration includes a description of the land on which the buildings are located, a description of the building and improvements to land, a description of the common areas, a statement as to the value of each unit, a statement as to the permitted uses of each unit, the voting writes of owners in the condominium council of co-owners, the restrictions on the use of the unit and common area, and other details necessary for the effective organization of the condominium.[9]

Usually a floor plan of each building and all respective units is filed with the declaration. This is similar to a subdivision plat. The declaration also states the requirements for the conveyance and recording of title for individual units.

The Horizontal Property Act enabling the development of condominiums also allows a unit owner to mortgage a unit or subject the unit to a lien. The individual owner cannot subject the entire regime to a mortgage or lien. Specific authorizing acts allow the management council of co-owners to subject the project to a lien for repairs or improvements of the common areas. The owner of an individual unit may discharge a units indebtedness for repair of common elements by paying his units proportional share of debt.[10] The proportional share percentage is established in the condominium declaration and master deed. In most cases, taxes and assessments are charged to and collected from each individual unit owner, and if they are not paid would allow the individual unit to be sold at tax sale.[11]

The general guidelines for the management of the condominium are established in the Horizontal Property Act. This usually allows for the appointment of a manager, or a board of trustees elected by unit owners, or the formation of a non-profit corporation.[12] In general, the management of a condominium follows the general management concept of a corporation.

The details of the management plan for the condominium and common areas is conducted by the corporation. Monthly assessments are made to each unit to cover the costs of maintaining common areas and facilities, trash removal, street and parking lot maintenance. Provisions are made for the enforcement of these rules and other matters necessary for the efficient operation of the condominium association.

History

The word 'condominium' is derived from the Latin word meaning joint ownership. This with some other evidence supports that condominium ownership began under Roman law. Beginning in the 12th Century, German cities saw the ownership of floors of buildings or separate rooms as common practice. This later spread to France and Switzerland. The Napoleonic Code stipulated the rights of floor and apartment owners.[13]

Usually shortages of housing have precipitated condominium ownership. This occurred in Europe since the 1930s and Israel since the 1950s.[14] Large populations, shortages of land and the desire for permanent home ownership are economic factors encouraging condominium development. England has had condominium statutes since 1925 and most European Countries enacted enabling legislation in the 1930s. Latin America has numerous condominiums.

The concept of condominiums was recognized in the United States in the 19th Century, but the first condominium law was not adopted until 1947 in New York. In 1958, Puerto Rico adopted condominium laws. Following the National Housing Act of 1961 which authorized the Federal Housing Administration (FHA) to insure mortgages on individual units in multi-unit structures, there were many states that adopted enabling condominium statues.[15] The first states to enact Horizontal Property Acts pursuant to the enabling statutes were states where the costs of housing were high, populations were large, and where individual housing was limited. Illinois and New York were two of the first states enacting condominium statutes in 1963 and 1964 respectively. Maryland had enabling legislation in 1967 and Virginia in 1974.

These laws were amended from time-to-time in attempts to cure deficiencies in the original condominium legislation. Some of the amendments were for full disclosure of the condominium declarations, by laws, and operating budgets, detailed floor plans of offerings, and the approval of changes to the condominium declaration or bylaws by a specified percentage of votes of the owners. Typically 100% of the unit owners are needed to amend the master deed or declaration and 75% are needed to change bylaws.[16]

In the 1970s, the United States saw the expansion of condominium developments in second home markets which were mostly in recreational locations. This growth began in Florida and it spread to many beach, lake, and skiing resorts throughout the United States. Initially, developers held ownership of some common areas, leasing these areas to the condominium association. This was especially true where extensive recreational facilities were located. Because of high lease fees, this practice is uncommon today or is prohibited by law.

As condominium developments age, it is important to review the financial records of the condominium regime. One needs to ascertain the current condition of the regime maintenance, the maintenance plan, and associated current and future costs of maintenance as they affect condominium common area maintenance charges. Since the expenses can be quite costly they may impact the market value of individual units. This reflects the economic principle of substitution and principle of increasing and decreasing returns. A buyer purchasing a unit with the potential of excessive maintenance fees has the choice offering the asking price, offering a lower bid price because of the maintenance condition, or may choose to purchase a similar unit in another condominium with better deferred maintenance.

Advantages and disadvantages of condominium ownership

Condominium ownership has many of the same attributes as single property ownership while being achieved in a multi-dwelling structure. This is a major advantage of condominium ownership. An owner may obtain financing and insurance for the individual unit, receives an individual tax bill and pays an individual share of operating costs.[17] Deductibility of real estate taxes and mortgage interest from individual income taxes is also a major advantage of this ownership concept. Many owners prefer that the management of common areas and maintenance of the exterior is handled by the condominium management. Also, owners achieve equity buildup, and they do not have to pay rent. Generally acquisition costs are lower than other single property homes of similar size.[18] Other favourable factors include a better living environment and improved recreational facilities.

Disadvantages of condominium ownership include the close proximity of other dwelling units, noise, high monthly maintenance and management fees, dealing with a management company or council of co-owners, poor condominium association management, neighbours pets, noisy or undesirable children, parking difficulties, poor construction, renters in other units, dishonest sales people who sold units, and thin party walls. Despite these disadvantages in some condominiums, this form of ownership is important in the housing market. It is important for the appraiser to observe the project, research individual condominium sales with both grantor and grantee, if possible, and confer with condominium association management regarding the above issues. Verification of the condition of sold units and considerations made by the buyer and seller should occur.

Single property appraisal issues

The focus of this discussion is with the appraisal of individual condominium units in a mass appraisal environment. Considering issues of single property appraisal and data analysis for condominium properties is important before computer assisted mass appraisal techniques are addressed. CAMA systems must incorporate good appraisal methods and techniques of single property appraisal in order that the system can be easily understood by the public. This includes the ability to produce value estimates from the three approaches to value, most comparable property routines, and property valuation reports.

All three approaches to value (cost, sales comparison, income approach) should be considered in valuing a condominium project or an individual unit.[19] Thus, the CAMA system should provide the capability for these approaches. In valuing individual condominium units, appraisers generally use and rely upon the sales comparison approach. Recent sales of units of similar size, location, and quality are the best indicators of value and preferably recent sales of units in the same condominium project reflect the current condition, maintenance and impact of condominium association fees.[20] The comparative sales approach often is supported by the income approach if rentals of units similar to that being appraised exist. In this methodology gross rent multipliers are developed by comparing monthly rents to actual sale prices. The gross rent multiplier is derived by dividing monthly rent into sales price. In estimating value by this income approach, the appraiser estimates monthly rent for the subject unit and multiples it by the applicable gross rent multiplier producing a value estimate.

The cost approach is generally not used for individual condominium unit valuation. To use it would require that the cost both direct and indirect for the entire project would have to be estimated and then allocated to the unit being appraised. A total cost estimate is difficult to determine and the allocation to an individual unit may be somewhat subjective. Even with the difficulties cited, one should not overtly discard the cost approach in the mass appraisal process especially when market sales transactions are limited. The cost approach could provide a model that could assure uniform treatment of similar condominium units.

As stated previously, resales of similar units in a condominium or a similar condominium project are the best indicators of value. This is because differences exist in common area charges, design, recreational facilities, size, and quality. The appraiser should realize that comparative sales from projects that are not similar will be difficult to adjust. As with other residential subdivision property, prices of new units may be analyzed and used as comparables in the appraisal process. However, careful examination of resales prices should occur because they may be different than sales of new units.[21] In mortgage appraisals, lenders may require an analysis of an entire project in order to value an individual unit. Special attention should be paid to common area charges and the rate of change in these charges over time. Similar units in different condominium regimes may have different common area charges.

Many forms of residential condominiums exist. The most common are owner occupied individual units that can be found in highrise, midrise, quadruplex, and townhouse configurations. Condominium developments vary in form, price level, unit size, and design.[22] This provides a wide range of appeal to buyers. Most condominium owners desire living in a multi-family environment having the benefits of property management being provided by others and individual home ownership. Typically single property appraisal would require a description of all rooms and the interior finish and equipment present in the condominium. Data needed for analysis would include unit characteristics or attributes dealing with size, bedrooms, baths, heat and air conditioning, design, and location of the unit within the project. Additional items to be considered in data analysis are porches and patios, car storage, swimming pools, storage, common elements, recreational facilities, and monthly assessments.

When analyzing common area assessments, items for consideration are taxes for common areas, heating expenses, garbage disposal, elevator maintenance, water meters, and laundry facilities. Building maintenance items for common areas should be reviewed from a condition standpoint and the impact on future common area fees. Items to be considered are roof, basement, and mezzanine maintenance, entry lobby and furniture, a garage and garage attendants, doormen, management fees, hallway decoration, exterior paint and repairs including maintenance of brick exterior, yard maintenance, driveway maintenance, snow removal (cleaning and repair), pool and sun deck maintenance, janitorial expense, common area electricity, janitor living quarters, common area heating and insurance.

In mass appraisal applications, it is often easier to group similar condominium projects into groups with a unique identifier, to identify condominium projects by a unique numeric identifier and to establish unique model number for each model within the project. One method of accomplishing this is by the formation of a series of CAMA Set numbers for each group of similar condominium projects, and developing a series of CAMA Subset numbers for each condominium project. Finally, a series of model numbers for each model in the CAMA Set should be developed. This numbering and grouping system allows data analysis by similar condominium, and unique model within each specific project, while allowing for comparison of models in other projects.

Amenities should also be analyzed in that they impact value. In an individual unit, there should be general flexibility in room composition and size including desirable location for kitchen and bathroom facilities.[23] Generally, the unit should provide 'agreeableness and pleasantness'. There should not be functional deficiencies. As with all real estate, location is of great importance in a condominium. The neighbourhood must be desirable. Zoning laws must be enforced and building code and deed restrictions enforced. The appraiser should look at site coverage as it relates to the attractiveness and desirability of the living areas. Lot coverage of the condominium project must be kept to a minimum necessary for permanent protection of access to light, air, and view. Design is an important factor to consider. This includes the size and layout of rooms. Generally, larger rooms are found in condominiums as compared to rental apartment projects. There should be approximately 10% to 20% more space in a condominium and bathrooms should be larger than in a rental project.[24] Rooms should be designed to take advantage of the most desirable view. Terraces and porches are preferred amenities. Buildings with individual heating units are considered to be preferable to central building systems which have costs that are hard to control. It is preferred that utilities including water, gas and electricity be individually metered.

Functions of mass appraisal

The International Association of Assessing Officers identifies three basic functions of a mass appraisal system. These are reappraisal, data maintenance, and value updates. Reappraisal offers an opportunity to initiate a new appraisal system, or enhance an existing system. One will find that these systems will evolve over time from reappraisal to reappraisal. A manager's key goal is to have mass appraisal systems evolve over time instead of being reinvented. The following steps of a reappraisal and related major issues are listed below.

1   Performance Analysis - sales/value ratio study on existing values;
2   Reappraisal Decision - based on statute or performance analysis;

3	Analysis of Available Resources - staff, budget, data, computers;
4	Planning and Organizing - organization, production, critical event charts;
5	System Development - database, procedures, methods, software development;
6	Pilot Study - the pilot study tests the new system;
7	Data Collection - field review, data entry or transfer, quality control;
8	Value Production - analysis, model application, edits, quality control;
9	Final Performance Analysis - sale/proposed value ratio to evaluate work;
10	Assessment Roll - assessment notice production, assessment roll, appeals.[25]

It is assumed that the reader is familiar with real property appraisal methods, mass appraisal systems, and reappraisal programs. Should a detailed review of these issues be needed refer to *Property Appraisal and Assessment Administration* published by the International Association of Assessing Officers, Chicago, Illinois.

Valuation via CAMA

In computer assisted mass appraisal for ad valorem purposes, a cost approach, a modified cost approach or a market derived model is often used. Although this methodology may not be as sophisticated as other market oriented approaches such as multiple regression and adaptive estimation, they provide a standard basis for valuing similar properties. These approaches usually have tables for land valuation, replacement cost new, depreciation, or market rates and model identifiers. These approaches consider building quantitative data and quality data. Additionally, land is considered using land quantity information, as well as, land quality information. Finally, a total property quality or market adjustment may be made. These models allow for sale analysis listings showing land and building values for all properties that sold and allows for comparison of land and building values of non-sales properties with the sale of properties.

Condominium properties and townhouse properties are particularly well suited to a market comparison approach because of they are relatively homogeneous and have few characteristics that affect value.[26] Typically, a total property valuation approach would be used and a land value established through allocation.

Database development is one of the first steps in CAMA system development and model building. The database should have individual property characteristics quantified that would be needed to value a property. The database should include the individual units physical and quality characteristics. This may include the square footage of the unit, the number of bathrooms, the number of half-baths, the number of fireplaces, the number and size of porches, the floor level, the design of the unit including double frontage or view, corner or end unit, adverse location (near elevator shaft, noisy traffic area, trash dumpster area), heat type, air conditioning, quality of construction, and individual unit condition. Considerations for the entire project may be location to amenities, neighbourhood, individual condominium building or regime, general regime quality and condition, year built, parking, and amenities including boat slips, golf cart parking, and other recreational facilities.

Initial database development is key to a mass appraisal CAMA system. One should consider the quality of existing information, identify the factors or data elements previously quantified, and where possible develop categorical listings for each potential choice under each data element. The number of CAMA data files should be limited in any appraisal system. It is recommended that residential condominium properties be included in one large CAMA database file to control and minimize file maintenance processing. If all residential properties are in one CAMA file, it allows access and printing of residential records for administrative purposes. At the time of reappraisal subordinate files for valuation purposes can be created; however, these files should be kept to as few as possible for management reasons. By having a dwelling type factor, one can identify a condominium property from other individual residential parcels. The CAMA program allows differentiation of properties using a cost approach and others using a market model.

Residential CAMA database

One of the best ways to understand database development is to observe existing CAMA databases. Table 12.1 is a summary from a main file residential CAMA database used in a market calibrated residential cost approach to value system.

This database includes all residential, vacant land, condominium, and agricultural parcels. When residential condominium parcels are valued, the total property values are applied by model type with a percentage allocation of total property value for land value. This factor table and associated categorical levels allows the quantification of building characteristics for a residential cost approach. With slight modification the cost analysis program and individual factor itemization a limited number of factors could be identified for condominium attributes which are different from factors needed for the cost approach.

In this particular case, two property factors are needed for condominium valuation which are different from cost approach information. Factor 50 - number of bedrooms (condominium) v. number of family units (cost), Factor 51 - Floor level (condominium) v. number of dwellings (cost). All other factors in the

Table 12.1
Main residential file factor with condominium factors identified

No.	Name	No.	Name	No.	Name
1	Account No	56	Year Built	111	Market Value Index - MVI
2	Map	57	Effective Year Built	112	MVI OVERRIDE
3	Grids/Parcel	58	Model ID No	113	Total Dwelling Value
4	Plat/SEC/Block/Lot	59	Roof Cover	114	Total StRucture Value
5	Owner's Name	60	Dormer	115	OPEN
6	Situs Address	61	Dormer Linear Feet	116	Detached Garage #1 Type
7	Card Sequence No	62	Attic	117	Detached Garage #1 Size
8	Zoning	63	Attic Room - Square Feet	118	Detached Garage #1 Depr.
9	Use Code	64	Club Room - Square Feet	119	Detached Garage #2 Type
10	District	65	Heat Type	120	Detached Garage #2 Size
11	CAMA Set	66	Air Conditioning	121	Detached Garage #2 Depr.
12	MicroSolve No	67	Full Baths	122	ACCESSORY STRUCTURES
13	CAMA Subset	68	Half Baths	123	Lot Size
14	Last Update	69	Fireplace #1 Type	124	Land Units
15	Record Status	70	No of Fireplaces #1	125	Primary Land Adjustment
16	GEO Code	71	Fireplace #2 Type	126	Other Land Adjustment
17	Town Code	72	No of Fireplaces #2	127	Proposed Prefential Land
18	Prior Land Value	73	Porch #1 Type	128	Land OVERRIDE
19	Prior Improvement Value	74	Porch #1 Size	129	Land Status
20	Prior Total Value	75	Porch #2 Type	130	Land Type
21	Prior Curtilage	76	Porch #2 Size	131	Water & Sewer
22	Proposed Land Value	77	Porch #3 Type	132	OTHER LAND
23	Proposed Improvement Value	78	Porch #3 Size	133	Street Improvements
24	Proposed Total Value	79	Attached Garage Type	134	Topography
25	Proposed Curtilage	80	Attached Garage Size	135	Lot Location
26	Sale Date #1	81	OTHER CHARGES	136	Wooded
27	Sale Price #1	82	Sec. 1 Construction	137	Other Influence 1
28	Ground Rent	83	Sec. 1 No of Storeys	138	Other Influence 2
29	Transfer No	84	Sec. 1 Area	139	Lot Quality
30	# Parcels Conveyed	85	Sec. 2 Construction	140	Basement Adjusted
31	How Conveyed	86	Sec. 2 No of Storeys	141	Inspected by
32	Bad Sale Flag	87	Sec. 2 Area	142	Date Valued
33	Sale Date #2	88	Sec. 3 Construction	143	Valued by
34	Sale Price #2	89	Sec. 3 No of Storeys	144	Interviewed
35	Triennial Cycle	90	Sec. 3 Area	145	MRA Value
36	Remarks Flag	91	Sec. 4 Construction	146	Feedback Land
37	Future Use	92	Sec. 4 No of Storeys	147	Feedback Building
38	X Coordinate	93	Sec. 4 Area	148	Feedback Total
39	Y Coordinate	94	Sec. 5 Construction	149	Ratio No 1
40	Permit Type	95	Sec. 5 No of Storeys	150	Ratio No 2
41	Prior Appeal	96	Sec. 5 Area	151	Indicated MVI
42	Notice Date	97	Perimeter of Sec. 1	152	Notice No
43	Notified Land Value	98	Total Perimeter	153	Improvement Adjustment
44	Notified Improvements Value	99	Total Foundation Area	154	Factor C
45	Notified Curtilage	100	Total Enclosed Square Feet	155	Factor D
46	Preferential Land	101	Dwelling Base Value	156	Factor E
47	OPEN	102	Total - Other Charges	157	Factor F
48	OFFICE Use	103	Total - Base Value	158	Factor G
49	New Property Flag	104	Cost Index	159	Factor H
50	# of Family Units	105	Reproduction Cost New	160	Flag A
51	# of Dwellings/Floor Level	106	Physical Depreciation	161	Flag B
52	Dwelling Type	107	Physical Depreciation OVERRIDE	162	Flag C
53	Owner Occupancy	108	Functional Obsolescence	163	Flag D
54	Grade	109	Economic Obsolescence	164	Flag E
55	Condition	110	Depr. Reproduction Cost		

main file used in condominium valuation are used to describe the attributes of each unit and are the same as those needed for the cost approach. These are identified in Table 12.1 each factor number shaded. All data related to each of these factors must entered in the appropriate fields otherwise accurate data analysis cannot occur. The general CAMA model should allow the appraiser to group similar condominium projects into neighbourhoods, identify each individual project and model within the project. As previously stated a general grouping of homogenous projects might be identified as a CAMA Set and the individual condominium project might identified as a CAMA Subset. The limited number of factors needed to produce residential condominium values should be placed into each individual CAMA record.

Factors can be quantitative, categorical, and qualitative. Thus, quantitative data elements would be individually specified such as unit square footage, number of bedrooms, number of baths or half-baths, or floor level. Categorical factors such as dwelling type, or condition can be identified in only one factor for each with several possible types or conditions. Qualitative factors such as building quality or condition can also be identified in a categorical level factor. For later analysis, categorical levels should be linearized or equated to a numerical ranking. It is preferable that categorical listing and linearized values be in ascending or descending magnitude of value contribution.

Market analysis database

To enhance revaluation data analysis, a market analysis subordinate file can be created to be used in the sales comparison approach. This file can be created and data from the main file can be merged into the subordinate file. This file can be used for analysis of single family residential property, as well as, residential, commercial and industrial condominium properties. Table 12.2 is a summary of the market analysis database factor table for the subordinate file. One should review the factors listed to understand the data needed for valuation; because, this will be the primary file used in the remaining discussion.

This database does not consist of the detailed items need in a cost approach to value, but does contain raw data, model identifiers, binary data and data transformations which may be useful in market analysis applications. Raw data consists of quantitative data such a square feet, bedrooms, baths, and floor level. Model identifies consist of market value index or model numbers, office, retail, or warehouse model numbers. Binary data consists of a value of 0 or 1 in a data field to identify a unique characteristic for that property. A value of one (1) means the characteristic is present and a value of zero (0) indicates that the item is not present. Examples of binary variables in the subordinate market valuation

301

file are location matters such as ocean front, ocean front limited view, oceanfront side view, or amenity items such as indoor pool, security, slips, and golf. Data transformations are produced by transforming data existing in the database and storing it in factors in the database. Examples of data transformations are prior value, sale price or proposed value per square foot or per bedroom.

The sample valuation area

Maryland has a statewide assessment system for 1.9 million real property parcels in which all 24 counties are on one main frame computer and each county has a local area network (LAN) linked to the single mainframe. Each LAN has the same CAMA software and file structure. County CAMA files consist of from 14,000 to 265,000 parcels depending on the county. State law provides that all property be valued for assessment purposes once every three years. Thus, the properties are divided into triennial groups for valuation purposes.

The sample valuation area is a large ocean resort community generally identified as Ocean City, Maryland. This area is similar to other recreational communities throughout the United States in close proximity to waterfront or mountain resort facilities. This community is located on the Atlantic Ocean in Worcester County, Maryland which has approximately 52,000 total parcels of real property. The sample area is Triennial group 3 which has the majority of condominium parcels. Triennial Group 3 has 26,556 parcels of the total 52,000 parcels. These consist of 19,579 condominium units, 4,086 improved single family residential parcels, 1,651 vacant parcels, and 1,240 commercial and exempt parcels. Thus, 76% of the parcels being valued in Triennial Group 3 are condominiums.

The sample valuation area considered in this chapter deals with the 19,579 condominium units. Generally, these units are in condominium projects that are oceanfront highrise, midrise, and lowrise buildings. Another type of project is in close proximity to the ocean and considered to be in the ocean block (blocks) along the oceanside (east) of a heavily travelled highway. These units consist of lowrise and midrise masonry or frame condominium structures. On the west side of the Ocean Highway, there are typically lowrise condominium projects and townhouse condominium units. This area generally is referred to the as the bayside. There are canal front and bayfront condominium projects in this area which are typically townhouse or lowrise units.

The individual condominium projects were categorized into homogeneous groups or neighbourhoods for analysis prior to CAMA implementation. This practice continues and the neighbourhoods are called CAMA Sets. There are numeric codes which identify the condominium project or CAMA Subsets. Table

302

Table 12.2
Market data factor table

No.	Name	No.	Name	No.	Name
1	Account Number	42	Air Conditioning	83	Upper Interior
2	Map	43	Baths	84	Basement Interior
3	Grid/Parcel	44	Half-Baths	85	Basement End
4	Plat/Sec/Block/Lot	45	Fireplace	86	Outdoor Pool
5	Owner's Name	46	Porch Type	87	Indoor Pool
6	Situs Address	47	Car Storage	88	Security
7	Card Sequence No	48	Other Charges	89	Tennis
8	Zoning	49	Construction	90	Retail
9	Use Code	50	Storey	91	Club
10	District	51	Square Foot	92	Slip
11	CAMA Set	52	Other Charges	93	Ocean Front Location
12	MicroSolve No.	53	Functional Obsolesence	94	Boardwalk Location
13	CAMA Subset	54	Detached Garage	95	Ocean Front Limited View
14	Last Update	55	Accessory Structure	96	Ocean Front Side View
15	Record Status	56	Lot Size	97	Ocean Front No View
16	Town Code	57	Land Units	98	Ocean Block View
17	Prior Land Value	58	Land Overide	99	Ocean Block Limited View
18	Prior Improvement Value	59	Lot Location	100	Ocean Block No View
19	Prior Total Value	60	Lot Quality	101	Ocean Highway Ocean Block
20	Proposed Land Value	61	MRA Value	102	Ocean Highway Bay Block
21	Proposed Improvement Value	62	Feedback Land Value	103	Bay Side No View
22	Proposed Total Value	63	Feedback Improved Value	104	Bay Side View
23	Sale Date	64	Feedback Total Value	105	Bay Front
24	Sale Price	65	Ratio 1	106	Canal/Lagoon
25	How Conveyed	66	Ratio 2	107	Adverse Location
26	Bad Sale	67	Indicated MVI	108	Double Front
27	Remarks	68	Improvement Adjustment	109	North
28	Adjusted Sale Price	69	Office Model	110	South
29	X Coordinate	70	Office Square Feet	111	Location Factor
30	Y Coordinate	71	Office Rate	112	Design Factor
31	Notice Land Value	72	Warehouse Model	113	Condo Type
32	Notice Improvement Value	73	Warehouse Square Feet	114	Value Per Bedroom
33	Notice Curtilage	74	Warehouse Rate	115	Value Per Square Foot
34	Bedrooms	75	Retail Model	116	Sale Per Bedroom
35	Floor	76	Retail Square Feet	117	Sale Per Square Foot
36	Dwelling Type	77	Retail Rate	118	Prior Value Per Bedroom
37	Grade	78	Blocks to Beach	119	Prior Value Per Square Foot
38	Condition	79	Land %	120	Town House/End
39	Year Built	80	Lower End	121	Town House/Interior
40	Effective Year Built	81	Upper End		
41	Model No.	82	Lower Interior		

Table 12.3

Chart on CAMA sets, type of project, number of projects and units

CAMA Set	Type	Floors	Subsets	Models	Units
10.06	Townhouse	2/3			2,061
10.08	Ocean Front Highrise	>10	20	128	3,463
10.09	Ocean Front Midrise	5/10	56	163	2,555
10.10	Ocean Front Lowrise Masonry	1/4	40	82	598
10.11	Ocean Front Lowrise Frame	1/4	32	58	330
10.12	Ocean Block Lowrise Frame	1/4	132	201	2,250
10.13	Ocean Block Lowrise Masonry	1/4	120	227	1,146
10.14	Ocean Block Lowrise Frame	1/4	32	54	1,041
10.15	Ocean Block Midrise Masonry	5/10	10	11	367
10.16	Bay Front	1/5	49	116	1,258
10.17	Bay Side Canal/ Lagoon	1/5	55	132	1,585
10.19	Bay Side Inland 2	1/5	37	76	1,084
			660	1,451	19,579

12.3 identifies the CAMA Sets, the type of projects, the number of floors, the number of condominium projects within neighbourhood or CAMA Set, the total number of units and the number of unique models within the CAMA Set. Prior to automation through CAMA the following information would have required a tedious manual effort to compile. Through the database function of CAMA this only takes several minutes to produce.

It is important that one understands the organization and groupings of Neighbourhoods (CAMA Sets) and the use of Model Numbers for each style of condominium. Model numbers are assigned for each specific model in a project, but are numbered consecutively throughout the CAMA Set. Model numbers are assigned to units having similar unique characteristics within a condominium project. Model 1 might be a 1,122 square foot, 2 bedroom, 2 bath, ocean front unit. Model 3 might be a 1,440 square foot, 3 bedroom, 2 bath ocean front unit. In a CAMA Set model 1 and 2 may be in project or subset 100, model 3,4, and 5, may be in project or subset 101, and model 6 and 7 might be in project or subset 102. With this system, one can identify the project, or models within a project and can analyze sales by model type. If there is a distinct difference in sale price for a certain model that is different from a very similar unit in another project with a different model number, one can do further research to ascertain the reason for the difference. There may be a difference in condition of the units in one model or it may by a difference in condominium fees or maintenance as discuss earlier.

Previous manual mass appraisal system

The previous valuation system was manual. There were 19,579 individual property record cards which were posted with land and building values, individual unit models numbers and characteristics. A summary file folder was kept for each of 660 condominium projects which are now CAMA Subsets. These files contain model characteristics, model numbers, and previous model values. Typically, land values were computed as a standard percentage of total value. This is known as the allocation method.

Before CAMA mainframe computer sales listings would be produced in indexed order by condominium project. The assessor would manually post sales analysis listings for each project and compute data transformations, review the data per model, make field inspections, make final value estimates and post each individual record card with the land, building, and total value. Obviously, this manual effort was quite time consuming and there was little capability for automated data analysis, editing or statistical analysis.

The ratio study performance analysis that would be conducted prior to the valuation comparing current sales to prior value was conducted in the mainframe. It was produced overnight and a paper copy was printed on a remote printer in Worcester County. It is important that an administrator of a large multi-jurisdictional assessment jurisdiction understand that there are applications best suited for mainframe statistical analysis, and there are other applications that are best suited to CAMA analysis in the local area network. For example, the production of one statewide ratio report for 24 jurisdictions in the same format is best suited for the mainframe. Conversely, analysis of specific neighbourhoods, unique property analysis, graphics, or work requiring appraiser interaction with the system is best supported in a interactive CAMA environment based on a local area network (LAN).

Prior to implementation of CAMA in Worcester County, only a mainframe ratio report could be produced comparing current sales to prior value. Following the manual valuation and the data entry of new values to the mainframe, a performance analysis (ratio study) on the proposed values could then be conducted. Since this proposed value data did not reside on the mainframe and because this final performance analysis could not be produced until late in the year, it was difficult to conduct automated edits or statistical analysis that would improve the mass appraisal. Through the implementation of CAMA, these

305

problems have been eliminated and the valuation process has been speeded while allowing interactive analysis by the assessor. Other efficiencies include the illumination of paper records and the archival of all CAMA records on one compact disc.

Table 12.4 gives an example of the ratio study data that would have been produced from the mainframe for the condominium in the sample area just prior to the implementation of CAMA. The ratio studies were run in one comprehensive report for all sales from 1/1/92 to 1/1/93 which in the manual appraisal system would be the data that was the basis for the appraisal of properties having a notice date of 1/1/94. The main frame would also compare prior values to sales occurring during calendar 1994 for analysis of values as the valuations were being conduced. Finally, a mainframe ratio could be run on all sales or selected sales compared to proposed values. These ratio reports on proposed values could not be conducted in the mainframe until all values are uploaded. This system was good but was greatly enhanced by statistical and database capabilities of CAMA.

Table 12.4
Ratio study - condominium sales to prior value

Sale Period	CAMA Set	Total Sales	Value	Mean Ratio	Median Ratio	COD	Min Ratio	Max Ratio
1/92 -1/94	All	2,043	Prior	99%	99%	8.7%	61%	174%
1/92 -1/93	All	1,031	Prior	99%	98%	9.0%	66%	174%
1/93 -1/94	All	1,013	Prior	99%	99%	8.4%	61%	142%
7/93 -1/94	All	576	Prior	99%	99%	8.8%	61%	136%

These summary ratio statistics are for all condominiums. The report could be produced for all properties in the county, the triennial group, district, or property type such as condominiums. This program is hard coded in software that does not allow enhanced database capabilities or altering of statistical data requests without significant programming. Table 12.4 shows that the ratio statistics above on prior value were good. There was good uniformity shown by the coefficient of dispersion. However, the assessors wanted to lower the measures of central tendency (mean, median, weighted mean ratios) to under 100% and improve relative measures of dispersion. The sales listings provided from the mainframe in chronological order of sale date did not indicate inflation in property values from 1992 to 1994. Since most condominiums in this market are sold with furnishings which equate to about 5% of sale price, there was a tendency for the properties to by slightly overvalued when comparing current sales to prior values.

It was not until the mainframe was updated with the proposed new values that a ratio study could be produced on proposed value. This was the case in the manual mass appraisal system and continues to occur in the mainframe system when CAMA values are uploaded to the mainframe. The results of the proposed value mainframe ratio report are given in Table 12.5. Note that it is in the same format as the preceding report on prior value, but it cannot report ratio statistics on both prior and proposed value at the same time nor is it timely for assessor analysis. It is sufficient for statewide management control, but did not give tailored in-depth analysis at upper management levels.

Table 12.5
Ratio study - condominium sales to proposed value

Sale Period	CAMA Set	Total Sales	Value	Mean Ratio	Median Ratio	COD	Min Ratio	Max Ratio
1/92 -1/94	All	2,043	Proposed	96%	96%	6.2%	63%	191%
1/92 -1/93	All	1,031	Proposed	97%	96%	6.0%	63%	191%
1/93 -1/94	All	1,013	Proposed	96%	96%	6.3%	70%	158%

With the implementation of CAMA, added statistical analysis can be accomplished in a timely fashion both at the assessor level and at various management levels. An example of a jurisdiction wide and neighbourhood (CAMA Set) ratio study produced from a CAMA System on both prior and proposed values is presented in Table 12.6.

Note that one can compare prior and proposed value ratio statistics to judge the improvement of assessment levels by comparing measures of central tendency and comparing assessment uniformity by comparing the relative measures of uniformity such as coefficient of dispersion. It is also interesting to note that these reports can be prepared on demand in a matter of minutes.

Often jurisdictions do not move to automated CAMA systems for various reasons such as lack of funding, a champion for the cause, or employee reluctance for whatever reason. It is important that the appraisal manager understand that the extra efforts of a few persons in organizing and planning a mass appraisal system can provide quantum leaps in efficiency.

Table 12.6
Ratio study comparing condominium sales to prior and proposed value

Sale Period	CAMA Set	Total Sales	Prior v. Proposed	Mean Ratio	Median Ratio	COD	Min Ratio	Max Ratio
1/92 -1/94	All	2,043	Prior	99%	99%	8.7%	61%	174%
			Proposed	96%	96%	6.2%	63%	191%
1/92 -1/93	All	1,031	Prior	99%	98%	9.0%	66%	174%
			Proposed	97%	96%	6.0%	63%	191%
1/93 -1/94	All	1,013	Prior	99%	99%	8.4%	61%	142%
			Proposed	96%	96%	6.3%	70%	158%
7/93 -1/94	All	576	Prior	99%	99%	8.8%	61%	136%
			Proposed	96%	96%	7.2%	70%	158%
1/92 -1/94	10.06	210	Prior	98%	97%	9.1%	74%	138%
			Proposed	96%	95%	5.9%	73%	146%
	10.08	338	Prior	100%	99%	8.1%	73%	145%
			Proposed	96%	95%	5.9%	73%	146%
	10.09	205	Prior	102%	100%	7.4%	77%	149%
			Proposed	97%	96%	5.3%	69%	140%
	10.10	43	Prior	99%	97%	10.5%	66%	135%
			Proposed	95%	96%	6.0%	63%	135%
	10.11	18	Prior	108%	107%	10.4%	67%	149%
			Proposed	96%	97%	7.6%	75%	113%
	10.12	170	Prior	101%	101%	6.0%	77%	143%
			Proposed	98%	98%	4.2%	79%	124%
	10.13	122	Prior	100%	99%	9.1%	78%	136%
			Proposed	97%	96%	6.9%	73%	191%
	10.14	68	Prior	105%	102%	6.3%	87%	144%
			Proposed	94%	100%	4.0%	73%	163%
	10.15	37	Prior	96%	95%	6.4%	82%	115%
			Proposed	93%	94%	4.7%	81%	102%
	10.16	147	Prior	97%	96%	7.3%	75%	132%
			Proposed	96%	96%	6.4%	65%	158%
	10.17	283	Prior	96%	95%	9.4%	69%	174%
			Proposed	96%	96%	5.5%	76%	174%
	10.18	252	Prior	98%	99%	10.7%	69%	144%
			Proposed	96%	95%	5.2%	74%	130%
	10.19	154	Prior	100%	100%	8.2%	82%	128%
			Proposed	97%	95%	6.6%	80%	125%

With the statewide Maryland CAMA System being implemented in the early 1990s. Ocean City, Maryland was a ideal location to implement a condominium CAMA valuation system. It was decided to automate the existing manual valuation system to reduce the retraining of employee's. Once the database was developed additional applications could be implemented. Thus, the grouping of Condominium Projects (CAMA Subsets) into larger neighbourhoods (CAMA Sets) occurred, data entry commenced, listings of data were produced and edited, and model values were established. Model values are placed in a table within the CAMA system so that land, building, and total values can be applied to each record by model number.

The initial advantages of the CAMA system were not having to post and store almost 20,000 paper record cards or not having to enter land and building values for notices. This system allowed additional advances when the database was established. However, there had to be a staged implementation and all advances could not be achieved in the first year because of deadlines involved in an annual valuation cycle and initial data entry.

Steps in initial implementation

Once the database structure had been determined, initial data entry must occur. This may be accomplished in a combination of methods for efficient data entry. This includes the electronic transfer of data from existing mainframe files. In this case, all account ownership, legal description, and property transfer information was downloaded from the main frame computer and loaded into the CAMA file. Next, individual data entry can occur for each account. A unique feature allowing the copying for selected data elements may speed data entry especially with condominiums of similar model types. Optical mark sensing forms and scanners can allow persons to have a field document for each account which can be completed in the field, scanned at a central location, and converted to an electronic file that could be imported into the CAMA system.

After initial data entry, the power of CAMA system can be used to edit data, produce descriptive statistics about the total universe of properties, sale properties, or selected neighbourhoods or property types. CAMA also allows the production of various performance analysis ratio studies, frequency distributions, and data plots which allow the appraiser and appraisal manager to monitor the mass appraisal function. The full potential of CAMA has not been felt even with this first initial valuation. There are additional reports and capabilities which will need to be developed. Now that data is entered, data analysis reports, sales analysis, and ratio studies for nearly 20,000 accounts can be completed in from one to two weeks by one person. This analysis and valuation previously took about 6 months for 2 persons. Moving to other more sophisticated CAMA methods such as multiple regression analysis or adaptive estimation feedback to calibrate the CAMA model or to value the properties could speed the valuation analysis to less than two weeks in the future.

One can quantify data and develop descriptive statistics providing more confidence in the analysis, understanding of the universe of properties being valued, and supporting the values produced. Descriptive statistics are the gathering, condensing, arranging, graphing of data, or the developing of mathematical statistical data which allows an understanding of a universe of data or sample of data. Table 12.7 is an example of enhanced data analysis in chart form compares the neighbourhoods by type, number of properties in each neighbourhood, the number of sales, and the percentage that the sales are of total units. This chart is really a narrative representation of a several frequency distributions of two data elements which are the number of condominiums and the number of sales. The interval for each frequency is each CAMA Set.

Table 12.7
Sales as a percentage of total condominiums 1/92 -1/94

CAMA Set	Type	Units	Sales	%
10.06	Townhouse	2,061	203	10%
10.08	Ocean Front Highrise	3,463	338	10%
10.09	Ocean Front Midrise	2,555	205	8%
10.10	Ocean Front Lowrise Masonry	598	43	7%
10.11	Ocean Front Lowrise Frame	330	18	5%
10.12	Ocean Block Lowrise Frame	2,250	170	8%
10.13	Ocean Block Lowrise Masonry	1,146	122	11%
10.14	Ocean Block Lowrise Frame	1,041	68	7%
10.15	Ocean Block Midrise Masonry	367	37	10%
10.16	Bay Front	1,258	147	12%
10.17	Bay Side Canal/ Lagoon	1,585	284	18%
10.18	Bay Side Inland 1	1,841	251	14%
10.19	Bay Side Inland 2	1,084	153	14%
		19,579	2,039	10%

A frequency distribution or histogram is a two way scatter diagram that graphically depicts the distribution of data. To develop an understanding of information about numerous individual properties or sale properties the information is condensed into the number of occurrences within each frequency and displayed in one chart. CAMA software should have a routine which produces frequency distributions on user defined data. To use the routine and develop the frequency, the user identifies the data element, produces standard descriptive statistics consisting of measures of central tendency, dispersion, and the minimum and maximum values of the range of data. In using a frequency distribution routine, the user identifies the data element, identifies the beginning of the lowest value in the first interval, the size of each interval, and how many data items will equal one unit of measure in the frequency graph. The computer would then develop the frequency distribution.

Table 12.8 illustrates the enhanced descriptive statistics capabilities provided by CAMA. These compare the total of all condominiums units by the year built, the percent that the frequency is of the total units, and various sales data for each frequency. In this case, it indicates the majority of units were built over a 15 year period and are about 20 years old, and that there is a fairly uniform percentage of sales to total units by each frequency. Table 12.9 indicates the number of units and sales by number of bedrooms for all condominiums in Ocean City. This same information could be run for each CAMA Neighbourhood (CAMA Set) to understand the make-up of each CAMA Set.

Table 12.8
Units year built v. sales 1/92-1/94

Year Built	Units	Units v. Total	Sales	Sales v. Units Yr Blt	Sales v. Total Units
<1956	817	4%	13	1%	2%
1956-1960	230	1%	26	1%	11%
1961-1965	926	5%	78	4%	8%
1966-1970	5,269	27%	438	21%	8%
1971-1975	3,288	17%	325	16%	10%
1976-1980	5,483	28%	606	30%	11%
1981-1985	3,176	16%	341	17%	11%
1986-1990	390	2%	212	10%	54%
Total	19,579		2,039		10%

311

Table 12.9
Bedroom type v. sales 1/92 - 1/94

Bedroom	Units	Units v. Total	Sales	Sales v. Unit Type	Sales v. Total Units
Studio	3,112	16%	248	12%	8%
1 Bedroom	4,395	22%	488	24%	11%
2 Bedroom	10,002	51%	1,131	55%	11%
3 Bedroom	2,042	10%	172	8%	8%
4 Bedroom	28	0%	0	0%	0%
Total	19,579		2,039		

Computer Assisted Mass Appraisal systems allow great flexibility in using descriptive statistics utilities within the CAMA software, or developing statistical data with special programs written for that purpose in the CAMA software. If needed extract routines of data can be developed to export the data to other third party statistical software. The CAMA software used in Maryland allows descriptive statistics on any data element that includes mean and median values, standard deviation, coefficient of variation, coefficient of dispersion from median, variance, coefficient of skewness, coefficient of kurtosis, minimum and maximum values. This with the capability to quickly compute assessment ratios and to produce assessment ratio studies places significant analysis power in the hands of the assessor.

Additional understanding about assessment ratio studies can be gained by producing histograms or frequency distributions of ratio data. Figure 12.1 is a frequency distribution of assessment ratio studies based on sales from 1/92 to 1/94 compared to the prior value and proposed values after the valuation was complete. The individual ratio statistics are the same as produced from Table 12.4. CAMA allows the ratio statistics to be produce on demand based on prior value or proposed and allows ratios studies to be used by the assessor in the analysis for the reappraisal. Prior to CAMA, there was no user friendly interactive analysis system that could produce analysis reports or descriptive statistics. A complete ratio study performance analysis can be produced in CAMA and various descriptive statistics can be produced by the user.

The statistical module in the CAMA software allows for advanced statistical analysis and graphing capabilities. It allows for correlation analysis of two factors and produces a correlation coefficient. A correlation coefficient closer to 1 indicates that the factors are highly correlated. There is capability to produce

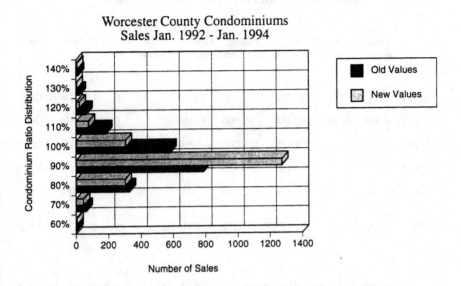

Figure 12.1 Frequency of ratios on prior value and frequency of ratios on proposed value

two population t-tests and a paired t-test of two factors which compares the means of ranges of data in two populations and which estimates the significance of the difference in mean values between the populations.

Market data information and valuation analysis

Generally market sales in this locale are quite brisk in the spring and summer. There are short term real estate cycles and long term real estate cycles. These usually relate to relationships to business cycles.[27] The primary determinants of short-term demand are the availability of credit, and interest rate levels. As interest rates rise, real estate demand plummets, as rates decline, demand increases. The Ocean City, Maryland real estate market has had short term and long term cycles.[28] Currently, there is little appreciation and large inventory of units for sale. There has been a decline in value in some areas.

Certain market analysis data can be produced for the entire market area or CAMA Set. Table 12.10 illustrates total units and total sales descriptive statistics which are then stratified by bedroom count showing various market and statistical

313

Table 12.10
Total units bedroom type and CAMA set 10.08

	Total Units	Total Sales	Average Sale Price	Median Sale Price	Median Ratio	COD Median	Std Dev Mean	Min	Max
Total									
Studio	3,122	248	56,039	55,700	107%	12	0.165	87%	142%
1 Bed	4,395	488	96,254	99,000	101%	6	0.071	85%	118%
2 Bed	10,002	1,131	123,118	120,000	98%	7	0.095	78%	145%
3 Bed	2,042	176	115,159	106,855	101%	12	0.148	72%	141%
4 Bed	28	0	0	0	0%	0	0.000	0%	0%
Set 10.08	3,463	338	121,785	118,250	99%	8	0.109	73%	145%

data. It also gives the overall data for one CAMA Set 10.08 which will be used to illustrate more refined neighbourhood analysis.

The market analysis reports produced by the assessor for valuation analysis and estimation of model values are produced by each CAMA Set in an indexed order of model type. This significantly speeded the process from the manual analysis process. This analysis consists of sales and data reporting for each model type, comparison of prior value transformations such as prior value per square foot or per bedroom to current sales prices per square foot or per bedroom. This report can be produced for development of proposed model values and after the proposed model values are applied can be reproduced giving a complete summary. The assessor does have to develop model rates for models which had no comparable sales. This is done by reviewing comparables units of similar models in other projects and reviewing sales of other models in the same project. The output report gives average statistics for various data in each model type for decision purposes. These are underlined in Table 12.11 for market analysis of ocean front highrise garden condominium units in CAMA Set 10.08. This report was produced on 338 property sales by model type for analysis purposes and is used in developing model values to be used to value all other properties.

Additional descriptive statistical data can be easily developed to gain insight into the market data about a neighbourhood. The following chart identifies descriptive statistical data by bedroom types of unit sales in CAMA Set 10.08. Note this data gives information on sale price, square footage, sale price per square foot, sale price per bedroom, prior value and prior value ratio.

Table 12.11
Sales analysis edit report CAMA Set 10.08 Ocean Front highrise

Record	Sale Date	Sale Price	Sale	Prior	Proposed	Bed Rm	Sale/Bed	Prior/Bed	Prop/Bed	Bath	Land	Improvement	Total	Prior Ratio	Prop/ Ratio
54	9303	134,900	120.23	135.47	115.86	2	67,450	76,000	65,000	1	65,000	65,000	130,000	1.127	0.954
53	9304	155,000	138.15	135.47	115.86	2	77,500	76,000	65,000	1	65,000	65,000	130,000	0.981	0.839
55	9311	145,000	129.23	135.47	115.86	2	72,500	76,000	65,000	1	65,000	65,000	13,000	1.048	0.897
			129.20	135.47	115.86		72,483	76,000	65,000					1.052	0.900
292	9310	205,000	142.36	103.47	103.47	3	68,333	49,666	49,667	1	74,500	74,500	149,000	0.727	0.727
			142.36	103.47	103.47		68,333	49,666	49,667					0.727	0.727
302	9202	114,000	111.76	102.94	105.88	2	57,000	52,500	54,000	1	54,000	54,000	108,000	0.921	0.947
295	9212	128,500	125.98	102.94	105.88	2	64,250	52,500	54,000	1	54,000	54,000	108,000	0.817	0.840
296	9312	131,900	129.31	102.94	105.88	2	65,950	52,500	54,000	1	54,000	54,000	108,000	0.796	0.819
			122.35	102.94	105.88		62,400	52,500	54,000					0.845	0.869
291	9202	102,000	100.00	98.04	98.04	2	51,000	50,000	50,000	1	50,000	50,000	100,000	0.980	0.980
303	9203	95,000	93.14	98.04	98.04	2	47,500	50,000	50,000	1	50,000	50,000	1,000,0	1.053	1.053
301	9205	118,000	115.69	98.04	98.04	2	59,000	50,000	50,000	1	50,000	50,000	100,000	0.847	0.847
294	9206	101,000	99.02	98.04	98.04	2	50,500	50,000	50,000	1	50,000	50,000	100,000	0.990	0.990
299	9207	105,000	102.94	98.04	98.04	2	52,500	50,000	50,000	1	50,000	50,000	100,000	0.952	0.952
289	9210	121,000	118.63	98.04	98.04	2	60,500	50,000	50,000	1	50,000	50,000	100,000	0.826	0.826

Table 12.11 (contd)
Sales analysis edit report CAMA Set 10.08 Ocean Front highrise

Record	Sale Date	Sale Price	Sale	Prior	Proposed	Bed Rm	Sale/Bed	Prior/Bed	Prop/Bed	Bath	Land	Improvement	Total	Prior Ratio	Prop/ Ratio
287	9303	107,000	104.90	98.04	98.04	2	53,500	50,000	50,000	1	50,000	50,000	100,000	0.935	0.935
296	9303	106,000	103.92	98.04	98.04	2	53,000	50,000	50,000	1	50,000	50,000	100,000	0.943	0.943
288	9312	96,500	94.61	98.04	98.04	2	48,250	50,000	50,000	1	50,000	50,000	100,000	1.036	1.036
297	9312	105,000	102.94	98.04	98.04	2	52,500	50,000	50,000	1	50,000	50,000	100,000	0.952	0.952
			103.58	98.04	98.04		52,825	50,000	50,000					0.951	0.951
290	9208	114,000	111.76	88.24	88.24	2	57,000	45,000	45,000	1	45,000	45,000	90,000	0.789	0.789
293	9209	83,000	81.37	88.24	88.24	2	41,500	45,000	45,000	1	45,000	45,000	90,000	1.084	1.084
			96.57	88.24	88.24		49,250	45,000	45,000					0.937	0.937
387	9201	128,000	104.49	91.43	107.76	2	64,000	56,000	66,000	1	66,000	66,000	132,000	0.875	1.031
385	9205	135,000	110.20	91.43	107.76	2	67,500	56,000	66,000	1	66,000	66,000	132,000	0.830	0.978
392	9311	138,000	112.65	91.43	107.76	2	69,000	56,000	66,000	1	66,000	66,000	132,000	0.812	0.957
			109.11	91.43	107.76		66,833	56,000	66,000					0.839	0.989
384	9205	106,500	86.94	87.76	81.63	2	53,250	53,750	50,000	1	50,000	50,000	100,000	0.939	0.939
390	9309	100,000	81.63	87.76	81.63	2	50,000	53,750	50,000	1	50,000	50,000	100,000	1.000	1.000
391	911	115,300	94.12	87.76	81.63	2	57,650	53,750	50,000	1	50,000	50,000	100,000	0.867	0.867
			87.56	87.76	81.63		53,633	53,750	50,000					0.935	0.935

Stratification of homogeneous units and the development of descriptive statistics allows the appraiser to gain insight into the market data and any valuation uniformity problems with the groupings. This information can be developed easily within the CAMA system statistical module. In this case, the typical value per square or bedroom gives indicators of value. Statistics on prior value and sale price indicate the difference between prior appraisal levels and current sales levels. When stratifications of similar properties, comparisons of ratio data measures of central tendency show differences in value levels by type of property. Similarly, where measures of dispersion are high further analysis should occur. Because of higher dispersion levels in the three bedroom strata in Table 12.11 is indication that further research should be conducted on theses units to determine the cause for reasons for the differences in values related to prior value.

Table 12.12
Unit bedroom type descriptive data for sales 1/92-1/94
CAMA set 10.8

Type	Factor	Mean	Median	COD	Type	Factor	Mean	Median	COD
Studio	Sale	56,039	55,700	13	1 Bed	Sale	97,461	100,000	11
	Sq Ft/#	425	453	6		Sq Ft/#	774	810	8
	Sale/#	131.91	131.47	10		Sale/#	127.10	126.67	14
	Sale/Bed	56,039	55,700	13		Sale/Bed	97,461	100,000	11
	Prior Value	60,889	64,000	5		Prior Value	97,736	96,000	10
	Prior Ratio	111	107	12		Prior Ratio	101	101	6
2 Bed	Sale	123,118	120,000	14	3 Bed	Sale	171,657	162,500	17
	Sq Ft/#	1,071	1,078	15		Sq Ft/#	1,499	1,488	9
	Sale/#	114.79	114.34	14		Sale/#	115.16	106.86	16
	Sale/Bed	61,559	60,000	14		Sale/Bed	57,219	54,167	17
	Prior Value	120,271	116,000	15		Prior Value	175,383	172,000	16
	Prior Ratio	98	98	7		Prior Ratio	103	101	12

Multiple regression analysis

CAMA software should allow for other advanced market modelling techniques. While the main method of valuation for the Ocean City condominiums was a user defined market model approach, other market modelling methods should be used to cross check and speed the modelling process. In the Ocean City Condominium mass appraisal software Multiple Regression Analysis capabilities are present and are being used for quality control and market modelling purposes. Multiple Regression Analysis (MRA) is the process by which statistical analysis using several variables is used to predict another variable that relates to them. The variables you are trying to predict are dependent variables.[29] In CAMA, the dependent variable would be predicted sales price. The variables that may influence the dependent variable sales price are known as independent variables. These independent variables may be unit square footage, bedrooms, unit quality and condition, location and so on. MRA determines the coefficients or values in an equation of independent variables which will produce the closest estimate of the dependent variables value.

In appraisal the goal is not true predictions or estimation of a values behaviour, but the estimation of the value when similar values are known. One usually wishes to estimate the values of properties in a neighbourhood, given the known selling prices of properties within the neighbourhood that occurred over the preceding year.

The MRA setup and run takes longer than the actual valuation of all properties via MRA. The first step is to build a cross products matrix file which does the arithmetic needed by the MRA run before it is used to value all properties.[30] You must set the parameters for the specific regression problem to be run and must specify the same variables used in the building of the cross products matrix file. You must indicate the total number of steps to be used in the stepwise process. You must also set a threshold F-value that the program can use in determining whether a given variable should be included in the run. The F-value is the statistical measure of the strength of the association or correlation between the independent variable and the dependent variable. The variable with the highest F-value on a particular iteration or run is then used in the equation.[31]

In the initial MRA run, the computer first calculates the correlation coefficients or values for all variables in the cross products matrix for all properties that sold over a specified period with a neighbourhood. The computer then analyses the independent variables and determines those that are the most significant in estimating property value. These are independent variables having the highest F-value. The computer runs stepwise through the data in iterations using one independent variable at a time and checks the current F-values. It then selects

318

the next most significant variable. At each iteration the F-values are recomputed. If the F-value of the independent variable already in the equation falls below the predetermined threshold, the variable is removed from the equation. When the required iterations or steps have been run or there are no further variables available with sufficiently high F-values, the MRA run is complete and the final coefficients are printed.[32] The MRA equation is saved to a computer file so that it can be run against all properties in the neighbourhood to estimate property value.

The MRA procedure can be used to value properties for ad valorem purposes or it can be used for calibrating other CAMA valuation models such as the one described in Ocean City.

Additionally, a mass appraisal quality control section could use MRA to test mass appraisal results on current sales or using sales data following the mass appraisal completion. Listings of model values and property characteristics from the mass appraisal can be compared to the estimated MRA value and differences analyzed. The assessor could produce MRA value estimates and compare these to the market analysis listing described for CAMA Set 10.08 to help in developing model values.

Although MRA valuation models may seem complex and hard to explain, they can be rather straight forward. The best way to become familiar with multiple regression is to work through the valuation of various neighbourhoods on a test basis. For detailed understanding of multiple regression consult *Property Appraisal and Assessment Administration*, a statistics text book, or an appropriate CAMA software manual. One will find that results will be affected by the same things that impact other mass appraisal models or single property appraisals such as errors in property attribute data, grade, or condition.

MRA run documentation and model explanation is difficult to explain most property owners. Thus, it should be used with care if it is going to be the only method of valuation. This is especially true when one considers the job of the assessor is to produce value estimates that are easily understood and explainable to the public. However, one should use all methods of mass appraisal to achieve the advantages provided by each technique. The advantages that MRA provides is in assisting in mass appraisal model calibration and speeding value estimation.

This can be illustrated when considering the valuation of the ocean front highrise condominium units in CAMA Set 10.08. The CAMA mass appraisal model that was previously described for Ocean City was used to produce the proposed value and assessment ratio study data documented earlier. In the case of CAMA Set 10.08, the ratio analysis and descriptive statistics produced a mean ratio of 95.5% and a median ratio of 95.1% with a coefficient of dispersion of 5.9% on 338 property sales. The mean and median sales price was $121,765 and $118,250 respectively. The mean and median proposed values were $116,145 and $112,000. These statistics are good. The CAMA market analysis model

319

described earlier works quite well, and the speed with which the actual valuation can be completed has been greatly enhanced so that the valuation of 13 CAMA Sets can be conducted in two weeks excluding field review.

The use of MRA will speed model calibration and potentially speed even the current CAMA market analysis and valuation. In a test MRA valuation of CAMA Set 10.08, 338 sales were used to develop an MRA Model. This model was developed using sales prices unadjusted for personal property and was applied to the 3,463 ocean front highrise units. The sale ratio study comparing MRA values to sale price produced a mean and median ratio or 102.3% and 102.5% (adjusted for personal property approximately 98%) and a coefficient of dispersion of 12.1%. When separate MRA model runs were developed for each bedroom style (studio, one, two, or three bedroom) and the values applied to all 3,463 units, the ratio study results improved to a mean and median ratio of 101.9% and 101.6% and the coefficient of dispersion improved from 12.1% to 10.7%. Although, the ratio study on MRA value estimates is not as good as the ratio results produced from the mass appraisal market model in CAMA Set 10.08, the MRA results were acceptable and could be refined.

It is important to understand the speed with which the test MRA model was developed and applied. The development of the first MRA run using all sales, the development of the four separate models for each bedroom style MRA run, the application of all MRA equations to all 3,463 units, and the production of ratio and descriptive statistics took less than one half hour. Thus, the valuation of 13 CAMA Sets potentially could take one day. By removing extreme outlier sales, and data editing unit quality and condition, the MRA model values could be improved. This would result in improved ratio statistics especially regarding dispersion.

By using MRA to calibrate CAMA market model analysis reports, the assessor can quickly speed the valuation process. This test has shown that there are data quality issues that must be addressed in the next physical inspection dealing with accurate and systematic documentation of building quality, unit condition, and unit location or view. When this is complete MRA modelling results should improve.

Other CAMA techniques

Other sophisticated CAMA valuation techniques are Adaptive Estimation Procedure (AEP or Feedback) and Artificial Neural Network Mass Appraisal Systems. AEP is another method used to estimate the value of group of properties for which representative recent sales data are available. This process is a trial and error process that tries sample values in an equation used for estimating property value and compares the estimated value to actual sales price. It adjusts the initial component values according to the discrepancy in value and applies the equation again. It repeats the process again until the discrepancies are small. AEP uses mathematical procedures called filtering algorithms.[33] These algorithms test the possible weights of factors relevant to the prediction of value, testing the predicted value against actual sales price. The process filters out all factors that do not impact value and weights the factors that do affect value.[34] Once the algorithm process is run on sale properties, the component values or coefficients are applied to the entire neighbourhood.

AEP is strongly affected by the initial dollar values and weights assigned before the algorithm process is run. Although these initial values and weights are tentative, it is important that the assessor use experience of market derived contributory value components when setting the initial component values to be used in the process and the value of the component. The model learns from experience as it passes the database on each successive run until the equation is adjusted to bring the model more closely in line with actual sales prices.[35]

The data elements that are used in AEP are building quantitative and qualitative factors, land quantitative and qualitative factors, and total property qualitative factors. Thus, initial value rates are established for value per square foot of improvement and land, contributory improvement value for other building components, and adjustments for quality of improvement, land, and total property.

When substantiated by other market analysis of contributory values, AEP is more easily understood by the general public than MRA or Artificial Neural Network value estimates. Thus, mass appraisal operations can be enhanced by AEP applications. AEP will be used in quality control testing and market model calibration in the next valuation of condominiums in Ocean City and expanded to other locations for the same purposes.

AEP seeks to minimize the average absolute deviation between variables while MRA minimizes the sum of the squared errors through the least squares statistical method. Thus, the MRA value estimates are influenced more by outlier property sales than the value estimate produced by AEP. MRA can be used in selecting the significant variables to be used in AEP.[36]

Within the last three years many Artificial Neural Network Mass Appraisal Applications have been developed. Papers on test applications have been presented to the mass appraisal industry. Clearly, any improvements in mass appraisal that can be achieved from new technology should be pursued. From limited initial review, this approach shows promise. However, the artificial computer intelligence architecture and the 'black box' concept of developing value estimates or contributory component values must be improved so that the results are easily documented and explained to the typical property owner.

Archival of CAMA records

The initial implementation of CAMA in Maryland was completed on local area networks. The first series of revaluations could be stored on the disk storage of the LANS. It became important to develop an efficient method of archival of property records and remarks. This was accomplished by modifying the CAMA software so that it would operate in a read only mode instead of the usual read and write method where data can be changed. This has allowed an efficient and cost effective method of archival. CAMA archival files with applicable archival computer programs are recorded on compact disc media. One compact will hold approximately 240,000 records. The appropriate number of discs are recorded for each county. In each location there is a compact disc reader so that archived records can be viewed or record cards printed. Of course, the current files remain on the LAN. In a multi-jurisdictional assessment environment, the backup CAMA files from each county and the compact disc technology allow all CAMA data to be centrally located for management review, and quality control processing for analysis reports. The files can be copied to the quality control LAN and can be processed in the normal CAMA operating software.

Conclusion

Condominium property valuation is easily adaptable to computer assisted mass appraisal systems. An overview of the concepts and appraisal issues relating to residential condominium appraisal was made in relation to valuation in a statewide computer assisted mass appraisal system. Care should be exercised in the design and development of CAMA databases so that the required data for valuation is present.

The assessor should exercise judgement when procuring CAMA software. It should allow user programming capability, a powerful database capability, an integrated statistical, and a graphing utility. The appraisal staff should be involved with development and system management. Although, normal operation resources are usually scarce, the assessment administrator should move to CAMA and advanced model building if this type of system is not already available. Clearly, efficiencies will accrue. It is extremely important that adequate training in the software operations be provided to the appraisal staff and there should be an adequate plan and organization for the mass appraisal operation.

This implementation has shown the benefits of CAMA in mass appraisal operations, the development of a user defined model and database structure, the use of descriptive data and ratio analysis, and the use of advanced CAMA methods in market model calibration and quality control.

Notes

1. Eckert, J.K. (1990), *Property Appraisal and Assessment Administration*, The International Association of Assessing Officers, Chicago.
2. Ibid, p 8.
3. Nunnink, K. (1994), 'How Realworks became the Backbone of an Appraisal Firm', *The Quarterly Byte*, The Appraisal Institute, vol. 10 no. 4, Fall.
4. Heuer, K.L. (1987), *The Appraisal of Real Estate*, Ninth Edition, American Institute of Real Estate Appraisers, Chicago.
5. Babcock, H.A. (1970), *Appraisal Principles and Practices*, Richard D. Irwin, Inc. Homewood, Illinois.
6. Boyce, B.N. (1984), *Appraisal Terminology*, Ballinger Publishing Company, Cambridge, Massachusetts.
7. Lusk, H.F., *Law Of The Real Estate Business*, Richard D. Irwin, Inc., Homeland, Illinois.
8. Ibid.
9. Ibid.
10. Ibid.
11. Boyce, B.N. and Kinard, W.N. (1984), *Appraising Real Property*, Lexington Books, Lexington, Massachusetts.
12. Lusk, H.F., *Law Of The Real Estate Business*, Richard D. Irwin, Inc., Homeland, Illinois.
13. Friedman, E.J. (1978), *Encyclopedia of Real Estate Appraisal*, Third Edition, Prentice-Hall, Inc, Englewood Cliffs, N.J.
14. Werczberger, E. (1988), 'The Experience with Rent Control in Israel', *The Journal of Real Estate Finance and Economics*, vol.1 no. 3.
15. Friedman, E.J. (1978), *Encyclopedia of Real Estate Appraisal*, Third Edition, Prentice-Hall, Inc., Englewood Cliffs, N.J.
16. Harrison, H.S. (1978), *Appraising The Single Family Residence*, American Institute of Real Estate Appraisers, Chicago, Illinois.
17. Friedman, E.J. (1978), *Encyclopedia of Real Estate Appraisal*, Third Edition, Prentice-Hall, Inc., Englewood Cliffs, N.J.
18. Harrison, H.S. (1978), *Appraising The Single Family Residence*, American Institute of Real Estate Appraisers, Chicago, Illinois.
19. Eckert, J.K. (1990), *Property Appraisal and Assessment Administration*, The International Association of Assessing Officers, Chicago, Ill.
20. Heuer, K.L. (1987), *The Appraisal of Real Estate*, Ninth Edition, American Institute of Real Estate Appraisers, Chicago, Illinois.
21. Harrison, H.S. (1978), *Appraising The Single Family Residence*, American Institute of Real Estate Appraisers, Chicago, Illinois.

22. Boyce, B.N. and Kinard, W.N. (1984), *Appraising Real Property*, Lexington Books, Lexington, Massachusetts.
23. Friedman, E.J. (1978), *Encyclopedia of Real Estate Appraisal*, Third Edition, Prentice-Hall, Inc., Englewood Cliffs, N.J.
24. Ibid.
25. Eckert, J.K. (1990), *Property Appraisal and Assessment Administration*, The International Association of Assessing Officers, Chicago, Ill.
26. Ibid.
27. Fanning, S.F., Grisson, T.V., and Pearson, T.D. (1994), *Market Analysis for Valuation Appraisals*, Appraisal Institute, Chicago, Illinois.
28. Brooks, D.H. (1994), *Ocean City Revisited 23 Edition*, Paul L. Faulstich, Worchester Information Network, Lipman, Firzzell and Mitchell, LLC, Baltimore, MD., June.
29. Eckert, J.K. (1990), *Property Appraisal and Assessment Administration*, The International Association of Assessing Officers, Chicago, Ill.
30. Schreiber, J. (1985), *MicroSolve CAMA Users Manual*, MicroSolve, Inc., Waltham, MA.
31. Ibid.
32. Ibid.
33. Eckert, J.K. (1990), *Property Appraisal and Assessment Administration*, The International Association of Assessing Officers, Chicago, Ill.
34. Schreiber, J. (1985), *MicroSolve CAMA Users Manual*, MicroSolve, Inc., Waltham, MA.
35. Ibid.
36. Eckert, J.K. (1990), *Property Appraisal and Assessment Administration*, The International Association of Assessing Officers, Chicago, Ill.

13 TAXES: Residential property valuation for local tax purposes in the Netherlands

G.M. ten Have, A. G. op't Veld and J. E. Janssen

Introduction

Within most markets public or private demand for information on products and prices can be met immediately and accurately (for example food stores, equities market, electronic equipment markets). The information available on Dutch real estate markets, however, differs from those markets (just as in other countries). One reason, of course, is the fundamental relationship of real estate with its location. Another aspect is commercial revenue related with local or regional information on real estate supply and prices. The market information on residential properties in the Netherlands is sometimes inaccurate, frequently incomplete, divergent and distributed among many places. For other types of real estate such as offices and retail, the registration (input) and information (output) is even worse. The main reason for this fundamental market imperfection is that there is a limited number of suppliers of market information. These suppliers want to play a dominant role in the local or regional market, thus making it difficult or even impossible to accomplish an effective and efficient application of real estate information for a range of purposes. The same applies for the levy of taxes. There are more than 600 local governments in the Netherlands who are responsible for the levy and collection of local government taxes.

The main issue which local governments have to deal with is the valuation of all real estate within their boundaries inside a short space of time and within limited budgets. Therefore, can Computer Assisted Mass Appraisal (CAMA) techniques play an effective role in solving these problems? Obtaining knowledge of market prices for residential property should not prove difficult to obtain by local governments because the Dutch National Land Registry Office has the responsibility to register all transactions. One problem at present is whether the transaction is executed correctly by the land registry office and what type of information or aspect of valuation does it refer to? There are many inconsistencies with the present system which would suggest that the Dutch legal cadastral registration is not a proper basis for tax levies.

To overcome this specific problem the Dutch parliament passed an act which makes it possible to register property information for taxation at a land registry office. At the beginning of this year (1995) the draft act became law. The name of the act is 'Act for Assessment of Real Estate'. The effect of the Act goes beyond the taxation problem including impact on the registration of real estate in general.

In this chapter attention is paid not only to the function of the specific act but especially to the different techniques that are now in progress to overcome mass appraisal problems. Expert system development for residential property is also highlighted. The chapter begins with a short explanation of the Dutch act on the assessment of real estate, followed by a theoretical approach of the CAMA systems. Then some practical examples of computerized systems on real estate in the municipalities of Amsterdam, Rotterdam and the Hague are briefly demonstrated. Furthermore, attention is paid to the development of the expert system TAXES by the Dutch association of real estate agents (NVM) and the Dutch Organization for Applied Scientific Research (TNO).

The Dutch act for the assessment of real estate (1995)

Dutch local government have two principal sources of income. The first and most important one is the national government funds scheme, whereby every local government receives a general share and a specific share depending on municipal criteria (number of inhabitants, number of people living beneath a certain welfare level etc.). The second source of income is completely independent of other authorities; it is income derived from local levies on property, water, sewerage systems and all kinds of licences. This source of income is a small proportion of the total income of local governments (less than 20% as an average). Nevertheless, the local levy on property contributes a high proportion of this the second source of income.

To overcome the problem of interpreting the value of properties for different fiscal purposes an act on real estate valuation was introduced. The name of the act is, 'Act for Assessment of Real Estate'. The value, which is estimated in respect of the Act, is applicable to the income tax, capital gains tax, the local property tax and the levy of the Water Board. The Act also serves as a kind of mediator between the values which are required for the different taxes. The Act submits the basic information for the other taxes. Of course, the value should not for example simply be related to the local property tax. Several corrections should be applied. But the basic value is available. These corrections are regulated in the acts which regulate the taxes. The registration of values and property should, according to the act, be completed by the local government. They submit the information to the Water Board and to the National Revenue Service. Each body has its specific requirements and will only get the information it actually requires. There is a board which is an independent public institution controlling the quality of the registration by local government. The name of the board is 'Dutch Council for Real Estate Assessment'. The Ministry of Finance can give additional rules for the registration.

Land registry

The following items are registered in respect of the act:

- Tax objects. These are the built and unbuilt parts of objects, combination or combinations of parts of objects all within one municipality.

- Subjects. Personal information, like the address of the owner or tenant.

- Identification of the owner/tenant. This forms the connection between the information on the subject and the tax object. There could be a tenant and an owner or different tenants and owners related to one tax object.

- Legal cadastral identification of the tax object. This object contains the lot number of the legal land registry etc., and is the connection between the tax object and the legal cadastral object.

The values are recorded for the tax object. The values prescribed by the Act are as follows:

- for dwellings - market value.
- for monuments - market value.
- for objects which are neither dwellings nor monuments the maximum of the market value or corrected replacement value.

For dwellings a market value is required which is obtained by applying the comparative method. For the comparative method the instruction of the Board requires the provision of a table. This is a table of reference prices and reference objects. These are then used as an benchmark for the valuation of other objects.

327

Comments

With regard to the registration of real estate the following comments can be made:

• The Dutch concept of the fiscal cadastre has relevance to other countries.

• The registrations which are used for the fiscal cadastre are important to several other bodies, e.g. for real estate agents, investment corporations, planning authorities etc.

• Several companies who are specialized in gathering data will lose their position in the market, as anyone seeking information will be able to obtain it.

• There still remains the problem of object segregation. Due to this problem one object could be given different values.

For local tax purposes efficient systems are required by local government to register market data, value properties and administer taxes. A mass appraisal system, whether computerized or manual, has four subsystems as shown in Figure 13.1.

1   a data management system;
2   a sales analysis system;
3   a valuation system;
4   an administrative system.

The data management system is the heart of the mass appraisal system and should be carefully planned and designed. Quality control is vital, because the accuracy of values depends on the reliability of the data from which they are generated. Therefore registration of data has to undergo quality tests.

Moreover, data collection, conversion and maintenance constitute the most expensive aspects of most valuation systems. The investment in making this inventory can be 75% of the cost of a revaluation. Design decisions taken in these areas will more than anything else, determine the operating costs of the system. Several European countries have had to deal with these severe problems and the assessment results depend very much on the quality of the data.

In the Netherlands, however, there is a significant amount of available data allowing the mass appraisal system to be built around the data, instead of building the data around the system, as so often happens.

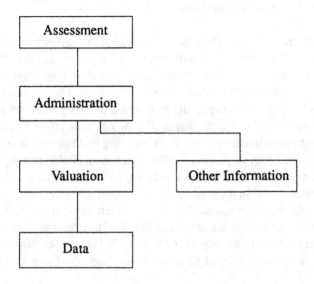

Figure 13.1 Valuation in relation to assessment in most countries

Within the Dutch system the approach for assessment and administration is the same. Besides, there is a large quantity of data that enables the execution of a valuation. This data can among other things serve as input for the assessment.

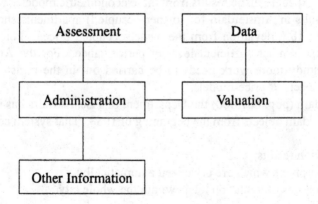

Figure 13.2 Valuation in connection with assessment in the Netherlands

CAMA systems in the Netherlands

To what extent are CAMA techniques of relevance in the Netherlands? CAMA techniques are of interest to local authorities because they have the obligation to levy local taxes on almost all the properties within their municipal boundaries. The four largest cities in the Netherlands (Amsterdam, The Hague, Rotterdam, Utrecht) have the financial capability to develop or to organize research in this field. It is interesting, however, that until now no cooperation has taken place between these municipalities. They are all relying on their own investment and strategic planning. Developments in other cities in this field are marginal. Most cities and small municipalities are relying on work done by professional companies specialized in local administration systems.

In this chapter the practical aspects of implementing systems in Amsterdam, Rotterdam and The Hague are presented briefly. In Amsterdam (pop. 850,000) there are more then 400,000 objects of which 320,000 are residential. All these objects and their fiscal related households are registered within a computer-system.

For residential valuations there are three methods used in combination with computerized registration. The first is the traditional valuation methodology used for approximately 2,000 residential objects in the city centre. The second is a combination of traditional valuation, computerized control and traditional assessment (90,000). The third is a fully computerized valuation and administration system dealing with some 230,000 objects. For Amsterdam apartments, models have been developed which are fully computerized valuation techniques (applying multiple regression analysis). The local authorities in Amsterdam expect realistic results from these econometric models. Modelling research results in Amsterdam for (owner-occupied) apartments showed that there was an 18% deviation from the owner-occupied prices. For valuation purposes this is not a sufficient level of performance. For the Amsterdam modelling study more work needs to be carried out in the registration and analyzing aspects of price-models.

In Rotterdam (pop. 601,000) the Department of Fiscal Affairs has registered all the Rotterdam objects from the beginning of 1988. That system consists of:

* valuation results;
* market prices which are organized automatically;
* calculations of valuation totals within the whole city.

The city has set up a reference system for residential properties which contains 180 primary properties, a total number of 19 sub-networks (1,300 properties) and more than 100 sub-sub networks (39,500 objects).

The capital The Hague (pop. 440,000) has two systems for the valuation of residential properties. The Hague has the advantage of having more than 15% owner-occupied houses while Amsterdam and Rotterdam have less than 10%. The integral fiscal system (IBS 2000) from the Hague contains the basic data for the valuation of properties. The other system (WGS) is developed especially for CAMA purposes. WGS is a system that creates the opportunity to value a large number of properties within one building complex. Firstly, there is a segmentation between housing types. Each type is valued in the traditional way within each neighbourhood and then the computer generates values for the other properties within the same type. In this way much of the valuation process in The Hague is standardized.

There is only one other organization developing CAMA techniques, the Netherlands Association of real estate agents (NVM).

The NVM and it's CAMA research developments

There are not many Multiple Listing Systems (MLS) in the Netherlands. The only MLS worth mentioning is that owned by the Netherlands Association of Real Estate Agents (NVM). The NVM is by far the most important association of real estate agents in the Netherlands. The association has approximately 2,300 members, and its aim is to promote the interests of its members and of the property broker's profession in general. Up to February 1994 there were standard conditions and rates, but at present there is free competition. Education and training for real estate agents, and their specific specialisms, such as financing and valuation, are developed to a high level.

One of the major conditions for becoming a member of the NVM is to comply with the obligation to exchange information. This implies that every individual property broker is compelled to report directly any properties offered for sale or to let in the multiple listing system of the NVM. Once this information has been put into the multiple listing system, every NVM member is able, within 48 hours, to view all the data regarding the properties offered by other NVM real estate agents. This enables individual agents to inform colleagues about available properties quickly and to provide appropriate information to interested parties.

The large number of users provides an extensive database and a great effort was made to perfect the system. Gradually, the system was changed from a paper and microfiche system to a fully computerized data communication system, based on the use of PCs in all NVM estate agencies. By January 1992 all NVM agents were computerized. From that date it was no longer possible to be a member of the NVM without being linked to the computer system. The latest automation development, which was introduced in January 1993, is the computerized ordering of photograph leaflets of properties. The system enables members to combine automatically all data on the property for sale or to let with an order for the production of a photograph of it.

The NVM Real Estate Agents Service Centre has designed several programmes for an integrated office computerization especially developed for estate agencies, allowing better and more efficient operating of the NVM broker's practice. The masterplan consists of a central address file which is connected to all other program modules, such as purchase/sale, accounts, insurance, etc. Extensive statistical programs are also a standard tool of each property broker. By means of a CD-Rom system, information on previous transactions with respect to a certain property is available. It is often possible to trace the number of times that a house has been sold, sale price, and how many days it took to sell the house. At present, many real estate agents use the NVM CD-ROM disk, containing the history of nearly one million houses. A management data system will be built around the entire system allowing every NVM member rapid monitoring of the size of his own market share.

The NVM multiple listing system is extremely successful. One of the main reasons is that NVM members are obliged to enter new data quickly. The NVM is authorized to fine individual offenders who fail to report new properties for sale or to let. Another important aspect of the multiple listing system's success is its reasonable price. Each NVM member participates in the system and the cost per participant is very low which contributes to the general satisfaction with the system. The system permanently contains some 30,000 to 40,000 properties and processes hundreds of transactions every day. No less than 80% of NVM members state that it is the number one reason for their NVM membership. Transactions through colleagues are extremely important in order to acquire a large portion of the property market. The NVM's multiple listing system is clearly the best means to this end.

TAXES: how the decision support system works

On the instruction of the NVM, the Netherlands Organization for Applied Scientific Research (TNO) developed a intelligent computer system entitled 'TAXES' which helps real estate agents to determine the current market value of a house. TAXES provides a valuation of the house using the comparative method. The most up-to-date reference data may date from 48 hours before the valuation. It therefore gives a recommendation about the current market value.

The system now being developed will for the time being only be used for houses. The multiple listing system for commercial property is operational, covering approximately 60% of the market, but the heterogeneity of such properties and the reliability of the data are for the present additional complicating factors. It should also be realized that the quantity of the data is of importance for the system to be able to function reliably. Perhaps a different division into geographical regions will have to be considered. As soon as the development of the system for houses has been successfully completed, it will have to be assessed to consider the feasibility of developing a similar model for commercial properties.

Theoretical background

With the exception of unmarketable property, valuations are always made from a frame of reference, in which a link is made between the selling prices (y) on the one hand, and the accompanying factors or circumstances affecting value (x) on the other. In general there will be several factors and circumstances which affect the value. These circumstances are the calibration points for the frame of reference. An application of a valuation method on the basis of this frame of reference will in general result in an assessed value (v) which deviates from the selling price (y).

The valuation process can be represented as follows:

$$v = f(x)$$

where

v = value
f = the function, which contains the ratios
x = the set of factors affecting value.

f is determined with the help of selling prices (y) and their accompanying set of x. For the valuer this is mostly a technical and subjective frame of reference. This process has to be made suitable for computer use. In doing so the usually subjective frames of reference of the valuer need to be converted into mathematical techniques. The three variables y, f and x can easily be converted into mathematical concepts. The aim being to achieve mathematical concepts which result in a clear and correct valuation. The model will then determine the appropriate form of f with the help of the data (y and x).

A requirement for the valuation of property is the determination of a group of properties with comparable characteristics in a defined region which appeal to the same group of buyers and therefore have a similar price composition.

Division into regions

In view of the large differences between the regional housing markets, the Dutch housing market had to be divided into regions. These regions were determined with the help of:

333

1   data on removals from the Central Bureau of Statistics;
2   the registration codes in the multiple listing system;
3   the principle that sufficient market information should be available for each region.

The key criterion is homogeneity in price ranges and in types of houses and has resulted in a division comprising 80 regions.

The segmentation method

Within each of the housing market regions a further subdivision is made enabling the house to be valued to fall into a group of reference houses. This division into market segments is undertaken by a segmentation method, which can be different for each region. The segmentation method is based on statistical techniques using the multiple listing system file of the region concerned and dividing the houses in terms of their selling prices and related variables. Each group is divided up again until no further division is possible. The tree thus formed has a group of houses at the ends of all the branches to which no further distinctions can be made with respect to the selling prices on the basis of the characteristics of the house known within the system. Represented schematically the segmentation method is as follows:

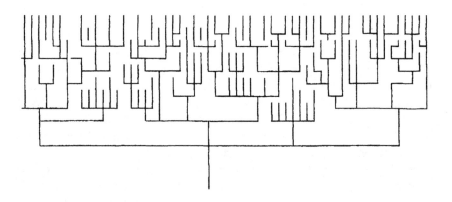

Figure 13.3 The segmentation method

The segmentation method thus obtained will be fixed for this region for a period of 3 to 6 years. It only needs to be adjusted if there is a change in consumer preference. In practice, it appears that this only takes place gradually, because consumer preference is also determined by the supply of houses. In qualitative

334

terms the supply is practically stable and can only be influenced by large new developments and renovations. From the analysis of the regions which has already been carried out, it appears that the segmentation method, or consumer preference, is different for each region. The outcome of the analysis results in an order of importance of various housing characteristics.

Figure 13.4 shows the relevance levels utilized within the analysis:

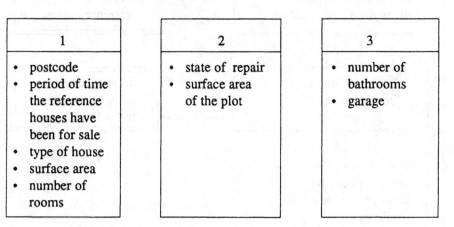

Figure 13.4 Relevance levels

With respect to the postcode it is perhaps interesting to know that the Netherlands is divided into an intricate network of postcode areas. Each street or even part of a street has its own unique postcode, which is related to the postcode in the immediate surroundings. Also, the selling time of the reference houses is an important characteristic. This period is registered by the computer in the multiple listing system and forms the period between the date on which the property is offered for sale through the multiple listing system and the date on which the house is registered as sold.

Reference houses

The segmentation method, developed for each region, is then an important tool for finding reference properties. As soon as the property to be valued is put into the computer, the computer begins looking for the most relevant characteristics in the segmentation method. The group of relevant characteristics found subsequently forms the basis for the reference properties in the multiple listing system file. Represented schematically, the TAXES programme is as shown in Figure 13.5.

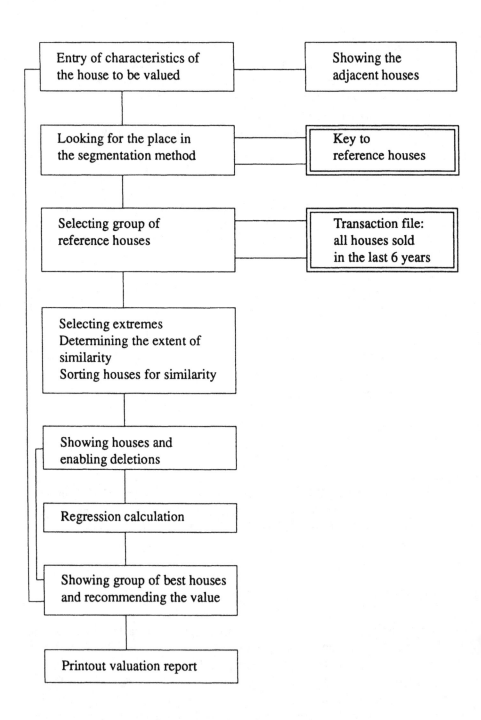

Figure 13.5 TAXES - Valuation procedure

336

In practice

For the valuer who works with TAXES, there are only four screens, a main menu, a screen to be filled in, a screen with adjacent houses and a screen with the reference houses and the recommended value. The connection between the four screens is shown in Figure 13.6.

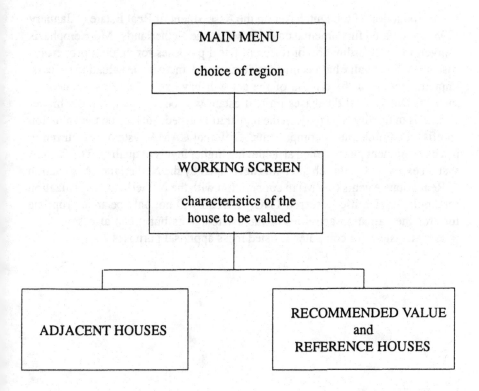

Figure 13.6 Menu structure of TAXES

TAXES: conclusions

Under certain conditions the segmentation method used in TAXES can offer great opportunities for the valuation of owner occupied houses and rental houses. It enables real estate agents to achieve cost savings on daily routine activities. A number of problems will still have to be solved, but these problems seem to be of secondary importance.

For the estate agents of the NVM, this change means that more time can be spent on quality control and on service activities, which after all are the most important issues for them.

Summary

The introduction of the Dutch Act on the Assessment of Real Estate (1 January 1995) has created fundamental changes within the Netherlands. More emphasis is given to the coordination of different fiscal purposes for valuing properties. Also, the market value has become the dominant element in the valuation process. Implementation of the criteria of the act will have significant consequences, such as, Dutch local databases on real estate will be required to meet higher standards of quality. Not only on the registration aspect but also on the valuation and fiscal administrative components. Different CAMA systems are currently in a development phase aimed at achieving higher levels of quality. The CAMA system explained in this chapter was developed by the Netherlands Association of Real Estate Agents (NVM) in cooperation with the Netherlands Organization for Applied Scientific Research TNO. TAXES will not only be an appropriate tool for the valuation activities of the estate agents but it can also serve as a potential system for computer assisted mass appraisal purposes.

14 Mass appraisal for property tax purposes in Singapore

L.S. Leng

Introduction

Property tax is a tax levied on immovable properties. The property tax system in Singapore is basically an annual value system. Annual value is defined in the Property Tax Act (Chapter 254, 1985 Edition) as the gross rent at which the property can reasonably be expected to be let from year to year, the landlord paying the expenses of repair, insurance, maintenance or upkeep and all taxes. The tax is currently levied based on a standard tax rate of 15% per annum on the annual value. A concessionary tax rate of 4% is granted for owner-occupied residential premises.

The Inland Revenue Authority of Singapore (hereinafter referred to as the Authority) is the organization responsible for the administration of taxation in Singapore. The division within the Authority that provides the professional valuation service is the Property Valuation and Assessment Division (PVAD). This is one of the eleven divisions in the Authority.

Methods of assessment

The principal methods of assessment in the determination of the annual value are briefly described as follows:

Buildings

1   Rental Comparison Method

This method is adopted for properties such as houses, flats, factories and offices, and other properties which are commonly let. The annual value of a property is derived by comparing the subject property with the letting of other similar properties in a similar economic situation.

Since properties are seldom comparable to the extent that they are identical, adjustment would have to be made to account for factors such as location, size, terms of tenancy and for the lapse of time between the dates at which the rents of comparable properties were determined and the date of assessment of a property.

The valuer has to sieve through the various factors affecting the rental value and make a judgment on how each factor influence the value and the extent of the influence.

2   Contractor's test

For properties where actual or comparable rentals are rare e.g. shipyard, gas station, the contractor's test method is normally used. The application of the contractor's test involves five stages:

(a)   Estimate the costs of buildings and improvements.

(b)   Adjust cost of construction from Stage 1 to reflect physical depreciation and functional obsolescence of the improvements.

(c)   Estimate the land cost based on its existing use in accordance with market conditions and planning regulations.

(d)   Apply appropriate rate to the effective capital value of the property (which is generally taken to be the sum of the land value and the value of improvements) to arrive at what it will cost the occupier, in annual terms, to provide the accommodation for himself, rather than to lease it.

(e)   The last stage takes into account the cost of repairs, insurance, maintenance or upkeep and property tax.

3   Profit's basis

The annual values for properties owned by public utilities and port undertakings are determined by the profit's method. This approach is applicable in the case where a hypothetical tenant would relate his share of profits from the business he conducts on the premises.

This method of assessment makes use of the accounts of the actual occupier to ascertain the gross receipts of the business. Working expenses are then deducted from the receipts to leave a balance which is divided between the hypothetical tenant and the landlord. The tenant's share must be sufficient to induce him to carry on the business, and the residue, after deduction of the tenant's share is deemed the gross rent which the hypothetical tenant is willing to pay.

Land

For vacant land, the annual value is statutorily determined by adopting 5% of its capital value. The capital value is the amount at which the vacant land could reasonably be expected to sell, or the price it would fetch in the open market by a willing seller to a willing buyer as at the date of assessment. The capital value is based on the evidence of vacant land sales in the vicinity. A similar basis of assessment is adopted for land in the course of development.

Valuation list

Under the Act, the Chief Assessor is required to publish annually a Valuation List containing all assessed properties in Singapore with their annual values. As at 1 January 1995, the composition of the Valuation List is shown in Table 14.1.

Table 14.1
Composition of Valuation List

Type of Property	Number
Commercial	41,776
Industrial	11,695
Private Residential	125,939
Public Residential	595,619
Others (e.g. clubhouses, hospitals)	4,580
Land	2,919
TOTAL	782,528

A Valuation List remains in force until superseded by a new List on 1 January of the ensuring year. Amendment to the Valuation List may be made by the Chief Assessor when there is any change in material particular of a property. Some circumstances where such amendments are made are:

341

1   When the rental or sale evidence of a particular or similar properties indicate that the annual value of the property is inaccurate; and

2   When any building is rebuilt, enlarged, altered or improved.

It is essential to keep the Valuation List up-to-date so that tax collected based on the annual value is reflective of the prevailing market conditions.

Efforts to enhance efficiency

The property tax administration system has been continuously improved upon in Singapore to cater for the rapid economic and social changes. It is a challenge to maintain an up-to-date Valuation List in view of the volatility of the Singapore property market.

For example, between 1988 to 1992, the property price index for the residential sector showed an increase of nearly 70%. With such dynamic market movement, annual values get out of date quickly and therefore creates pressure for frequent reassessment.

As the annual value is determined based on the annual expected gross rent at the time of assessment, a reasonable time period between assessments would be one year. This means that in an up-to-date Valuation List, all properties should be assessed at least once every year.

The Authority has turned to computerization and re-engineering of its work processes to expedite the reassessment of properties. Some of the areas where computer technology is employed to assist the Authority in achieving a annual reassessment cycle for all properties in the Valuation List are described as follow:

Computerized database

In the past, a significant amount of time is spent on retrieving the necessary information required for assessment. These information, contained in correspondence, floor plans and official records are accessible only through the slow and laborious paper filing system.

In 1989, a computerized database was established for all taxable properties in Singapore. The system allows the retrieval of information such as floor area, building type, year of construction, date of last reassessment, records of all valuation notices sent and rental contracted in a specific period from the users' work stations. As a result, reliance on paper records is reduced.

Computer assisted mass assessment

With a computerized database, the next challenge is to make use of these records to perform mass appraisal of properties to further enhance our efficiency.

PVAD has been sending its assessors regularly to the United States, Australia, New Zealand and Canada to observe the tax authorities at work. These authorities seem to be moving away from case-by-case valuation and have been using the computer to assist in mass assessment of properties for the collection of property tax.

Having observed the mass assessment techniques as applied in other tax authorities, PVAD decided to develop its own model to facilitate mass appraisal.

Imaging system

As a further enhancement to data collection, storage and retrieval, the Authority has embarked on a project to test the use of imaging technology in 1992. After the successful pilot project, work is currently in progress to create more than 1.2 million electronic images of all paper assessment files. The conversion process is scheduled for completion in September 1995.

The basic feature of an imaging system is akin to an electronic filing cabinet. It enables simultaneous access to the same document by different users and therefore allows action to be taken on the same document concurrently. This system also provides the capability of automatic assigning of documents to the relevant user's work station for actions.

Computer assisted telephone answering system

In November 1992, an automatic telephone answering system called Inland Revenue Information Service (IRIS) was introduced. It is linked to IRAS's database and responds to taxpayer's enquiries on income tax and property tax matters with prerecorded messages.

Through this service, which on the average attends to 3,000 calls per day, the Authority has been able to provide general tax information with minimal manpower during and after office hours.

Teleview

Teleview is a two-way video text information retrieval and transactional system to enable photographic quality pictures of products, services and information to be displayed on personal computers or television screens. Service providers are organizations from both the public and private sectors. Users can access Teleview from their homes of offices through their personal computers. They received information from the service providers via the telephone line or television antenna.

The Teleview system is owned by Singapore Telecom. Subscribers can obtain information on property annual value, property tax rate and property owner's name. They can also obtain general income tax information such as tax rates, relief and rebates, and guidance for the completion of income tax return.

There is also a tax preparation software that Teleview user can down-load to their personal computers to help them compute their income tax liability.

Electronic data interchange

Currently lawyers can submit legal requisition through computers in their office to enquire on the ownership, existing annual value and the tax status of all properties in the Valuation List. Lawyers are also encouraged to file the notices of transfer electronically whenever properties are transferred.

As there is no physical exchange of paper documents, faster response to the legal requisition submitted and savings in cost is possible as the need to translate and code information contained in paper documents to the mainframe database is no longer necessary.

Development of computer assisted mass appraisal (CAMA) System

Properties to be assessed

We noted that mass appraisal is normally used for the assessment of homogeneous properties in other tax authorities. The Multiple Regression Analysis (MRA) technique is commonly used to estimate or predict the capital value. The regression equation is normally modified for local conditions. PVAD has decided that the use of MRA techniques is not feasible in our context for the following reasons:

1   large amount of data is required to derive a regression equation. Resources would also be needed to collect and maintain the data;

2   additional work is also required for the regular updating of the weights and factors so as to take new factors into consideration; and

3   higher administration cost is likely to be incurred due to the additional system and manpower requirements.

344

As we analysed the composition and distribution of properties in our Valuation List, we find that the properties can be broadly classified into 4 main groups:

- *Highrise public residential apartments* About 80 per cent of Singapore's population live in Government subsidized housing built by the Housing and Development Board (HDB). These properties constitute about 76% of the total property stock in the Valuation List. Their annual values are determined by the rental comparison method. It is a statutory requirement that such properties be owner-occupied; approval for the letting out the whole flat is granted only under special circumstances.

  As a result, these properties are not exposed to the volatile changes in the rental market and their annual values remain relatively stable from year to year. The Division had not encountered problem on the annual assessment for this group of properties.

- *Highrise private residential apartments, factories, warehouses and offices* Annual values of these properties (which makes up about half of the remaining property stock) require constant review as they are exposed to the dynamic changes in the rental market. Owners are free to decide whether to let out their properties or to remain in owner occupation.

  For properties that are let, the lease term usually ranges from two to three years. In cases where the lease term is longer, a clause to allow rent review at regular interval e.g. every two years, is normally included in the tenancy agreement. They are assessed using the comparison method as there is an abundant of actual or letting of similar properties.

  The main reason that contributes to the volatility of the annual value of these properties is the changes in the market conditions and supply and demand forces.

- *Private residential houses, landed factories/warehouses and shops* These properties are also assessed using the comparison method. One major difference with highrise properties is that building area changes from time to time as each owner carries out additions and alterations to his property.

  Constant monitoring is required to account for physical changes. In the case of shops, the actual use may also vary from time to time.

- *Others (e.g. clubhouses, hospitals and land)* These group of properties are non homogeneous. Mass assessment is unlikely for these properties as special skills and knowledge are required.

The highrise private residential apartments, factories, warehouses and offices offer the most potential for the application of mass assessment method. Our CAMA system is thus developed specifically for this group of properties.

Our CAMA system is designed in recognition of the market behaviour and characteristics of the properties identified for mass assessment.

Characteristics of properties In general, annual value for any property are affected by four broad categories of factors namely: physical, legal, social and economical. The factors affecting the rental value of highrise and homogeneous properties is compress into two groups: all factors other than demand and supply forces and factors of demand and supply.

By grouping similar properties together, the net effect of the first group of factors can be held constant since:

- physical attributes of the properties rarely change due to structural constraint; and

- influence of social preference and bias applies uniformly to all properties of the same type and class within a block or a small neighbourhood.

Our analysis based on actual rentals contracted also shows that for comparable properties subjected to similar market forces, the market rents for properties within a block or a small neighbourhood based on unit floor area usually vary within a small range.

Submarket group In our CAMA model, comparable properties are grouped together to form a submarket group (SMG). A SMG comprises homogeneous properties of the same use within a small geographical location. Properties within the SMG should be subjected to similar market forces. Rental for properties within the SMG move in tandem with changing market conditions. One example of a SMG would be prime office developments within the central business district.

Identifying properties to be included in a SMG is a very important process in our CAMA system. A SMG would have a common base rental rate or value. With the correct grouping of similar properties, the same ratio of change could then be applied to the whole group of properties.

The process of forming SMG is a valuation function as knowledge of the properties, its characteristics and rental value is needed.

Benchmark property and base rate Groups of property are selected as benchmarks from each submarket group. Normally, the benchmark properties are extensively let so that changes in their annual value can be readily detected. The benchmark properties are valued based on the normal valuation processes and the assessment rate to be adopted for the benchmarks is termed the base rate.

Relativity factor The influence of physical factors such as size, orientation is determined for other groups of properties with reference to the benchmark property and is compressed into a single factor expressed as a ratio of the base rate. This factor is called the relativity factor.

The relativity factor takes into account the relative advantage or disadvantage as compared to the benchmark property. In principle, the determination of the relativity factor is no different from the adjustments that valuers apply to a property relative to the comparable properties in the market comparison method.

So long as the physical, social and legal factors affecting the values do not change, the valuation judgment in the determination of relativity factors need not be repeated.

Suggested annual value As a result of the formation of submarket groups and the relationship that exists between properties within a group (measured by the relativity factor), the computerized system is able to compute the annual value for properties based on the following formula:

$$\text{Suggested Annual Value} = \text{BR} \times \text{RF} \times \text{FA}$$

where
BR = Base rate of the SMG
RF = Relativity factor of the subject property
FA = Area to be assessed for the subject property

CAMA basic design

The CAMA environment

The CAMA system is designed to make use of the computer's ability to process vast amount of information to carry out mass assessment.

The CAMA system performs its function in a environment separated from the mainframe database system. The separation is to ensure that no valuation notices can be issued by other officers when an CAMA exercise is still in progress.

While a CAMA assignment is in progress, the property and rental data for the submarket group will be extracted from the mainframe database on a predetermined date. This date is termed the schedule date for each CAMA assignment. Any amendments made to the mainframe database after the schedule date will not be reflected in the CAMA environment. The reasons to have a set of fixed data are as follow:

1   to ensure consistency in data analysis and processing of suggested annual values during the assignment; and

2   to allow users to assess the impact of changing the base rate and relativity factors.

It is important that all the necessary data be accurately coded to ensure that annual values are computed correctly. This will also minimized the need for user to update the property data in the CAMA environment when an assignment is in progress.

Main functions

The 7 main functions in the CAMA system are as follows:

1   Security control

Under this option, the CAMA manager is able to:

•   Create the identification code and description for individual submarket group. Each code is unique to a group and is allocated by the system based on certain built-in rules,

•   Schedule CAMA exercise and appointment of officer-in-charge for each assignment. The system will verify the password of the user before access to the data is allowed. There is also a check in the system to ensure that a new assignment of the same submarket group cannot be created until the current assignment has been completed,

•   Terminate or abort the CAMA assignments when necessary, and

•   Monitor the status of each assignment and the printing of reports for project management and audit purposes.

2   Project management

Programs under this panel allow users to :

•   Display history of assessment of any submarket group according to users' requirement e.g. if any officer is reviewing the assessment of a office development, he may request the system to list out all commercial submarket groups located within the vicinity of the subject submarket group for comparison;

•   Monitor the status of an ongoing assignment e.g. officer-in-charge, schedule date and approving officer etc.; and

- Display all current assignment sorted by officer-in-charge or within a specific period as required.

3   Maintenance of submarket group

Properties to be assessed under the CAMA system are tagged with a code for identification purpose. Programs under the submarket group maintenance menu allows the addition and/or deletion of properties to the group. This can be done by either property-by-property or en-bloc basis. The identification code will be displayed in the mainframe data base.

4   Data preparation

Although the data in a submarket group is frozen after the schedule date, the system would still allow users to change the area to be assessed if necessary. This is to ensure that data is up-to-date and annual values are computed correctly.

5   Rental analysis

The programs under this menu enable the users to prepare statistics (e.g. mean, median, mode) on the rental contracted within the submarket group by selecting any of the options as follows:

- Property type;
- Range of relativity factor;
- Range of rental commencement date; and
- Range of floor area.

The results of the statistical analysis could be viewed on screen or printed.

6   Processing of suggested annual values

The annual value computed by the system is termed the suggested annual value (SAV). The menu provides for the following transactions to determine the SAV:

- Specify base rate to be used;

- Compute relativity factor;

- Compute the SAV;

349

- Enter the effective date for the Valuation Notice to be issued;

- Adjustment of SAV computed by the system;

- Suppress the issuing of Valuation Notice when necessary, for example, when the annual values of properties have not changed.

7   Approval in the CAMA system

After the suggested annual values are finalized for all properties in the submarket group, the processed information will be 'locked' in the CAMA environment and copied over to the mainframe system. Based on these input, the main system will update the relevant data fields and issue valuation notices to the taxpayers.

Workflow

Workflow under the CAMA system is shown in Figures 14.1 and 14.2. The flow can be classified into 6 main processes:

1   Identification

Properties are grouped into submarket groups. Knowledge of the properties, its characteristics and its rental values are essential. Benchmark properties are also chosen at this stage. This is a valuation function that will determine the accuracy and consistency of the relativity factor, base rate and suggested annual values later on.

2   Extraction of data from existing mainframe system

Information like rental details, floor area, property type which are already residing in the mainframe is extracted. The data have to be thoroughly checked to ensure that annual values are computed correctly.

3   Determination of base rate and relativity factor

The base rate is the assessment rate to be adopted for the benchmark properties within each submarket group. The valuer determines the base rate through the normal valuation process.
    The relativity factor is designed to account for the relative advantage or disadvantage of the subject property as compared to the benchmark property. The determination of the relativity factor is no different from

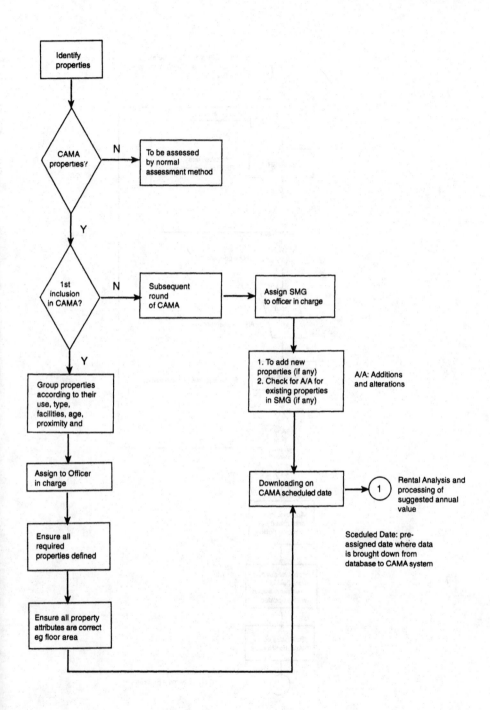

Figure 14.1 Work flow

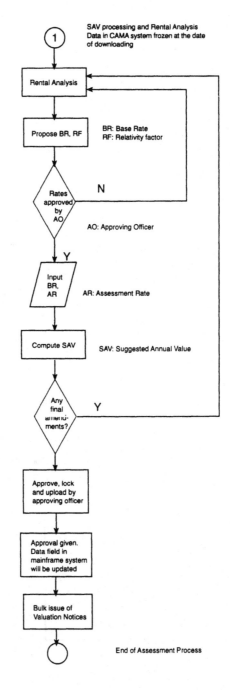

Figure 14.2 Flow chart of assessment process

the adjustments that a valuer will make to a property relative to comparable properties in the market comparison method.

As a start, historical assessment rates accepted by the taxpayers were analysed with reference to the benchmark property. In this way, preliminary relativity factor are worked out for different property within the submarket group.

4   Computation of suggested annual values

Once the base rate (BR) and relativity factor (RF) are determined, the system can compute the suggested annual values (SAV) based on the following formula:

$$SAV = BR \times RF \times Floor\ area$$

5   On-line approval

The proposal will be sent to the necessary officers for checking and approval. The approving officer can view the suggested annual values of all the properties in the SMG from his work station and decides whether any further amendment is necessary.

6   Update mainframe system

Once approval is given, the information in the CAMA environment will be updated into the mainframe system. Assessment details such as the date of commencement and completion of each CAMA assignment are recorded to enable scheduling of subsequent review. Valuation notices will also be issued to taxpayers based on the approved annual values and effective dates.

Evaluation of CAMA system

Our CAMA system makes use of the characteristics and market behaviour of highrise properties to facilitate mass assessment. It is restrictive in its application and users have to ensure that the correct type of properties are assessed using this system.

There were concerns that the professional standard of valuation had been compromised to achieve higher productivity. In our model, we have not replaced valuers with the computer. The system makes use of the valuer's knowledge by transferring his input into the formation of submarket groups and the determination of the relativity factor and base rate. The valuers can make adjustments to the suggested annual values computed, and are still accountable for the final annual values. Objections and appeals to the valuation are resolved by producing market evidence to substantiate our valuations.

The use of CAMA has improved our productivity in two aspects:

1   the saving in the valuer's time as he need not repeat the process of factoring the difference between properties every time a submarket group is due for review so long as the change in annual value is due only to changes in market conditions; and

2   there is no need to update individual property record and to issue valuation notice on a property-by-property basis, as the system is able to do bulk updating and processing.

Due to productivity gained as a result of the CAMA system, all properties can be reviewed annually to attain an up-to-date Valuation List. More time is also available for valuation of properties that requires special skills and knowledge e.g. the assessment of land, shipyards and hotels.

Since properties in a submarket group have a common base date and changes in the market conditions are accounted for on a year-to-year basis, the need for ad-hoc reassessment is minimized. This ensures that similar properties in the same estate or development have an uniform assessment rate.

The CAMA system also enables easier scheduling as assessment cycles can be managed on submarket group-by-submarket group basis instead of property-by-property.

The CAMA system cannot be applied to the assessment of properties not grouped into submarket groups. However, there is a possibility of extending the project management approach based on groups of properties to other non homogeneous properties. For example, cinemas in different locations may be grouped to form a submarket class (SMC). The whole SMC can then be reviewed when there are changes in the factors that will affect annual values of properties within the SMC.

Conclusion

Since the implementation of CAMA in August 1992, we have identified and categorized almost 98,000 properties into 341 submarket groups (or 57% of the total private property stock of 173,000) to be assessed under this system. All the submarket groups are already in the second or third round of the annual assessment cycle. By using the CAMA system, the productivity is about three times higher than the normal assessment process.

The purpose of implementing the CAMA system is to assist PVAD in achieving annual reassessment and thereby maintaining an up-to-date Valuation List. While PVAD tries to hasten the valuation process to achieve higher efficiency through the use of CAMA, we are also aware of the limitations of the system and do not sacrifice accuracy in determining the annual values of properties.

With the help of CAMA, annual values in the Valuation List are reflective of the prevailing market conditions and this has helped us to accomplish fairness in our assessments.

(The views expressed in this paper do not necessarily represent those of the Inland Revenue Authority of Singapore or the Government of Singapore.)

Index

least squares - *see* multiple regression

Malaysia 103-130
market area model 260
market value - *see* value
model 3, 51, 62, 83, 107, 125, 219, 258, 263, 276, 296, 304, 320, 353
modindex 16, 216, 231
multi-layered perceptron 65
multiple listing system 17, 331, 335
multiple regression
   additive 11, 19, 51, 219, 240, 263
   backward selection 7
   backward stepwise 7
   bayesian 272
   constrained 7, 271
   constrained nonlinear 7
   double-log 43
   forward selection 7
   forward stepwise 7
   functional form 2, 70, 83
   Gauss-Newton nonlinear 7
   hybrid 4, 19, 223, 264
   least squares 7, 81, 262, 321
   linear 7, 36, 82, 235, 278
   log on log 37
   loglinear 263
   multiplicative 16, 37, 219, 262, 269
   nonlinear 7, 263, 271
   regression based indexation 12, 27, 42
   stepwise 7, 215, 239, 318

neighbourhood 13, 17, 32, 94, 154, 237, 260, 275, 297, 309, 331
Netherlands 325-338
network 6, 13, 67, 90, 198, 320
neurons 63, 89, 265
New Zealand 211-232
Northern Ireland 59-78

office 12, 34, 52, 111, 126, 345
outlier 51, 100, 215, 265, 321

parallel distributed processing 89, 101
performance analysis 297, 312
predict 13, 19, 42, 98, 221, 344
predictive accuracy *see* accuracy
property characteristic 11, 46, 81, 218, 270, 319
property inspection 218
property tax 14, 29, 60, 137, 152, 245, 326, 344
proportionality model 16, 235, 252
prototyping 129

rateable value - *see* value
rating 29, 103, 187, 234
ratio study 297, 320
ratio tables 171
real estate market 18, 62, 207, 325
reference assessment 12, 33, 52
relativity factor 18, 347, 354
replacement 41, 135, 175, 267, 296, 327
research 6, 13, 15, 16, 19, 114
revaluation 2, 12, 28, 52, 103, 117, 130, 188, 217, 235, 253, 270, 301
robust model 237
rule based system 5, 10, 69

sample size 47, 67, 93, 260
scientific approach 22, 60, 72
segmentation 331, 334, 335, 336, 337
services 134, 146
shopping complex 104, 106, 107, 109, 111, 121, 127, 128, 129
Singapore 339-355
single property appraisal 1, 17, 60, 289, 290, 291, 295, 296, 319
size 10, 15, 32, 47, 61, 79, 109, 139, 176, 218, 242, 263, 269, 297, 332

Printed in the United States
by Baker & Taylor Publisher Services